42 $\frac{50}{}$

PORTALS, PILGRIMAGE, AND CRUSADE

in Western Tuscany

PORTALS, PILGRIMAGE, AND CRUSADE

in Western Tuscany

DOROTHY F. GLASS

PRINCETON UNIVERSITY PRESS

Library of Congress Cataloging-in-Publication Data

Glass, Dorothy F.
Portals, pilgrimage, and crusade in western Tuscany / Dorothy F. Glass.
p.   cm.
Includes bibliographical references and index.
ISBN 0–691–01172–9 (cloth : alk. paper)
1. Relief (Sculpture), Italian—Italy—Tuscany.   2. Relief (Sculpture), Medieval—
Italy—Tuscany.   3. Christian art and symbolism—Medieval, 500–1500—Italy—
Tuscany.   4. Lintels—Italy—Tuscany.   5. Crusades.   I. Title.
NB1282.G58   1997
730'.945'509021—dc20   96-33486
CIP

This book has been composed in Linotronic Sabon by
The Composing Room of Michigan, Inc.

Princeton University Press books are printed
on acid-free paper and meet the guidelines
for permanence and durability of the Committee
on Production Guidelines for Book Longevity
of the Council on Library Resources

Printed in the United States of America by
Princeton Academic Press, Lawrenceville, New Jersey

10 9 8 7 6 5 4 3 2 1

FOR ALL THE MEMBERS OF

THE DEPARTMENT OF MEDIEVAL ART AND THE CLOISTERS,

THE METROPOLITAN MUSEUM OF ART,

WITH AFFECTION AND GRATITUDE

CONTENTS

LIST OF ILLUSTRATIONS

ABBREVIATIONS

ActaSS	*Acta Sanctorum Bollandiana*
Biehl	Walther Biehl, *Toskanische Plastik des frühen und hohen Mittelalters*. Italienische Forschungen, Kunsthistorisches Institut in Florenz, n.s., 2 (Leipzig, 1926)
BS	*Bibliotheca Sanctorum* (Rome, 1961–70)
Crichton	George H. Crichton, *Romanesque Sculpture in Italy* (London, 1954)
DBI	*Dizionario biografico degli italiani* (Rome, 1960–)
Heydasch-Lehmann	Susanne Heydasch-Lehmann, *Der 'Taufbrunnen' in San Frediano in Lucca und die Entwicklung der toskanischen Plastik in der 2. Hälfte des 12. Jahrhunderts*. Europäische Hochschulschriften, series XXVIII, History of Art, vol. 123 (Frankfurt am Main, 1991)
LCI	*Lexikon der christlichen Ikonographie*, ed. E. Kirschbaum et al. (Rome, 1968–76)
MGH SS	Monumenta Germaniae Historica, Scriptores
PL	*Patrologiae cursus completus, Series Latina*, ed. J.-P. Migne
RDK	*Reallexikon zur Deutschen Kunstgeschichte*, ed. Otto Schmidt et al. (Stuttgart, 1937–)
Salmi	Mario Salmi, *Romanesque Sculpture in Tuscany* (Florence, 1928)
Schiller 1	Gertrud Schiller, *Iconography of Christian Art*, vol. 1, *Christ's Incarnation-Childhood- Baptism-Temptation-Transfiguration-Works and Miracles*, trans. Janet Seligman (Greenwich, Conn., 1971)
Schiller 2	Gertrud Schiller, *Iconography of Christian Art*, vol. 2, *The Passion of Jesus Christ*, trans. Janet Seligman (Greenwich, Conn., 1972)

Schiller 3   Gertrud Schiller, *Ikonographie der christlichen Kunst*, vol. 3, *Die Auferstehung und Erhöhung Christi* (Gütersloh, 1971)

Schmarsow   August Schmarsow, *S. Martin von Lucca und die Anfänge der toskanischen Skulptur im Mittelalter*. Italienische Forschungen zur Kunstgeschichte, vol. 1 (Breslau, 1890)

Toesca   Pietro Toesca, *Storia dell'arte italiana*. Vol. 1, *Il Medioevo* (Turin, 1927; reprint, 1965)

Venturi   Adolfo Venturi, *Storia dell'arte italiana*. Vol. 3, *L'arte romanica* (1904; reprint, 25 vols. in 11. Nendeln/Liechtenstein, 1968)

FOREWORD

The genesis of this small volume lies in a seemingly simple question. That is, anyone who has studied Romanesque art, even at the most elementary level, is aware that the three major pilgrimage centers are Santiago de Compostela, Rome, and Jerusalem. Indeed, the first mentioned site may even be said to lie at the very heart of the study of Romanesque art, for more than two generations ago, such scholars as Paul Deschamps and Arthur Kingsley Porter posited that stylistic features were transmitted along the primary pilgrimage roads leading from France to Santiago de Compostela and vice versa. Hence, I began to wonder why the Via Francigena, the primary pilgrimage route to Rome, had not been examined in the same way. Rome, after all, is the very seat of Christianity.

I soon discovered that the route was well known to historians, but with the exception of Arturo Carlo Quintavalle, it had been little studied by art historians, who have tended to focus on a particular locale rather than to trace the entire route from what are now the borders of France and Switzerland to Rome itself. Thanks to an American Philosophical Society Grant-in-Aid awarded for the summer of 1988 and a Western European Regional Fulbright Fellowship awarded in 1989–90, I was able to travel the entire route while taking copious notes and photographs. I am grateful to the sponsoring organizations for their generous support of a then rather amorphous project.

Unfortunately, the masses of material I had gathered, although not without interest as individual units, did not amount to the proverbial hill of beans. In sum, the Via Francigena did not generally function in the same way as the routes to Santiago de Compostela did. Casting about for a way out of my dilemma, I lit upon the rather old-fashioned notion that concentration on a particular work might induce some coherence in my own thought if not in the material itself. Once I began to focus on the portal from San Leonardo al Frigido now at The Cloisters in New York, some pieces of the puzzle began to fit together and the endeavor began to have some shape. This phase of the undertaking, as well as most of the research for this book, was made possible by a two-year (1991–93) Jane and Morgan Whitney Senior Research Fellowship awarded by The Metropolitan Museum of Art and held in the Department of Medieval Art and The Cloisters. There I was greeted cordially, treated collegially, and made to feel welcome both intellectually and personally. That this study is dedicated to all the members of the department is but a small measure of the extent to which I am in their debt. I thank them individually and collectively.

While I was working on this project, I received a number of invitations to lecture on the material. The penetrating questions and thoughtful observations of my various audiences helped me to sharpen my arguments and refine my thoughts. For such intellectual hospitality and convivial evenings, I thank Brendan Cassidy, formerly of the Index of Christian Art, Princeton University, and now of the University of Saint Andrews; the Robert Branner Forum of Columbia University; George Gorse of Pomona College; Madeline Caviness of Tufts University; Nurith Kenaan-Kedar of Tel Aviv University; and Jaroslav Folda of the University of North Carolina at Chapel Hill. I am particularly indebted to the last mentioned for insisting on the need to rethink some of my notions about the Crusades and their relevance to Tuscany.

The manuscript, in its penultimate form, was read by Jaroslav Folda, Deborah Kahn, Charles Little, Mary Shepard, and Christine Verzár. I am grateful for their keen observations, thoughtful queries, and generosity of spirit. Any and all remaining insufficiences are solely my responsibility. I am obliged to Timothy Wardell, formerly of Princeton University Press, for expressing early interest in the manuscript and for shepherding its acceptance. At the Press, the manuscript was greatly improved by Elizabeth Johnson's meticulous editing. Her good humor, as well as Sara Bush's, often soothed the anxious author. The handsome design of the book is the work of Carol Cates and Laury Egan.

Others have helped in countless ways—by prodding me, by listening to me, by offering advice and bibliography, by reading various drafts. Although I hope that the following list is comprehensive, it is written with the fear that I have inadvertently omitted a name; for that I offer apologies in advance. Thanks are due Elizabeth Bartman, Barbara Drake Boehm, Katharine Brown, Irene Brückle, Lisbeth Castelnuovo-Tedesco, Carmelle J. Côté, Sharon Dale, Eve D'Ambra, Jerilynn Dodds, Karin Einaudi, Helen Evans, Vera von Falkenhausen, Maria Teresa Filieri, Ilene H. Forsyth, Julian Gardner, Paula Gerson, Mary Weitzel Gibbons, Adelaide Bennett Hagens, the late Jane Hayward, Timothy Husband, Michael Jacoff, Deborah Kahn, Shari Kenfield, Daniel Kletke, Charles Little, Elizabeth Parker, Arturo Carlo Quintavalle, Willibald Sauerländer, Nancy Ševčenko, Pamela Sheingorn, Mary Shepard, Alison Stones, Christine Verzár, Maria Wenglinsky, and William Wixom.

I am also indebted to many libraries and librarians for the use of superb resources and help gladly given. Special thanks are due the staffs of the Thomas J. Watson Library of The Metropolitan Museum of Art; the Avery Library and Butler Library, both of Columbia University; the Index of Christian Art at Princeton University; the New York Public Library; the Bibliotheca Hertziana in Rome; the Biblioteca Apostolica Vaticana; and the Interlibrary Loan Office of the State University of New York at Buffalo. I am grateful to this last institution for the released time granted to take advantage of the opportunities afforded me.

Dorothy F. Glass
Buffalo, New York
Palm Sunday, March 31, 1996

PORTALS, PILGRIMAGE, AND CRUSADE

in Western Tuscany

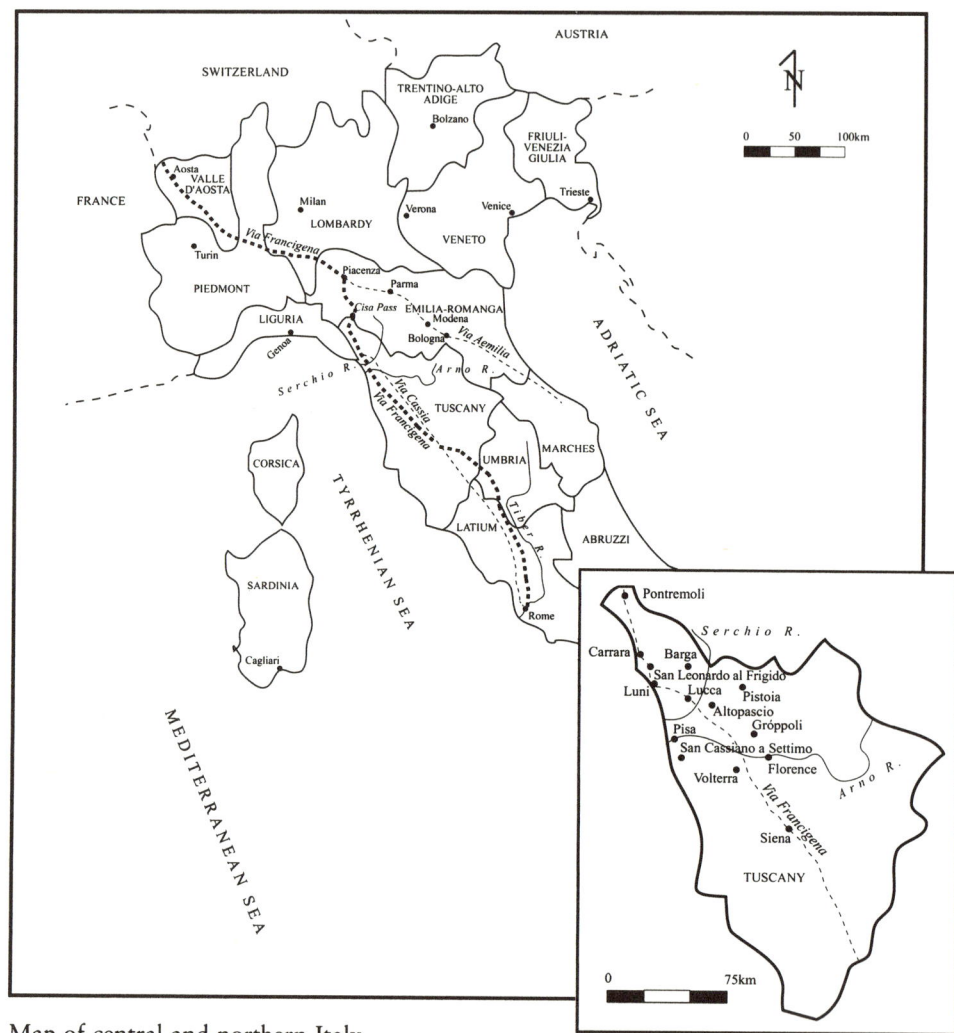

Map of central and northern Italy

Chapter One

Time and Place

Tuscany, the zenith of Renaissance culture, evokes visions of Florence and Siena, of gently rolling hills dotted with vineyards and olive trees. The ascendancy of these two cities in the thirteenth century overshadowed the significant role played in Tuscany just one hundred years earlier by such prosperous cities as Pisa, Lucca, and Pistoia. Yet a combination of historical circumstances and geographical location launched these and neighboring cities into the forefront of medieval commerce, culture, and travel.

One of the primary features of western Tuscany is its extensive Tyrrhenian coastline, home to Pisa, a prominent port often in competition with Genoa, its Ligurian archrival 150 kilometers to the northwest. From Pisa, Tuscany's principal port, expeditions sailed for Amalfi, Sicily, Sardinia, North Africa, Turkey, and the Holy Land, as well as the more western parts of the Mediterranean world. Located at the mouth of the Arno, Pisa's port also served inland water routes.[1] Surely aware of its importance, Pisa's archbishop controlled the city's bridge over the Arno during the twelfth century.[2] Similarly, the Serchio River and its tributary, the Auser, provided convenient water routes in the area around Lucca.

Medieval western Tuscany was also endowed with a serviceable network of roads dating to the Roman era.[3] The coastal route, the Via Aurelia and its extension, the Via Aemilia Scauri, stretched from Rome to Gaul. Inland, the Via Cassia traversed Tuscany from Rome to Pisa.[4] To these were added, during the Lombard era, the Via Francigena.[5] Denied access to the Adriatic by the Exarchate of Ravenna, the Lombards were apprehensive about using the Tyrrhenian Coast because they feared the frequent incursions of the Moslems and other hostile parties.[6] The Via Francigena cut across the Appennines at the Cisa Pass between Piacenza on the ancient Via Aemilia and Pontremoli, about thirty-five kilometers north of Carrara. South of Pontremoli, the Via Francigena turned inland to Lucca, Siena, and thence toward Rome. North of Rome, at Bolsena, it joined the ancient Via Cassia. Throughout the Middle Ages, the Via Francigena was the primary but not exclusive means by which northern pilgrims reached the Eternal City.[7] Because it largely avoided the perils of the coast, the Via Francigena and its extensive network of hospices was also an attractive route to merchants and other voyagers.[8]

Lucca, Pistoia, and Pisa were the three most prominent cities in twelfth century western Tuscany.[9] Lucca's position was established early on, for the city was the capitol of the Lombard kingdom north of Rome. Throughout the Middle Ages, Lucca, famed for her textiles, was one of the primary points from which caravans of traders departed by land for northern Europe. Although the rival cities of Pisa and Lucca are separated by a mere twenty kilometers, travel between them was not easy, for in that distance the flat terrain of the bed of the Arno River gave way to the rocky Monte Pisani, because of which, in the words of Dante, "the Pisans cannot see Lucca."[10] Less than forty kilometers northeast of Lucca and about thirty kilometers northwest of Florence, lies Pistoia, at the foot of the spiny and precipitous Appennines. Pistoia was strategically important because of its location at the beginning of the routes to Modena and Bologna, cities of exceptional importance on the eastern side of the Appennines.[11]

In the earlier years of the Middle Ages, Tuscany had been dotted with numerous *pievi*, small baptismal churches having local jurisdiction. Built on mountains, in valleys, and along roads, the *pievi* served as the center of their small respective territories and thus provided a web of social structure in their communities.[12] The intense commercial activity in Pisa, Lucca, and Pistoia, fostered by the communal form of government, engendered urban life, for nodes of communication and services were necessary for the conduct of business. The economies of the three cities benefitted from virtually unfettered trade. Unlike cities to the north and east, such as Milan and Verona, the three Tuscan cities did not suffer from the incursions and subsequent control of Frederick Barbarossa.[13] The common internecine feuds in western Tuscany were of a much smaller scale and rarely impeded trade for a long duration.[14]

Commercial ventures were not the only source of wealth in Pisa, Lucca, and Pistoia, for all three cities were also famed pilgrimage centers that attracted hordes of visitors. Having traversed the Via Francigena, as well as other routes, pilgrims stopped in western Tuscany to venerate the relics, stay in one of the numerous hospices in the area, and then often proceed to Rome or the Holy Land. To arrive at the latter, pilgrims embarked from such ports as Pisa or Bari. The pilgrimage history of the three Tuscan cities is neither synchronous nor of equal magnitude.

Pisa, although not on the Via Francigena, seems to have attracted pilgrims from an early date, for it was one of the coastal stops on the sea route to Rome described in the mid-twelfth century by both al-Idrisi, the Arab geographer of Roger II of Sicily, and by Rabbi ben-Jonah of Tudela.[15] Ligurinus, in his *De Rebus Gestis Friderici* (i.e., Barbarossa) refers to Pisa as "a station well known to pilgrim boats."[16] Legend has it that Saint Peter himself, having founded the church at Antioch, then sailed toward Pisa and disembarked at San Piero a Grado on the outskirts of the Tuscan port. On that site he built a church, thereby establishing the first Christian community in Italy. The stone altar of the church was consecrated by Clement I (ca. 91–101 A.D.).[17]

Lucca, one of the primary sites on the Via Francigena,[18] houses the celebrated Volto Santo.[19] Although the date of its arrival in Lucca is debated and the current statue is clearly a copy of an earlier one, it is known that the relic was venerated in Lucca from at least the early twelfth century: the first papal bull to mention the *sacrarium vultus* is that of Paschal II in 1107, and the first donation from a pilgrim also occurs in the early twelfth century. Just east of Lucca, the famed hospice at Altopascio seems to have become active at about the same time, perhaps to serve pilgrims en route from Lucca to Rome. The first incontrovertible document concerning the hospice is dated to 1084.[20]

Like Pisa, Pistoia is located on the Roman Via Cassia and is bypassed by the Via Francigena.[21] Yet because of the initiative of Pistoia's bishop, Atto, who held the see from 1133 until 1153, Pistoia too became a significant pilgrimage site, albeit at a later date than Lucca.[22] In response to grievous wounds to his prestige inflicted by the independent-minded consuls of Pistoia, Bishop Atto sought to augment both his image and his power. To this end, he sought the help of Rainerius, formerly a cleric at San Zeno, the cathedral of Pistoia.[23] Educated at Winchester and a master of the chapter school at Santiago de Compostela, Rainerius ultimately persuaded Archbishop Diego Gelmirez of Santiago de Compostela to give Bishop Atto a piece of the head of Saint James the apostle.[24] Two trustworthy men, Mediovillanus and Thebaldus, escorted the treasured relic on the long journey to Pistoia.[25]

The date of the arrival in Pistoia of the piece of Saint James's head is not known, but it is thought to have been before the death of Archbishop Gelmirez in 1140 as well as before the dedication of the chapel housing the relic, on July 25, 1144. The chapel, destroyed in 1786, was built into the first two bays in the south aisle of the cathedral at Pistoia.[26] On November 22, 1145, while at Viterbo, Eugene III issued two bulls: one granted seven days indulgence to pilgrims who visited the oratory of Saint James the Great at Pistoia and the other urged the bishops of Siena, Volterra, Florence, Lucca, and Luni to send their parishoners, both male and female, to the oratory.[27] At a later date, an enormous and richly decorated gold dossal was made. The earliest work thereon, the Virgin and apostles, dates from 1287 with additions being made at least until the end of the fourteenth century.[28]

Although the cult of Saint James in Pistoia has left few tangible remains, its clear documentation serves to enfold Pistoia in the international nexus of pilgrimage and crusade, be it to Santiago de Compostela, Rome, or the Holy Land. Pistoia's acquisition of a piece of the head of Saint James thus seems to have been conditioned not by the city's location on a primary pilgrimage route, but rather by the initiative of Bishop Atto and his highly placed friends, who may have sought both to rival the sites on the route itself and to respond to the city's intransigent consuls. In any case, the cult of Saint James seems to have taken a firm hold in Pistoia, for we know of a hospice for pilgrims established there in 1148.[29]

Western Tuscany also prospered because of the seemingly uncanny ability of its leaders to choose the appropriate political alliance at a given moment. While many of the secular inhabitants of Pisa and Pistoia welcomed Frederick Barbarossa, western Tuscany still enjoyed the careful attention of the papacy during the second half of the twelfth century because so many of the pontiffs were natives of that area. Eugene III (1145–53), a Pisan, was a Cistercian and an intimate of Bernard of Clairvaux, and with Bernard's encouragement and guidance, a fervent proponent of the second Crusade.[30] Alexander III (1159–81), born in Siena, was a professor of canon law at Bologna and later canon at Pisa,[31] while Lucius III (1181–85), a Cistercian, was from Lucca. The papacy's strong interest in the area might have its roots in the late eleventh century when Countess Matilda of Tuscany (ca. 1046–1115) willed her allodial lands to the papacy. The area also enjoyed a degree of independence because of the disinclination of the powerful Cluniac priory at San Benedetto Polirone, southwest of Mantua, to extend its possessions much beyond North Italy. Indeed, in Tuscany there were only three monasteries, all in the area of Lucca, dependent on Polirone.[32] In sum, western Tuscany was bolstered by trade, pilgrimage, independence, and papal interest.

No city is more representative of medieval western Tuscany than is Pisa. Pisa's seafaring ventures to distant ports began at an early date; commercial relations were initiated with Africa in the second half of the eleventh century, and Pisa was also in the forefront of triumphant expeditions to Reggio in 1005, Mogahid in 1016, Bona in 1034, Palermo in 1063, al Mahdiya and Zawila in 1087, and the Balearics in 1113–15. Pisa's wealth and resultant importance were thus achieved prior to the first Crusade. Not only did Pisans participate in that Crusade, but Daimbert, who was made bishop of Pisa in 1088 and later served as a papal legate in Corsica, became patriarch of the newly settled Latin kingdom of Jerusalem in late December 1099; he held the post until his death on June 15, 1107 during a journey to Messina.[33] Hence Pisa's interests in the Holy Land were well tended.

Because the Latin kingdom of Jerusalem did not have a navy of its own, the sea power of the Italian maritime colonies was constantly in demand; Pisa thus had ample opportunity for enrichment through both trade and pillage.[34] Having assisted Alexius I in his battle against Bohemond of Antioch, the Pisans were invited, in 1111, to trade in Constantinople. The colony there flourished and was sufficiently large to require two churches, those of Saint Nicholas and Saint Peter. Pisa, rivalled by Genoa, was a more significant force in the Levant during the early twelfth century than was the quiescent Venice. A Pisan administrative official in the East is mentioned for the first time in 1157 and soon each community had a consul who tended to the administration of that colony and reported to Pisa. The sheer number of Pisans present in the East was impressive; for example, during the trading season, as many as one thousand resided in Constantinople. Some became permanent residents. Moreover, the presence in the East of such famed Tuscan translators as Leo Tuscus, his brother Hugo Eterianus, and Burgundio of Pisa is also noted during the latter half of the twelfth century.[35]

Emblematic of Pisa's wealth and international power is her vast cathedral complex, the construction of which extended over more than two centuries.[36] It is composed of the cathedral itself, its campanile (the renowned Leaning Tower), the baptistery, and the Campo Santo or burial ground (fig. 1).[37] The cathedral, begun in 1063 after the city's momentous victory in Palermo, was funded in part by the revenue produced by its merchant colonies abroad. The bulk of the funds from the Pisan colony in Constantinople belonged to the Board of Works of Pisa's cathedral complex. The enormous size of the cathedral, 100 meters long and almost 70 meters wide at the transepts, attests to the vast resources available to the project. Pisa's Board of Works is also believed to have been the best customer of the quarries at Carrara during the Middle Ages.[38]

Pisa's cathedral, the first part of the complex begun, is symptomatic of the wide-ranging taste that might be expected of a city prominent in international trade. The imposing five-aisled structure is reminiscent of Roman basilicas, and its Romanesque nave is capped by a dome.[39] The continuous side aisles suggest French pilgrimage churches, while the interior's screened effects evoke Byzantine monuments in Saloniki as well as Hagia Sophia.[40] Islamic pointed arches in the interior coexist with capitals that are either ancient or primarily classicizing and nonfigurative.[41] Similarly, the lower parts of the facade are decorated in an abstract manner more typical of Islamic than of western Romanesque ornament. The whole was capped by an enormous metal griffin, a trophy perhaps of Egyptian or Spanish origin (fig. 2).[42] *Spolia*, both local and imported, are employed abundantly, while Bonanus, a local artisan, made the bronze doors of Pisa's cathedral.[43] Built of alternating courses of black and white marble, the cathedral at Pisa not only speaks to the importance of that city, but also declares the architectural style that was to reign, with minor variations, in western Tuscany throughout the late eleventh and twelfth centuries and even into the thirteenth century.[44] This style, both classicizing and abstract, gave little importance to architectural sculpture.

Like Busketus and Rainaldus—the architects of the Pisan cathedral— the sculptor Guglielmus, who carved the cathedral's first pulpit, is commemorated by an inscription on the building's facade. This pulpit, the key sculptural monument carved during the earlier years of the cathedral's history, dates to between 1159 and 1162.[45] It remained in the cathedral until it was replaced by Giovanni Pisano's pulpit, carved between 1302 and 1310. At that time Guglielmus's pulpit was shipped to the cathedral at Cagliari on the island of Sardinia, where Pisa was continuously trying to impose her political and commercial hegemony.[46] The pulpit was rebuilt in Cagliari in 1312; later, in 1670, it was divided into two sections, one for the gospel and one for the epistle. The two reconstituted pulpits are now located on either side of the interior of the west wall of the cathedral in Cagliari, and the four lions that supported the original pulpit are installed at the entrance to the choir. Thus the monument that seems to mark the beginnings of Romanesque sculpture in western Tuscany has long been virtually inaccessible, rarely photographed, and known primarily through casts stored in Pisa.

The Cagliari pulpit is rich iconographically and revealing stylistically. Because it has been refashioned into two pulpits, the original disposition of the scenes has not been definitively ascertained. The pulpit designated for the gospel currently portrays the *Magi before Herod*, the *An-*

nunciation and the *Visitation* (fig. 5), the *Holy Women at the Tomb*, the *Last Supper*, the *Massacre of the Innocents*, the *Nativity*, the *Soldiers at the Tomb*, and the *Betrayal*. The epistle pulpit now depicts the *Ascension*, the *Transfiguration*, the *Baptism*, the *Adoration of the Magi*, the *Presentation in the Temple*, and the *Departure of the Magi*. The *Crucifixion* is conspicuously absent, while the Magi are emphasized through their appearance in three scenes. The panels focus on the earliest and latest events in Christ's life; such scenes as the miracles, central to Christ's life on earth, are omitted.

The scenes, each identified by inscription, are arranged horizontally two to a panel in a format reminiscent of antique sarcophagi. Each is a self-contained narrative conveying only minimally its relationship to the episodes that surround it. The antique format of the individual panels is often combined with a rather jarring decorative intent, perhaps of Islamic origin, as seen in the backgrounds composed of rosettes within vines and embellished with black paste in, for example, the *Annunciation*, *Nativity*, and the three episodes concerning the Magi. Save for the *Presentation in the Temple*, there is little interest in architectural setting. The stocky figures usually extend virtually the entire height of their respective panels. They are swathed in heavy drapery reaching to the ankles or to the ground itself. Movement is often signified by a bent knee, and communication between figures is indicated by the figures' leaning toward each other.

Regardless of the oft-debated origins and training of Guglielmus, there can be no doubt that the pulpit now in Cagliari is the *fons origens* of Romanesque sculpture in western Tuscany.[47] Such sculptors as Adeodatus and Gruamons can be stylistically traced to the workshop of Guglielmus. The young Biduinus is thought to have been trained there also.[48] The shop initiated by Guglielmus in the mid-twelfth century seems not to have had a lengthy history in Pisa, for the numerous projects centered around the cathedral were interrupted at various stages and work must have become scarce. For example, the campanile, begun in 1174, was temporarily halted at the third story, and the baptistery endured a similar pause. Although there is no further trace of Guglielmus, those sculptors who putatively trained with him seem to have left the city and found employment nearby, at Pistoia and Lucca. It is with these works that this extended essay is primarily concerned.

Chapter Two

Adoration and Participation

SANT'ANDREA AT PISTOIA

Pistoia's acquisition of a piece of Saint James's head may have provided the crucial impetus toward making Pistoia one of the significant pilgrimage centers in western Tuscany, for it linked the city spiritually to both Santiago de Compostela and the Via Francigena, the road to Rome. Only two decades after the advent of the relic in Pistoia, three of the town's churches, all originally built during the Lombard era and all named for apostles, began to be rebuilt and all three, that is, Sant'Andrea, San Giovanni Fuorcivitas, and San Bartolomeo in Pantano, embody and reflect the central importance of pilgrimage in Pistoia. The lintels of the three churches comprise the only narrative Romanesque lintels in the city; moreover, there are no figurative Romanesque tympana in Pistoia. Sant'Andrea at Pistoia, the *plebs magna* and second in importance only to the cathedral, will be the focus of this chapter. San Giovanni Fuorcivitas and San Bartolomeo will be discussed in chapter 3.

Sant'Andrea was founded in the eighth century.[1] Little is known of it until it became one of the many Pistoian churches enlarged and in part rebuilt during the latter half of the twelfth century. Unusually oriented— its apse is in the west—it has been restored in order to remove the later additions to the upper part of the facade which now appears to be denuded (fig. 3).[2] The lower part of the facade, typical of western Tuscany, is divided into five arched sections, of which the center is the highest and widest. The left and right edges of the facade are each emphasized by a pilaster, while more plastic colonnettes topped by capitals and supporting arches in relief articulate the remainder of the lower part of the facade. The mural surface of all but the central vertical segment is broken at the top by the insertion of a three-stepped diamond pattern composed of white marble and *verde di Prato*. The center door is emphasized not only by its height but also by its more elaborate decoration. Each end of its archivolt is supported by lions; the one at the left wrestles with a serpent, while the one at the right does battle with a supine man. The acanthus

outer archivolt grows from a single sculpted head on both the left and the right.[3]

The inscriptions on various parts of the main portal of Sant'Andrea at Pistoia provide an extraordinary amount of information concerning chronology, hand, and iconography (fig. 4). The date of the lintel, 1166, is given in a still-legible inscription on the lower side of the lintel, the side facing the ground: "Then there were the workers Villanus and Pathus, son of Tignosius, 1166 A.D."[4] The lower border of the front face of the lintel identifies the sculptors: "The good master Gruamons and his brother Adeodatus did this work."[5]

A one-line inscription carved in far smaller letters on the narrow upper edge of the lintel describes, in rather verbose fashion, the scenes carved on the lintel, the *Magi before Herod* and the *Adoration of the Magi*:

> Behold the Magi come following the royal star. You, Herod, were deceived, because you wanted to destroy Christ. The star directs the Magi, Melchior, Caspar, and Balthasar. They give the child three gifts.[6]

The capitals of the center portal bear equally informative inscriptions. The left capital depicts the *Annunciation to Zechariah* on the front and the *Visitation* on the inner face. The inscription on the front reads, "Do not be afraid Zechariah for your prayer is heard" (Luke 1:13), and, on the inner face, "Elizabeth your wife [will bear a son]" (Luke 1:13).[7] The capital at the right depicts the *Annunciation to the Virgin* on its front face and Saint Anne on its inner face. Here, the inscriptions reveal both the subject matter and the sculptor. The inner face is inscribed, "Saint Anne," and on the front, "Hail Mary, favored one, [the Lord] is with you [Luke 1:28]. Master Henricus made me."[8]

The inscriptions, in addition to identifying the subject matter, thus suggest that at least part of the facade was built by Villanus and Pathus in 1166, that the Magi scenes on the lintel were carved by Gruamons and Adeodatus, while the right capital was carved by Henricus at an unknown date, but certainly at about the same time as the lintel. On stylistic grounds, the left capital is surely by the same sculptor as the right.

Inscriptions designating the contents of individual scenes can also be found on Guglielmus's pulpit now in Cagliari. Like so much Romanesque sculpture in the western part of Tuscany, the style of Gruamons and Adeodatus is rooted in his work. The patterned background of the lintel is comparable to such scenes on the Cagliari pulpits as the *Annunciation*, the *Nativity*, and the *Adoration of the Magi* (fig. 5). The rhythm of the figures, their stockiness, and their drapery are also similar, as are such specific details as the levitating angel in the *Annunciation* scenes. But, the inscriptions identifying similar scenes at Sant'Andrea in Pistoia differ textually from those on the Cagliari pulpit.[9]

Historiated capitals supporting narrative lintels are a comparative rarity in Romanesque western Tuscany; the portal formerly at San Leonardo al Frigido and now installed at The Cloisters offers the only other example.[10] At Sant'Andrea, the narrative begins on the front of the capital at the left with the *Annunciation to Zechariah* (Luke 1:8–20) (figs. 4 and 6).[11] An angel with knees bent floats aloft and approaches a surprised Zechariah who, leaning on a staff, faces the heavenly messenger. A tree trunk topped by three leaves separates Zechariah from the inner face of the capital, which depicts a rather impersonal *Visitation*; Mary and Elizabeth touch but do not really embrace.[12] The narrative sequence is not contained within each individual capital, for after the *Annunciation to Zechariah* on the front of the left capital, the chronological account moves to the front of the right capital where a damaged angel is poised so that his feet float above the ground on the inner face of the capital while his left wing and upper body appear on the front face of the capital. The Virgin, holding a spindle, stands impassively at the center of the front face of the capital (figs. 4 and 7). Joseph, grasping the same sort of staff as Zechariah on the left capital, stands to the Virgin's left and is separated from her by the same type of tree that appears on the left capital.[13] The inner face of the capital is primarily occupied by the isolated, standing figure of Saint Anne, who looks somberly across to the *Visitation* on the inner face of the left capital.[14]

The two historiated capitals on the facade of Sant'Andrea at Pistoia, though depicting commonly known events, are unusual for a number of reasons. They are distinctively symmetrical because the front face of each capital depicts an *Annunciation*, while the inner face of each represents women standing quietly, confronting each other across the portal. The narrative order and convention have been sacrificed to visual symmetry. Not only is the *Annunciation to Zechariah* a comparatively rare scene, but also Joseph, though often present at the *Nativity*, rarely appears at the *Annunciation to the Virgin*. Saint Anne, the Virgin's mother, an apocryphal figure not mentioned in the biblical account, normally accompanies neither scene.[15] The repeated elements in the scenes—the older men with staffs, the angel with raised lower legs, the two identical trees, and the standing women—all suggest carefully planned pendant scenes. Early on, Saint Ambrose in his *Expositio Evangelii secundum Lucam* noted the parallelism between the doubts expressed by Zechariah and those voiced by Mary (Luke 1:12, 34). He likewise made an analogy between the fears of Mary and Joseph prompted by the unexpected miraculous events.[16] The notion of this particular set of parallelisms was surely well known by the mid-twelfth century when Sant'Andrea's capitals were carved.

The facade capitals at Sant'Andrea seem to be very much a local phenomenon; the closest comparanda are found in western Tuscany and the Emilia-Romagna.[17] This is not surprising because the Via Francigena traverses the Appennines from Piacenza in the Emilia-Romagna to Pontremoli in northwest Tuscany thereby providing a convenient route for exchange between the two provinces. The earliest member of the group seems to be a capital on the right side of the right portal of the cathedral at Parma, which probably dates from the third decade of the twelfth century (fig. 8).[18] Here, the *Visitation* appears on the front of the capital while Zechariah and Joseph each stand alone on one of the sides. The respective spouses thus frame a scene that not only suggests the antecedent *Annunciation* but also expands to include them as onlookers at an event in which they have no active part. A similar conceit is seen in a nave capital in the cathedral at Carrara on the other side of the Appennines (fig. 9).[19] There, the Virgin and Elizabeth embrace on the front of the capital while their respective spouses, each accompanied by an angel, stand individually on the left and right sides of the capital.

The pulpit formerly in the cathedral at Pisa and now in the cathedral at Cagliari (1159–62) carved by Henricus's presumed teacher, Guglielmus, is also part of the iconographic matrix. On the upper part of one panel of what is now the gospel pulpit, Joseph, holding the same kind of staff as seen on the Pistoia capital, stands at the left of the panel (fig. 5).[20] Next to him is the *Annunciation*, unusually composed with Gabriel arriving from the right.[21] The *Visitation*, in which Mary and Elizabeth grasp each other's hands but do not embrace, is at the far right of the panel. The patterned background, the presence of Joseph at the *Annunciation*, the pose of the angel, and the rather impersonal type of *Visitation* all serve to denote the relationship between Guglielmus's pulpit formerly in Pisa and the capitals by his pupil, Henricus at Sant'Andrea, Pistoia.

The fascination with this theme in western Tuscany continued until at least sometime around 1200 as can be seen in a relief from the last quarter of the twelfth century, formerly in Sant'Jacopo at Altopascio, a site famed for its pilgrims' hospice (fig. 10). The figures on the relief, now in the Museo Nazionale di Villa Guinigi at Lucca, are labelled on the upper edge of the panel: Saint Gabriel, Saint Zechariah, Saint Elizabeth.[22]

Zechariah looks toward the angel while a pensive Elizabeth stands calmly at Zechariah's side at the right of the panel. The Altopascio panel is thus not a literal interpretation of the *Annunciation to Zechariah* as related in Luke 1:8–20, for Elizabeth is present; in the text she is not with Zechariah at the moment of the *Annunciation*.

Similar liberties are taken on the reconstructed pulpit in the church of San Michele at Groppoli in the foothills of the Appennines just west of Pistoia (fig. 11).[23] Dated by inscription to 1193, it depicts on separate panels the *Annunciation* and the *Visitation*. The anomaly occurs on the far right of the *Visitation* panel where Joseph, with an angel perched on his shoulder, leans on a staff. The angel possibly alludes to the *Dream of Joseph*, which takes place after the *Nativity* but before the *Flight into Egypt*. Both scenes appear on the pulpit at Groppoli. Joseph is not, however, normally associated with the *Visitation*.

A related configuration occurs in a panel excavated in 1939 and now immured in a wall in the crypt of the cathedral at Pistoia (fig. 12).[24] Measuring 90 cm × 72 cm × 12 cm, it most likely once belonged to the cathedral's pulpit, dismantled between 1546 and 1563. Although its patterned background is comparable to Guglielmus's pulpit now at Cagliari and to the lintel and capitals at Sant'Andrea, Pistoia, this panel's looser, more monumental style seems to place it in the last decade of the twelfth century.[25] The panel depicts a most unusual *Visitation*. The top border bears an inscription reading: "The infant leaps as the Virgin greets the barren woman."[26] The center of the panel depicts Mary and Elizabeth, who grasp each other's hands but do not embrace; the pose is similar to the *Visitation* on the left capital of Sant'Andrea at Pistoia. At the right of the panel stands a male figure holding a large staff; an angel is perched behind his shoulder in the same configuration as the *Visitation* on the pulpit at San Michele in Groppoli. But because there are no surviving panels at Pistoia relating specifically to this narrative, it cannot be suggested that the figure has perhaps migrated from an adjacent scene as was perhaps the case at Groppoli. The *Visitation* in the cathedral at Pistoia is flanked at the left by a cleric, probably a deacon, holding a book; to my knowledge, this depiction is unique.

The unsigned and recomposed pulpit in the cathedral at Volterra, dating from about 1200, is also part of this series of distinctive depictions of the *Annunciation* and the *Visitation* (fig. 13).[27] One of its three surviving panels depicts both scenes. The names of all five figures are inscribed above their respective heads on the upper edge of the panel: Zechariah, Elizabeth, Mary, Gabriel, Mary. The angel of the *Annunciation* repeats the same curious pose seen at Cagliari and Sant'Andrea, Pistoia, while Zechariah, leaning on a staff, recalls both the left capital of Sant'Andrea at Pistoia and the figure tentatively identified as Joseph standing beside the *Visitation* on the pulpit at Groppoli. In sum, it seems that during approximately four decades, from ca. 1160 until ca. 1200, the *Annunciation* and *Visitation* not only enjoyed great popularity in western Tuscany, but were also depicted in unique ways that are worthy of further exploration.[28]

The lintel of Sant'Andrea at Pistoia depicts, at the left, the Magi's arrival at Herod's court (fig. 4). The crowned Magi are mounted on horseback, thereby signifying their journey, and a messenger kneels before Herod and announces their arrival. The right side of the lintel is occupied by the more traditional scene of the *Adoration of the Magi*. Here, all three Magi stand before the Virgin and child, behind whom stands Joseph leaning on a staff. The star mentioned in the inscription does not appear.[29] This scene is clearly based on Guglielmus's pulpit in Cagliari. Gruamons and Adeodatus learned their lessons well, for all the figures occupy the same positions as Guglielmus's figures and both scenes also share similar decorative backgrounds. At Cagliari, however, the *Adoration of the Magi* reads from right to left, opposite of Sant'Andrea, and the inscriptions on the two monuments are not identical. The left part of the lintel at Sant'Andrea, Pistoia, appears to be a conflation of two panels of the Cagliari pulpit. At Cagliari, an entire panel is devoted to the three Magi on horseback while a second panel depicts them dismounted and standing before Herod. In the latter panel, there is no messenger kneeling before Herod, but two additional figures stand to the right of the Magi.[30]

At Sant'Andrea, Pistoia, the kneeling messenger is a supernumerary figure who is not mentioned in the biblical text relating the episode (Matthew 2:7–12). The messenger appears in no other depiction of the episode known to me.[31] Early on, this kneeling figure was identified by K.A.M. Hartmann as the Nuntius who appears in medieval plays concerning the Magi.[32] The characterization, seconded by Hugo Kehrer and Hans Hofmann,[33] with which I agree, offers a tantalizing clue to the relationship between drama and art in twelfth-century Tuscany, an affiliation enhanced by the observation that the stage directions in the *Ordo ad Representandum Herodem* in the *Fleury Playbook* (Orléans MS. 201) specify that the messenger is to bend his knee as he reports to Herod.[34] In the play Herod is to clasp the messenger's hands between his own in a gesture that may be related to feudal vows.[35]

Saint Augustine averred that the Magi were the first born of the heathen to whom God revealed Himself, for their adoration is their recognition of the son of God manifest in the child.[36] This notion is also contained in one of the lections for Epiphany, Isaiah 60:1–4; therein, the glory of the Lord is revealed:

> Arise, shine; for your light has come, and the glory of the Lord has risen upon you. For, behold, darkness shall cover the earth, and thick darkness the peoples; but the Lord will arise upon you, and his glory will be seen upon you, and nations shall come to your light, and kings to the brightness of your rising. Lift up your eyes round about, and see; they all gather together, they come to you; your sons shall come from far, and your daughters shall be carried in the arms.

The Magi who have seen the light are thus contrasted with Herod still residing in spiritual darkness. An analogy fashioned to contrast the faithful Christians and the faithless Moslems may be intended.

Another unusual aspect of the lintel is seen on the thrones of Herod and the Virgin (figs. 14 and 15). On the former, a dragon is seizing a child, a motif interpreted by Salmi as the soul of Herod in the clutches of a demon.[37] Thus interpreted, the image would parallel related depictions of a devil perched on Herod's shoulder or constituting part of his crown.[38] The image may perhaps also serve as a premonition of the Massacre of the Innocents. On the Virgin's throne, there is a winged figure that flutters freely and appears to be offering a benediction, thereby perhaps suggesting a soul unfettered by guilt.[39] On the Cagliari pulpit, in the scene depicting the *Magi before Herod*, a small naked figure of uncertain identification appears in one of the arcades at the base of Herod's throne.[40]

The decision to depict the *Adoration of the Magi* on the lintel of Sant'Andrea at Pistoia, although clearly based on Guglielmus's dismantled Pisan pulpit now in the cathedral at Cagliari, may also have had a more contemporaneous resonance for the citizens of Pistoia. Bishop Atto, it will be recalled, made Pistoia a pilgrimage center by acquiring from Santiago de Compostela a piece of the head of Saint James a generation before the lintel of Sant'Andrea was sculpted by Gruamons and Adeodatus. The Magi have long been viewed as archetypical pilgrims;[41] indeed, they are sometimes depicted carrying pilgrims' staffs.[42] Their appearance at Pistoia may thus have had enriched associations for the pilgrims visiting there.

Moreover, interest in the Magi and their relics was intense during the seventh decade of the twelfth century, for Frederick Barbarossa, having entered Milan on March 26, 1162, ordered the Magi's relics translated from the vanquished city to Cologne. Little is known of the relics prior to their relocation to Germany. An eleventh-century legend maintains that Bishop Eustorgius of Milan had obtained the relics from Constantinople in the sixth century,[43] but there is no secure evidence for a cult of the Magi in Milan prior to their translation to Cologne.[44] After obtaining the relics of the Magi, on June 11, 1164, Barbarossa gave them to Rainald of Dassel, his chancellor and archbishop of Cologne. Shortly thereafter, on July 23, 1164, the relics arrived in that city, where they were enshrined in the cathedral of Saint Peter,[45] ultimately in a shrine made by Nicholas of Verdun in the 1180s.[46] The transfer of the relics was meant to desacralize Milan and thus minimize the importance of that city.[47] In Cologne, the Magi became the patrons of the city as well as the centerpiece of Barbarossa's imperial propaganda that sought the legitimization of the emperor's temporal sovereignty as it had once been held by Charlemagne. As part of this campaign, Charlemagne was officially canonized by Rainald of Dassel on January 8, 1166. The cult of the Magi at Cologne was to be promulgated like that of Charlemagne at Aachen.[48]

Two capitals in the western apse of the cathedral of Saint Jean at Besançon also suggest the importance of the translation of the relics believed to be those of the Magi. They depict the Magi arriving before Herod and the *Adoration of the Magi*. In the former, the Magi are dressed as pilgrims. The two capitals, believed to have been ordered by Archbishop Herbert who had followed Frederick Barbarossa on his campaign in Italy, are dated stylistically to the third quarter of the twelfth century.[49] Although Rainald of Dassel's precise itinerary is unknown, it is certain that he passed through the Comté, for shortly after leaving Pavia with the relics of the Magi, he announced in Vercelli on June 12 his departure for Cologne by way of Turin and Mont Cenis.[50] Later, in 1189, before departing on the third Crusade, Barbarossa founded an altar in the cathedral at Besançon and had it dedicated to Saint George, certainly an appropriate warrior saint of Eastern origin.[51]

That Pistoia would wish to be associated with the policies of Frederick Barbarossa during this era is not surprising, for the city had remained loyal to the emperor.[52] Indeed, Bishop Traccia who ruled the see from 1153 until 1167 was specially favored by the emperor,[53] and as late as 1181, Frederick was the guest in Pistoia of Bishop Rinaldus.[54] In emphasizing the Magi on the lintel of Sant'Andrea, it is possible that Pistoia also underscored her privileged relationship with the emperor, a union of great importance because Pistoia, given her location, controlled the routes to Bologna and Modena and thus access to the Veneto.

The lintel and capitals of the center portal of Sant'Andrea at Pistoia constitute the earliest historiated portal in western Tuscany. As such, their declarative intent is important for it introduces principles that were elaborated upon and embellished at least until the turn of the thirteenth century in sculpture of the area. That intent is seemingly garbed in easily understood episodes recognized by all classes of the populace: *Annunciations* to the Virgin and Zechariah, the *Visitation*, the *Journey of the Magi*, and the *Adoration of the Magi*. The portal sculpture is significant precisely because it transmutes episodes from the gospels into images that could have been perceived by medieval viewers in terms of events witnessed and known in twelfth-century Pistoia. The stagelike organization of the capitals calls to mind the liturgical drama associated with Epiphany, while the lintel evokes the significance of the relics of the Magi and the importance of the amicable relationship between the Pistoiese and Frederick Barbarossa. In their adoration and participation, the Pistoiese fuse biblical history and contemporary events into a comprehensible whole specifically relevant to time and place.

Chapter Three

Preaching and Serving

SAN BARTOLOMEO IN PANTANO AND
SAN GIOVANNI FUORCIVITAS AT PISTOIA

SAN BARTOLOMEO in Pantano at Pistoia is, in many ways, a close relative of Sant'Andrea in the same city (fig. 16).[1] Both facades are divided into five segments by arches and framed by pilasters. Lions support the center portal archivolt of both churches; at San Bartolomeo in Pantano, the lion at the left grapples with a basilisk while that at the right wrestles with a man. But, at San Bartolomeo in Pantano, the lower part of the facade is not adorned with alternating bands of white marble and *verde di Prato* and the Corinthian capitals under the sculpted lintel at San Bartolomeo in Pantano are not historiated. The narrative is thus confined to the lintel.

San Bartolomeo in Pantano, a Lombard foundation that was throughout the entire high Middle Ages a dependency of San Giovanni Evangelista at Parma, was rebuilt by the priest Buonus in 1159.[2] Its lintel can be dated precisely, for an inscription on the underside of the lintel, that facing the ground (i.e. in the same position as at Sant'Andrea), reads: "The worker Rodolfinus. A.D. 1167."[3] Rodolfinus, not known to have been a sculptor, may perhaps have been the contractor or simply, as the inscription states, a worker.

The lintel of San Bartolomeo has been the subject of scholarly equivocation for two reasons: its subject matter and its attribution (figs. 17 and 18). The iconography is denoted as the *Incredulity of Thomas* (John 20:24–28) or the *Mission of the Apostles* (Matthew 28:16–20). The lintel has been attributed to Guglielmus himself, to Gruamons, as well as to the youthful Biduinus.[4] Stylistically, the patterned background of the lintel firmly places it in the circle of Guglielmus, for such backgrounds are used on both the Cagliari pulpit and the lintel of Sant'Andrea at Pistoia. The three monuments are also linked by the sculptors' propensity for large heads and awkward bodies swathed in heavy drapery. Yet, the figures on the lintel of San Bartolomeo in Pantano are generally more stolid and rectangular and less well articulated than those at Sant'Andrea. In my view, the lintel is not attributable to Guglielmus or to Gruamons, but rather to a more minor figure within that circle. Likewise, the lintel does not bear a convincing resemblance to Biduinus's work in any phase of his career.

At either end of the lintel is an angel framing the twelve apostles. The lower border of the lintel has a damaged one-line inscription; the last name at the far left and the two names at the center are no longer extant. From early records, the inscription has been reconstructed to read:

[Simon] Matthew Philip Matthias Bartholomew [Thomas]
[Jesus] John Peter Andrew Thaddaeus James James.[5]

In contrast to the left to right narrative of Sant'Andrea, the fulcrum of the composition appears at the center of the lintel where Christ, fully dressed and cross-nimbed, stands just to the right of center. He turns toward Saint Thomas and jabs his forefinger at the saint as if forcefully making a point. Clearly, Thomas is not probing Christ's wounds with his finger, as is conventional in depictions of the *Incredulity of Thomas*. Five apostles stand to the left of Thomas and six to the right of Christ, making a total of twelve; all hold scrolls or books. In sum, the relationship between Christ and Thomas at the center of the lintel suggests the *Incredulity of Thomas*, but the requisite actions are not depicted. The event portrayed must, however, postdate Christ's Passion, for Matthias rather than Judas is among the apostles.[6]

The mystery concerning the subject matter of the lintel of San Bartolomeo in Pantano is illuminated by a close reading of the inscription, partly gibberish or simply poor Latin, on the upper edge of the lintel:

Peace to you. I am I. I provide that by which it may be most firm. Look twice discerningly because I am God. Behold, see and touch me. In this way you ought love. Diseases having been driven out throughout the four quarters of the world. Convert the whole world [which is] washed by the holy fountain.[7]

The phrase "Behold, see and touch me"[8] clearly alludes to the *Incredulity of Thomas* and may explain the juxtaposition of Christ and Thomas at the center of the lintel. The remainder of the inscription seems to refer to the rarely depicted *Mission of the Apostles* for, in the inscription, Christ also urges the apostles to go to the four corners of the earth to spread his word.

It is, rather, through the inscription that we are meant to understand that both the *Incredulity of Thomas* and the *Mission of the Apostles* are intended. The union of the two scenes in this fashion is singular and the inscription is not a literal rendition of the biblical accounts of either event. Likewise, the specific use of the verb "convertit" does not appear in the biblical accounts and may be an allusion to one of the stated purposes of the crusades.

The *Incredulity of Thomas* is a subject closely associated with the Holy Land; it appears on a capital probably from the church of the Annunciation at Nazareth as well as on the famed ampullae from the Holy Land now at Monza and Bobbio.[9] Organized vertically, as seen for example in the famed ivory from Trier-Echternach, the scene is fraught with dramatic possibilities; Thomas fervently jabs his finger into Christ's wound thereby intensifying and focussing the emotion.[10] Sometimes, as in the scene depicted in the lower cloister of the monastery at Silos, the exchange between Thomas and Christ is framed by the other apostles, the format approximated at San Bartolomeo in Pantano.[11]

There is, however, one significant local parallel for the *Incredulity of Thomas*: the lintel of the now suppressed church of Sant'Ilario at Piacenza (fig. 19).[12] Believed to have been sculpted by a follower of Nicholaus,[13] the lintel depicts Christ in the center holding aloft a book in his left hand and raising his right arm so that Thomas, bending low, can probe his wound. There are four apostles flanking Thomas and six flanking Christ. The absence of Matthias, the apostle elected to replace Judas, differentiates the lintel from that at San Bartolomeo in Pantano.

At Sant'Ilario, the book held by Christ is inscribed "Because I am myself, touch and see."[14] On the lower edge of the lintel, the gravely deteriorated and scarcely discernible inscription, only partially decipherable, reads "Do not fear but [see or touch?] the wound on my side."[15]

The inscriptions at Sant'Ilario are thus partially related to those on the lintel of San Bartolomeo in Pantano. The two lintels are the only Italian ones of which I am aware that depict the *Incredulity of Thomas*. The connection between the lintel of San Bartolomeo in Pantano and that of Sant'Ilario at Piacenza is notable for the two cities are separated by sixty kilometers of torturous Appennines terrain. That Pistoia is on the old Roman Via Cassia rather than on the Via Francigena,[16] suggests that the latter was not the only means by which artistic influence was transmitted. The inscription on the lintel of Sant'Ilario at Piacenza is also significant because, with the exception of the word CUNCTIS, the inscription duplicates a portion of the text of *Peregrinus*, a liturgical drama contained in the *Fleury Playbook* and performed on Easter Monday.[17]

The unusual horizontal arrangement of the scenes at San Bartolomeo in Pantano at Pistoia is reminiscent of Early Christian sarcophagi.[18] Several depict the *Mission of the Apostles*: those in the Musée Lapidaire at Arles, in the cathedral at Ancona, in Sant'Ambrogio at Milan and in Aix-en-Provence, to name just a few (fig. 20).[19] In all cases, Christ is centralized and flanked by the apostles as he instructs them to go forth and preach his word. While the lintel of San Bartolomeo in Pantano differs from the Early Christian depictions in that Christ is not standing on a mound, the frieze-like arrangement, the horizontal shape, and the rather severe processional quality of the composition reveal the lintel's parentage, a lineage not uncommon in Romanesque Tuscany.

The *Mission of the Apostles*, although not regularly depicted in the West between the Early Christian era and the twelfth century, appeared significantly in Rome in the triclinium of Leo III (795–816) in the Lateran Palace.[20] The mosaic was still extant in the seventeenth century when it was copied and described by Grimaldi.[21] It depicted Christ standing on a hillock from which flowed the four rivers of paradise. In his left hand, he held an open book and he blessed with his right hand; he was accompanied by the apostles. The inscription below the figures is taken from Matthew 28:19–20:

> Go ye therefore and teach all the nations, baptizing them in the name of the Father, and of the Son, and of the Holy Ghost, and teaching them to observe all that I have commanded you; and lo, I am with you always, to the close of the age.

Leo III's mosaic thus followed the iconography of Early Christian sarcophagi, as does the lintel of San Bartolomeo in Pantano where both the reliance on tradition and the conservatism are noteworthy.

The local context of the Pistoian lintel is further enriched by examination of the now dismantled pulpit in San Bartolomeo in Pantano that is attributed to Guido da Como and dated to 1250.[22] One panel depicts the *Appearance of Christ to the Apostles* above the *Incredulity of Thomas* (fig. 21). The panel is inscribed on the top:

> Here (the wound) is laid bare, shown before the sight of the apostles.
> Thomas who was not there does not believe any of them.[23]

and on the bottom:

He tells the disciples that He is Christ, and Thomas believes everything when he touches; the mouth[s] of those who err is [are] stopped.[24]

That is, in the upper part of the panel, Christ appears to the apostles, but Thomas is not present.[25] In the lower section, Thomas probes Christ's wound to convince himself that Christ has indeed risen. The inscriptions relate the events, but are not quoted from a specific biblical or liturgical text.[26] I know of no other example of the juxtaposition of these two events on a pulpit. The two episodes are joined, however, in liturgical drama as seen in the text of the expanded version of the *Peregrinus*. Karl Young aptly summarizes the final moments of the drama:

> After the usual message has been reported to Thomas, Christ enters saying "Pax vobis" three times, the chorus responding with suitable sentences from the Psalms. He convinces Thomas by showing His wounds, and then charges the disciples to preach the Gospel throughout the world.[27]

Here, then, unlike in the Gospels, the *Doubting Thomas* and the *Mission of the Apostles* appear together as on the lintel of San Bartolomeo in Pantano. Like the pendant scenes comprising the capitals at Sant'Andrea at Pistoia and the Nuntius on the lintel of the same church, so here too, the liturgical drama appears to have been influential. The church of San Bartolomeo in Pantano at Pistoia seems to have displayed an uncommon amount of interest for more than seven decades in scenes rarely depicted in Italian medieval sculpture, for they appear on its lintel and, less than a century later, on its pulpit.

The notion of the significance of the *Mission of the Apostles* was deeply rooted in Christianity from its earliest years. Isaiah's second prophecy (52:7–11) was viewed by early Christian writers as a prediction of the *Mission of the Apostles*:

> How beautiful upon the mountains are the feet of him who brings good tidings, who publishes peace, who brings good tidings of good, who publishes salvation, who says to Zion, "Your God reigns."
>
> Hark, your watchmen lift up their voice, together they sing for joy; for eye to eye they see the return of the Lord to Zion.
>
> Break forth together into singing, you waste places of Jerusalem; for the Lord has comforted his people, he has redeemed Jerusalem.
>
> The Lord has bared his holy arm before the eyes of all the nations; and all the ends of the earth shall see the salvation of our God.

Depart, depart, go out thence, touch no unclean thing; go out from the midst of her, purify yourselves, you who bear the vessels of the Lord.

And Saint Jerome, in his *Commentaria in Isaiam*, states that Isaiah's prophecy:

makes it clear that the spiritual Jerusalem, namely the church, was erected by the apostles . . . the arm of the Lord is revealed to all the nations and that all of the ends of the earth see His salvation.[28]

Jerome then goes on to relate Isaiah's prophecy to the command that Christ gave to the apostles (Matthew 28:19): "Go ye therefore and teach all the nations, baptizing them in the name of the Father, and of the Son, and of the Holy Ghost."

That the meaning of Jerome's commentary continued to be understood in the era of the crusades is evidenced by Raymond of Aguilers, a participant in the first crusade who, when referring to July 15, 1099, noted:

On this day, moreover, the apostles were cast forth from Jerusalem and scattered over the whole world. On this same day the children of the apostles regained the city and fatherland for God and the fathers.[29]

The crusaders, identified as "children of the apostles," were thus meant to go forth and rescue anew Jerusalem from the infidels. Western Tuscans, long concerned with matters in the East, would surely have understood the contemporary meaning of the scenes depicted on the unusual lintel of San Bartolomeo in Pantano.

The Lombards also founded San Giovanni Fuorcivitas outside the walls of Pistoia in the eighth century.[30] Rebuilt in the mid-twelfth century, it was again enlarged in the second half of the fourteenth century (fig. 22). Its long, north flank contains, in the sixth bay from the west, a portal signed "The good master Gruamons made this work."[31] This inscription appears on the individual pieces of the alternating white marble and *verde di Prato* of the archivolt (fig. 23).[32] Gruamons is the same sculptor who, with his brother Adeodatus, carved the lintel of Sant'Andrea in Pistoia. At San Giovanni Fuorcivitas, however, the date is not indicated.

The lower parts of the north flank and portal at San Giovanni Fuorcivitas resemble those of Sant'Andrea in the same city. A pilaster frames each end of the structure, while the entire surface is animated by arches dividing the exterior into individual bays punctuated by the characteristic three-step inserted diamond. As at Sant'Andrea, the double archivolt, composed of one band of acanthus and one of alternating green and white stones, is supported by two lions; that at the left struggles with a bear and that at the right wrestles with a man. San Giovanni Fuorcivitas also resembles San Bartolomeo in Pantano in that there are no heads at the lower ends of each side of the archivolt and the capitals beneath the sculpted lintel are not historiated.

The lintel of Gruamons's portal depicts the *Last Supper*: it has the carved, patterned background favored by Guglielmus and his school.[33] The greater fluidity of the style intimates a later date than Sant'Andrea and San Bartolomeo in Pantano, perhaps ca. 1180, but it is difficult to be more precise.[34] The cloister, on the south side of the church, was most likely built at the same time that the lintel was carved.[35] This additional work may have been made possible by the newfound prosperity resulting from the monastery's association with the cathedral at Prato which began on March 4, 1119, and continued until the second half of the thirteenth century.[36]

Sitting behind a table that extends the entire length of the lintel are shown eleven apostles and Christ. At the center, John leans on Christ's breast as the latter reaches across the table to offer the sop to the kneeling Judas. The moment depicted then is the identification of Judas as the traitor who will betray Christ, as related in John 13:21–30. Yet the now virtually eradicated inscription that spans the length of the upper edge of the lintel does not describe the event depicted but instead states the meaning of Christ's action:

> While He is eating, Christ gives the disciples the words of greeting.
> While He is eating, He gives the new law and ends the old.[37]

In other words, the institution of the eucharist symbolizes the end of the old order and the beginning of the new order, an idea evoked by Luke in his account of the *Last Supper* (Luke 22:20–21):

> This cup which is poured out for you is the new covenant in my blood.
> But behold the hand of him who betrays me is with me on the table.

The solemn, theological character of the inscription is amplified and reinforced by the arrangement of the *Last Supper* on the lintel of San Giovanni Fuorcivitas. Other than the center vignette composed of Christ, John, and Judas, the remaining apostles sit solemnly erect at their places that are, in turn, clearly defined by the catenary folds of the tablecloth. Their subdued gestures are contained within the outlines of their bodies and the pristine table is not strewn with the various culinary implements that often appear in representations of the *Last Supper*. The pervasive mood is one of reverential stillness.

The *Last Supper*, so often painted in Italian refectories during the Renaissance,[38] rarely adorns the lintels of Italian medieval churches; indeed, it does not appear on a lintel elsewhere in Romanesque central and northern Italy.[39] Rather, the *Last Supper* is depicted most often on interior liturgical furnishings as seen for instance on the virtually contemporaneous *pontile* in the cathedral at Modena,[40] as well as in Tuscany, on the dismantled pulpit in the cathedral at Pistoia, the aforementioned pulpit by Guglielmus now at Cagliari, and on the recomposed pulpit in the cathedral at Volterra (fig. 24).[41] Only the Cagliari pulpit predates the lintel at San Giovanni Fuorcivitas. The distinctive arrangement of the *Last Supper* on the lintel of San Giovanni Fuorcivitas emerges clearly when it is contrasted with the three aforementioned pulpit panels where, in the Byzantine mode, Christ appears at one end of the table where Judas also kneels; the table is cluttered.[42] The inscription on the Last Supper on the Cagliari pulpit is merely descriptive: "While He dines, He gives himself as a symbol to Judas to eat."[43]

At Cagliari and especially at Volterra, the *Last Supper* is made more dramatic by the presence of the serpentlike figure denoting evil. On the Cagliari panel, the small figure seemingly floats above the prostrate Judas, while at Volterra, a beast larger than Judas bears down upon him and dominates the lower part of the front plane of the composition. In a broad sense, Judas is identified with evil; in a more literal sense, the presence of the serpent literally illustrates John 13:26–27:

> So when he dipped the morsel, he gave it to Judas, the son of Simon Iscariot. Then after the morsel, Satan entered into him.

This device is similar to that used at Sant'Andrea at Pistoia where the small devil depicted on the side of Herod's throne serves to mark him as wicked. In both instances, the devil draws the viewer to the scene by strongly contrasting the good and evil protagonists: Herod countering the Virgin and Child, Judas countering Christ.

The *Last Supper* on the lintel of San Giovanni Fuorcivitas at Pistoia also differs from French depictions where the Last Supper appears most prominently on mid- to late-twelfth-century sculpted lintels in Provence, such as at Saint-Gilles-du-Gard, Condrieu, and Beaucaire.[44] The three French depictions are similar to each other but differ in substantive ways from the lintel at San Giovanni Fuorcivitas. In all the Provençal lintels, Judas is seated on the same side of the table as Christ. The table is set with utensils and food; the apostles react physically to Christ's words. Moreover, as at Condrieu, for example, the *Last Supper* on the lintel is associated with a scene in the tympanum, in this case the *Crucifixion*.[45]

The unique solemnity of the lintel at San Giovanni Fuorcivitas, as well as its independence from a more comprehensive *Passion* cycle encourage speculation, for as Léon Pressouyre has noted, the scene is also an exemplum of the communal meal and was frescoed in the refectories of San Paolo fuori le Mura at Rome and Saint Martin at Dover as well as sculpted on the tympanum of Saint-Bénigne, Dijon.[46] Because San Giovanni Fuorcivitas was situated on a major medieval road through Pistoia, it is likely that passersby, especially pilgrims, were meant to perceive the significance of the new order stated in the inscription as they proceeded toward Rome, Santiago de Compostela, or Jerusalem. The liturgical meal would thus indicate to the weary traveller that the monastery also served as a hospice for those making the long journey. Carra Ferguson O'Meara makes a parallel suggestion in regard to Saint-Gilles-du-Gard, so prominent on the Via Tolosana, the southernmost route to Santiago de Compostela. She notes that, as part of the reform at Saint-Gilles, some of that wealthy abbey's funds were stipulated for charity; the monks were to feed thirteen paupers in the refectory each day, a number clearly evoking the *Last Supper*. And, at the same French church, the feeding of the poor was conducted annually on Holy Thursday in front of the edifice.[47] Hence, the public statement made on the lintel of San Giovanni Fuorcivitas serves to define the work of the monks resident there. The charity of the monks of San Giovanni Fuorcivitas additionally served as an example to the laity.[48]

The extensive work at Sant'Andrea, San Bartolomeo in Pantano, and San Giovanni Fuorcivitas is but part of the considerable number of building projects undertaken in Pistoia during the second half of the twelfth century. Also of note are the second ring of the city walls indicative of a growing and prosperous city and the aforementioned chapel to house the relic of Saint James in the cathedral.[49] A hospice to accommodate the pilgrims who came to worship that famed relic was established in 1148, and donations for such projects began to appear in wills.[50] This sort of activity also required vast amounts of building material; hence quarries were acquired at Gugliano, about ten kilometers northwest of Lucca, in 1163 and 1173.[51]

Because Bishop Atto had had the sagacity to acquire a piece of the head of Saint James from Santiago de Compostela, Pistoia became a part of the far-flung pilgrimage network comprising the Holy Land, Rome, and Santiago de Compostela. Visitors drawn by the Volto Santo at Lucca needed to travel only a few kilometers on the Via Cassia to arrive at Pistoia. Indeed, documents indicate that an exceptional number of pilgrims from all over Europe visited Pistoia; there is also ample evidence that Italians journeyed to Santiago de Compostela. Of the twenty-two miracles reported in the *Liber Sancti Jacobi*, four specifically concern Italian pilgrims, and the *Historia Compostelana* reports the existence of an Italian confraternity of ex-pilgrims to Santiago de Compostela founded in 1120.[52] Pistoia's distance from the Via Francigena seems not to have impoverished its significant role as a pilgrimage center.

Chapter Four

Marching to Jerusalem

PROCESSION AND INTERCESSION

THE WORK of Gruamons and Adeodatus in Pistoia is strongly dependent both stylistically and iconographically on the work of Guglielmus, their master. Their roots in his Pisan workshop are clear. Another sculptor associated with the extensive twelfth-century work on the Pisa cathedral complex is Biduinus, but compared to Gruamons and Adeodatus, he seems to be a somewhat younger and more independent figure.[1] His only work that is both signed and dated is the lintel of the center portal of the west facade of the *pieve* of San Cassiano a Settimo, a dependency of the bishop of Pisa during the Middle Ages, located a few kilometers southeast of Pisa (figs. 25–27).[2] Some of the *pieve*'s interior capitals have also been attributed to Biduinus.

The center lintel depicts the *Entry into Jerusalem*,[3] as well as the *Raising of Lazarus* (John 11:1–44) and a scene heretofore identified as the *Healing of the Blind*. The sarcophagus from which Lazarus rises bears an inscription: "Biduinus did in learned fashion this work you see,"[4] while a more lengthy inscription on the upper edge of the lintel reads, "1180 years have passed after the time when God was born of the Virgin."[5] The lintel was thus sculpted by Biduinus in 1180, the year in which one Amatus is documented as *pievano*.[6]

The north lintel of the facade of San Cassiano a Settimo depicts a procession of animals, some real and some mythical, accompanied by two shepherds (fig. 28). The south lintel portrays two confronting griffins on either side of a rather forlorn ram (fig. 29). These animal friezes are directly comparable to two friezes on each side of a door at the lowest level of the campanile of the cathedral at Pisa. Beneath one of the campanile reliefs is the date 1174 (fig. 30). Biduinus has also been credited with a similar animal frieze at the top of the first story of Pisa's cathedral.[7] It is thus generally accepted that Biduinus was trained in Pisa and, like Gruamons and Adeodatus, later left to pursue other commissions in western Tuscany.

The center lintel at San Cassiano a Settimo is dense and muddled. At the far left, on a separate block, is depicted the so-called *Healing of the Blind*. Reading from left to right, the *Raising of Lazarus* and the *Entry into Jerusalem*, both carved from the same block, follow. At the far left of this second block, immediately before the *Raising of Lazarus*, is a curious two-storied tower; a male pulling his beard and looking upward stands on the lower floor, while two figures stand between the turrets above. The *Raising of Lazarus* is joined subtly to the *Entry into Jerusalem*.[8] The penultimate apostle in the procession toward Jerusalem holds a palm frond over his right shoulder and turns toward the *Raising of Lazarus*. The last apostle in the cortege has turned completely from the cavalcade and, instead, supports Lazarus who stands upright in his sarcophagus. An angel, opposite the apostle, kneels on the top of the sarcophagus and reaches toward Lazarus thereby framing him effectively. To the left of the angel, a compositional fulcrum is provided by two vignettes. In the background, a plump, bearded figure looks toward Christ while resting his chin on his left hand and pointing toward the *Raising of Lazarus* with his right. This figure is probably Simon or another Pharisee who, according to the biblical text, witnessed the scene.[9] In front of the Pharisee, Mary and Martha kneel while supplicating Christ, who holds a double-barred cross in his left hand, rather than the thaumaturgic rod seen in earlier medieval depictions; with his right hand, he extends a blessing in the direction of Lazarus.

The center lintel at San Cassiano a Settimo is characterized by slender figures placed against a plain background, albeit now discolored. The vinelike pattern so prominent in the backgrounds of the works of Guglielmus and his most immediate disciples, Gruamons and Adeodatus, is nowhere evident. The figures, whose primary articulation is seen in their knees, are rather staid and lack the awkward, angular movements of many of the figures carved by Gruamons and Adeodatus. Their bodily stillness, emphasized by the regular repetition of drapery folds, is perhaps their primary stylistic feature.

The depiction of the *Raising of Lazarus* on the lintel at San Cassiano a Settimo is a logical choice, for the scene immediately precedes the *Entry into Jerusalem* in the gospel of John; moreover, the Lazarus episode takes place in Bethany, less than a kilometer from Bethpage, where the original procession toward Jerusalem began. The *Raising of Lazarus*, in the Greek church, is one of the twelve great feasts and is celebrated on the day before Palm Sunday.[10] The propinquity of the two events is evidenced by the tenth-century Romano-German pontifical, in which it is noted that a hymn concerning the *Raising of Lazarus* is sung during the Palm Sunday procession.[11] The Romano-German pontifical was, not surprisingly, known at least in Lucca from an early date;[12] indeed, Rangerius of Lucca, commented with pride on the liturgy of his native city: "It brings together both festival customs and stations, [a thing] which is not [the case with] all Tuscan churches."[13]

The *Raising of Lazarus* may be read at a number of relevant levels, not the least of which is its parallel with the *Resurrection of Christ*. As the *Entry into Jerusalem* begins Christ's Passion, it is well to remember that he will rise again. This notion is clearly evident in the text of the *Raising of Lazarus* that appears in the twelfth-century *Fleury Playbook*. There, at the beginning of the procession and after each stanza, the choir sings, "Oh, sons and daughters. The King of heaven, the King of glory rose from death today. Hallelujah!"[14] The Fleury play, which departs from the text of the Bible in many instances, emphasizes both Christ's humanity and his cosmic power;[15] Lazarus is thus an apt parallel to Christ's human aspects.

The signed and dated lintel from San Cassiano a Settimo must be viewed together with the lintel from Sant'Angelo in Campo now in the Palazzo Mazzarosa in Lucca (fig. 31).[16] Signed "This work was made by Master Biduinus,"[17] it too depicts the *Entry into Jerusalem*; no date is given. There are so many fundamental iconographical and even formal differences between the two lintels that, were they not both signed by Biduinus, one would be hard put to attribute them to the same sculptor. In the Lucchese lintel, three youths prepare to throw branches from the palm tree, and two figures place cloths on the ground in front of Christ while a third prepares to do so. Peter, bearing the keys, stands third in line behind Christ and hence does not lead the procession as he does at San Cassiano a Settimo. The apostles, some of whom hold palms and such liturgical objects as censers, form a liturgical procession, while the context of the apostles at San Cassiano al Settimo is more faithful to the narrative, for they hold only palms. At the far left of the Lucchese lintel, at the end of the apostles' cortege, the archangel Michael treads upon a very large serpent. Clearly, the image is meant to signify Sant'Angelo, the patron saint of the church for which the lintel is believed to have been carved.[18]

But the iconographical differences between the lintel now in the Palazzo Mazzarosa and that still *in situ* on the center portal of San Cassiano a Settimo pale in comparison to their stylistic differences. The former is clearly both more crude and more movemented. Its ground line is simply the bottom of the lintel and all twelve apostles follow behind Christ with movements that can only be characterized as abrupt and jerky; their heads are large and often awkwardly related to their bodies, the hips emphasized by the drapery folds. Though more slender than the figures on Gruamons's and Adeodatus's Pistoian lintels, Biduinus's apostles on the lintel from Sant'Angelo in Campo are similarly awkward and disjointed. Lacking documentation, the usual evolutionary approach would suggest that the lintel from Sant'Angelo in Campo predates that at San Cassiano a Settimo. Yet, simplification and greater movement is often characteristic of later work.

The relative chronology of the lintels from Sant'Angelo in Campo and at San Cassiano a Settimo is but one issue. Equally troubling is the seemingly abrupt change in Biduinus's style. It must be remembered, however, that the eclectic nature of Pisan culture did not encourage consistency of style. The influence of antiquity was mediated by both Byzantine and Islamic art as well as by work in other media such as Bonanus's bronze doors for the cathedral at Pisa.[19] Indeed, the Byzantine style, as evidenced by the early thirteenth-century work on the east portal of the baptistery and on the facade of San Michele degli Scalzi, both at Pisa,[20] co-exists with the classicizing style based on the close study of Roman antiquity. Moreover, Biduinus was farther removed from the work of Guglielmus. Biduinus's style seems to be more varied, perhaps because of his awareness of the continuing work on the cathedral complex at Pisa during the latter part of the twelfth century.

The portal from San Leonardo al Frigido, now at The Cloisters in New York, has also been attributed to Biduinus (figs. 32–34). The small and now much-restored church of San Leonardo al Frigido is just southeast of Carrara and outside the town of Massa in northwest Tuscany; the church lies on the banks of its eponym, the Frigido River.[21] The Frigido is now a murky stream clogged with industrial effluvium, while the nearby town of Massa is primarily devoted to the marble trade. Once, however, the area's beauty inspired Petrarch to note ecstatically in his diary of a journey from Marseilles to Naples, "Thence [flows] a river, cold in both fact and name, its water and sand shining; lower down it descends [into] the very pleasant country of Massa,"[22] while Repetti, writing in the 1830s referred to Massa as the "Nice of our Tuscany."[23]

The site, known as the Taberna Frigida in the Roman era, was first mentioned in pilgrimage literature in the account of Philip Augustus's return from the Holy Land in 1191.[24] San Leonardo al Frigido is less than twenty kilometers from Luni, as the twelfth-century Icelandic pilgrim Abbot Nikulas of Munkathvera noted, in which all roads leading north from Italy and ultimately to Santiago de Compostela joined.[25] The propinquity of San Leonardo al Frigido to the nexus of Italian medieval trade and travel lifts the portal from an obscure provincial monument to one of great significance, despite the fact that the heavily restored church, bombed during World War II, is a mere fifteen meters long and half as wide. The continuing importance of the location during the later Middle Ages is indicated by the fact that between 1218 and 1225, the churches of San Giovanni and San Sepolcro at Pisa contested for control of the hospice on the site of San Leonardo.[26]

The portal from San Leonardo al Frigido consists of a lintel depicting the *Entry into Jerusalem* placed on two capitals portraying apes (fig. 32).[27] The left doorpost has framed vignettes of both the *Annunciation* and the *Visitation*, while the right doorpost has a large figure of Saint Leonard holding the small figure of a prisoner. The recarved, postmedieval bases of both doorposts depict animals. Removed from its provenance and sold by a Florentine dealer, the portal was integrated into the Countess Benkendorf-Schouvaloff's Villa Monticello outside Nice during the late nineteenth century;[28] subsequently, it was purchased by The Cloisters in 1962 and first published by the museum in 1965.[29]

The figure of Saint Leonard, extending the entire length of the right doorpost, is, to my knowledge, highly unusual, all the more so since the left doorpost houses two distinct scenes. The presence of the French saint whose relics are housed at the abbey of Noblat is, however, explicable, for his cult was disseminated especially by the Benedictines of the abbey at Farfa in the Sabina south of Tuscany.[30] He was, *inter alia*, the patron saint of prisoners and is thus shown here holding a freed prisoner.[31] The mid-twelfth-century doorposts, recarved sarcophagi of *bardiglio nero* rather than marble, do not elicit persuasive stylistic comparanda in either Tuscany or Liguria, where figural sculpture did not flourish until the mid-twelfth century when Guglielmus and his school became active. Rather, the doorposts seem to resemble most closely a capital depicting Samson and Delilah on the exterior of the north apse at the cathedral at Parma (fig. 36).[32] The shapes of the heads, the features, and the articulation of the drapery are all comparable and suggest a date perhaps in the second third of the twelfth century. Such stylistic analogies are not surprising for it need only be remembered that the Via Francigena, the famed pilgrimage road leading to Rome, traversed in part a route from Piacenza, approximately fifty kilometers northwest of Parma, to Pontremoli, just north of San Leonardo al Frigido. Similarly, as noted earlier, a capital on the facade of the cathedral at Parma seems to have influenced the iconography of the *Visitation* capital at Sant'Andrea, Pistoia, perhaps by way of the cathedral at Carrara.[33]

The two ape capitals, carved from marble, as is the lintel, are easier to place in a satisfactory stylistic context, especially when it is remembered that the school of sculptors responsible for the lintels discussed here had its origins in Pisa. The ape capitals closely resemble a capital formerly on the campanile of the cathedral at Pisa (figs. 34 and 35).[34] Now in the collection of the Schloss-Glienicke in Berlin, the capital is iconographically and stylistically akin to the two capitals on the portal from San Leonardo al Frigido.[35] The depiction of apes in Romanesque sculpture is not highly unusual, for by the twelfth century they had become a familiar sight in western Europe and sculpted examples appear, *inter alia*, in Spain at Santiago de Compostela; at San Isidoro, Léon; at San Martin at Fromista; as well as at Jaca and Loarre. In France, apes can be found depicted at Saint Sernin at Toulouse, Saint-Gilles-du-Gard, and at Morlaas in the Basses-Pyrénées, and in Italy, in addition to Pisa, at the abbey of Sant'Antimo, also in Tuscany. Indeed, the ape may be viewed as but one exemplar of the greater knowledge of things foreign that was engendered by both the Crusades and pilgrimage, an era during which both apes and their trainers were imported from the East.[36]

After noting the presence of apes in Mediterranean Romanesque sculpture, one must also examine their complex and multifarious meaning. W. C. McDermott notes that in antiquity, apes were widely owned as pets and that those which appear in ancient art tied by chains or leashes or with collars around their necks are invariably pets.[37] Gregory of Nazianzus (ca. 330–ca. 390), on the contrary, understood the animal as evil, for he characterized pagans as apes.[38] Similarly, Janson argues that the Pisan ape capital from the campanile, inspired by a French prototype, betokens evil because it is chained and the chain is held in the beak of a demon's head.[39] Yet, in the same era, apes were used in theatrical performances and were owned by people in all walks of life.[40] The two capitals on the portal from San Leonardo al Frigido likewise seem to evoke a series of interpretations. That on the right depicts one ape seemingly feeding himself and the other having its left ear nibbled at by a basilisk, an imaginary creature associated with evil. The creatures on the left capital have tails and may more properly be called monkeys. The belts or leashes around their waists may indicate that they are pets. Hence, like the written lore that accompanies and precedes them, it would appear that the apes on the portal from San Leonardo al Frigido embody a number of meanings.

On the lintel from San Leonardo al Frigido, Christ rides astride an ass that is followed by a colt. The reins of the ass are held by a male figure and the group is approaching two figures who place garments on the ground to honor Christ while four youths in a tree prepare to throw palm leaves at the approaching entourage. Behind the ass bearing Christ are eleven apostles, the first of which is clearly Peter for he holds a large key in his right hand. The remaining, smaller figure at the end of the procession is tonsured, wears a turned-down hood, and carries a staff. It is generally agreed that he is Saint Leonard to whom the church is dedicated. Saint Leonard, like Saint Michael on the lintel from Sant'Angelo in Campo, is thus elevated to the status of the apostles as he proceeds with them toward Jerusalem. The apostles themselves serve dual roles. Most of them carry or once carried the palms expected in the *Entry into Jerusalem*, but those in the front row additionally bear a scroll, a book, or a censer as, with mouths wide open, they sing intensely. This community of apostles, as those on the lintel from Sant'Angelo in Campo, may thus be viewed as a liturgical procession.

The undated lintel of the portal from San Leonardo al Frigido has been attributed to Biduinus perhaps because its subject matter, the *Entry into Jerusalem*, is the same as the two lintels signed by him; similarly, it is from western Tuscany and shares a generally classicizing style. Moreover, the ape capitals, comparable to that formerly on the campanile at Pisa, where Biduinus worked at the lower levels, bring the upper parts of the portal from San Leonardo al Frigido into his circle and suggest a date between approximately 1175 and 1185. Of the two lintels signed by Biduinus, that at San Cassiano a Settimo is more similar to the lintel from San Leonardo al Frigido. In both, the apostles are relatively still, the shapes of the heads analogous, and the repetitious drapery folds related. At San Leonardo al Frigido, however, the carving of the drapery is very much on the surface, the folds broader, and there is less attempt to create a scene by the use of a ground line or foliage. The attribution to Biduinus himself, while possible, is to my eye unconvincing. The lintel does not resemble the work of any other known sculptor of the era, but may perhaps be attributed to an anonymous sculptor in the circle of Biduinus.

The fact that Saint Leonard appears twice on the portal, on the lintel as well as on the right doorpost, may indicate a program carved at two different times. The presence of Saint Leonard among the apostles on the lintel nonetheless suggests a degree of participation that is worthy of note. Not only is the humble saint included among the apostles, but also those viewing the portal could metaphorically join their local saint on the journey to Jerusalem and thereby participate in the momentous events of the era. Thus Saint Leonard functions in the same way that Saint Michael does on the lintel from Sant'Angelo in Campo. In both cases, the patron saint serves as the local reference to a specific event that took place outside the locale.

The aforementioned consistent position of the patron saint on the lintels from San Leonardo al Frigido and Sant'Angelo in Campo urges a reexamination of the so-called *Healing of the Blind* at the far left of the lintel of the center portal of San Cassiano a Settimo (fig. 27). Close scrutiny of the vignette reveals several oddities. Unlike the figure of Christ in the adjoining scene of the *Raising of Lazarus*, here Christ neither has a nimbus nor carries a cross. And, of the two supposedly blind men that Christ is about to heal, one is holding an open book. The episode is reminiscent of the depiction of Grammar among the liberal arts in the archivolt of the south portal of the west facade at Chartres cathedral (fig. 37). In sum, it would seem that the scene at San Cassiano a Settimo has been previously and consistently misidentified. For instead of Christ, the large figure at the left of the vignette should be identified as Saint Cassian of Imola, the schoolmaster celebrated by Prudentius to whom the church is dedicated.[41] He, alas, met an ignoble end for he was stabbed to death by his own students who, on the lintel, appear before him prepared for their lessons. The proper identification of the scene at the far left of the lintel of San Cassiano a Settimo suggests that the three lintels depicting the *Entry into Jerusalem* share a common practice. That is, the lintels are localized by the insertion of a saint doubtless familiar to local citizens. Through the patron saint, the viewer participates in the more universal Christian event, the *Entry into Jerusalem*. This sort of paraliturgical activity, often mimetic, appears to be central to Tuscan medieval religious practice, and may, indeed, anticipate the *lauda* performed later by confraternities.[42]

Chapter Five

Sailing from Byzantium

THE EFFICACY OF SAINT NICHOLAS

Aൗൺൾ Romanesque churches abound in both Pisa and Lucca, there is little figurative architectural sculpture in either city. Indeed, in the latter, San Salvatore in Mustiola, documented from the eleventh century, is the only church bearing narrative lintels (fig. 38).[1] The lintel over the door in the south flank depicts the *Bath of Saint Nicholas*, when, just hours after his birth, he stood upright and unsupported in the bath (fig. 39). The south, or right, lintel of the west facade depicts the story of the *Son of Getron*, one of the posthumous miracles performed by Saint Nicholas,[2] which is also among the four plays concerning the saint in the *Fleury Playbook* (fig. 40). The other two facade lintels are not sculpted.

The *Bath of Saint Nicholas* is signed by Biduinus.[3] On the round tub in which Saint Nicholas stands are inscribed the words "Biduinus made me, this work."[4] The inscription on the background itself, in the area of the basin, identifies the central figure as "Saint Nicholas presbyter,"[5] thus identifying the subject. Like Biduinus's signed lintel from Sant'Angelo in Campo, now in the Palazzo Mazzarosa in Lucca, the south flank lintel of San Salvatore in Mustiola is not dated. The nimbed infant Saint Nicholas stands upright with arms in orant position in a curved tub having rings for handles. A servant at each side, dipping a knee gracefully, holds onto the tub with one hand while delicately touching one of Saint Nicholas's elbows with the other. This scene is framed on each side by an extraordinarily detailed architectural representation. That on the left consists of a file of five twisted columns. A dome is centered on the middle three columns and is flanked at each side by a turret inhabited by one figure. Beneath the dome, a tonsured cleric appears to be holding a book, while the adjoining compartment contains a bell, or perhaps a lamp, supported on a transverse bar. The figure in the turret at the left brandishes a cross, while that in the right turret gestures with his right hand. The structure occupying the right third of the lintel is virtually identical to that at the far left; it is, however, more fully occupied. At the lower level, divided into four compartments, a man situated at the far left holds a narrow scroll. The center two compartments are occupied by a bear and a lion who confront each other on either side of a column. The figure at the far right holds a staff and faces Nicholas. Above, in the turrets, the figure at the left gestures in a way similar to that of his partner in the tower at the left of the lintel, while the figure in the right turret holds a book.

The narrow, inhabited towers link the lintel on the south flank of San Salvatore in Mustiola to Biduinus's signed and dated (1180) lintel on the center portal of San Cassiano a Settimo where a two-story inhabited tower, albeit not flanking a domed structure, appears at the left of the *Raising of Lazarus* (fig. 26). Indeed, that architectural detail and the presence of Biduinus's signature constitute the only similarities between the two lintels. Granted that the vastly different subject matter renders comparison troublesome, it is nonetheless difficult to believe that the same artist sculpted both lintels. Perhaps such an impression is not untoward since Biduinus's aforementioned signed lintel now in the Palazzo Mazzarosa at Lucca likewise differs from that at San Cassiano a Settimo.

The *Bath of Saint Nicholas* at San Salvatore in Mustiola is sparse; the background is composed of large, blank areas on either side of the central vignette and also flanking the towers. The garments of the women bathing the infant saint hang loosely on their bodies, the soft pleats revealing the legs. The lintel at San Cassiano a Settimo is, conversely, densely packed, not only with three scenes but also with a floreated groundline, a tree growing in the midst of the apostles' procession at the very center of this lintel, and the aforementioned additional figures in the *Raising of Lazarus*. The apostles' drapery is composed of numerous repetitious folds on both the bodies and the legs, so many, in fact, that the drapery tends to encase rather than reveal. The graceful motions, so obvious on the lintel at San Salvatore in Mustiola, are absent at San Cassiano a Settimo.

The south flank lintel of the Lucchese church would likewise seem to share nothing with the disjointed figures having jutting heads on Biduinus's other signed lintel from Sant'Angelo in Campo, now in the Palazzo Mazzarosa (fig. 31). We are thus confronted with three stylistically dissimilar lintels, all signed by Biduinus and one, at San Cassiano a Settimo, dated by inscription to 1180. If the evolutionary argument proposed for the date of the lintel from Sant'Angelo in Campo is adduced, the south flank lintel at San Salvatore in Mustiola would be dated still later, for its structure is even more loose. Nothing conclusive can be suggested.

The story of the *Son of Getron*, depicted on the south lintel of the facade of San Salvatore in Mustiola is also problematic (fig. 40). Unsigned and undated, it is usually attributed to the circle of Biduinus. Although the repetitious catenary forms of the drapery are similar to Biduinus's work on the center lintel at San Cassiano a Settimo, Biduinus's follower carves figures that are less lithe and clothed more schematically. The density of the facade lintel differentiates it from the south flank lintel. The popularity of the *Son of Getron* legend is evidenced by its virtual duplication, albeit more crudely and a bit later, on the flank of the cathedral at Barga, located a few kilometers north of Lucca in the foothills of the Appennines (fig. 41).[6]

To my knowledge, the *Bath of Saint Nicholas* had not been illustrated in any medium prior to that on the lintel of San Salvatore in Mustiola at Lucca. Although the saint is said to have stood upright on his feet for two hours during his first bath, indeed a miraculous occurrence, the infancy of Saint Nicholas is most usually represented by the saint at his mother's breast, for early on he gave indication of his beatific character by observing the canonical fast days; on Wednesdays and Fridays he refused to partake of his mother's milk more than once a day.[7] At San Salvatore in Mustiola, the infant saint is emphasized by his centrality and frontality, for he both occupies the center of the lintel and is flanked by buildings. While one can only hypothesize about the iconographical history of this rarely depicted bathing scene, its source is, I think, obvious; the infant Saint Nicholas standing upright in his bath immediately after his birth is easily derived from the commonly depicted scene of the Christ child being bathed by attendants. A conventional iconography has been adapted for a new purpose.[8] Here, however, rather than supporting, holding, or caressing the child, the two servants stand back and gracefully form what might be called parentheses emphasizing the small, erect figure of the newborn saint. The elaborate, inhabited architectural framing of the *Bath of Saint Nicholas* may simply be Biduinus's interpretation of local fortifications of which he would have been able to see many.[9] And, the centralized, domed structures may have been meant to evoke the wonders of the East, Saint Nicholas's birthplace, where such edifices were far more abundant than in the West. Or, the domes could have been mediated by Biduinus's study of centralized baptisteries or of Bonanus's contemporaneous bronze doors for the cathedral at Pisa (ca. 1180). There, domed architecture abounds. In any case, the *Bath of Saint Nicholas*, rarely depicted, does appear on an altarpiece, dating 1270–80, in San Verano at Péccioli, a small town south of the Arno and approximately midway between Pisa and Volterra.[10] The novel choice of subject matter requires examination of its textual sources in lieu of coeval comparanda in the visual arts, as well as of the reasons for the depiction of the subject in Lucca and environs in the latter part of the twelfth century.

The south lintel of the facade of San Salvatore in Mustiola at Lucca, although far more densely occupied than that on the south flank, also reveals the same concern for symmetry. It depicts the *Son of Getron*, a posthumous miracle performed by Saint Nicholas. The story tells of a pious couple, Getron and Euphrosina ("Grace") who, on the feast of Saint Nicholas, take their son Adeodatus ("God-given") to church. The infidel Marmorinus ("Stony") and his soldiers attack the church and capture the young Adeodatus who, all the while pledging faith to the Christian deity, is taken to the infidels' court and made a cup-bearer. The next year, on the feast-day of Saint Nicholas, Adeodatus's grieving parents again go to church, this time to pray for their son's return. Meanwhile, Saint Nicholas goes to Marmorinus's court, miraculously rescues Adeodatus, still clutching the king's goblet, and returns him to his grateful parents who, having returned from church, had prepared a dinner for schoolboys.

At the far left, at the end of a rectangular table, the king sits jauntily on a throne with his left leg crossed over his right knee. The queen and three courtiers, all seated behind the table, are enjoying a banquet, while at the right of the table, Adeodatus in his servant's role, approaches with a large cup. The narrative flows toward the right, as a nimbed Saint Nicholas grasps the hair of the youth as the latter is in the very act of serving at the table. The action is then punctuated by a slender fenestrated tower that appears in the background and is partially blocked by the figures in front of it. Immediately to the right of the tower, Saint Nicholas, still holding Adeodatus by the hair, has pivoted to return the lad to his mother who embraces both her son and the large cup that he still carries. To the right, three small figures appear to be sounding bells to signify the festive nature of Nicholas's return. The narrative concludes at the far right with Adeodatus's parents and their guests seated at a festively laden table, celebrating the return of their son. The symmetry of the narrative lies in the organization of the banquets at either end of the lintel. In both cases, the thrones, the table, and the arrangement of the figures at the table are essentially the same. Good has triumphed over evil.

The appearance on the lintels of San Salvatore in Mustiola of scenes from the life of Saint Nicholas is not surprising, for the extraordinary popularity of the saint's cult in Italy and elsewhere is abundantly documented.[11] Saint Nicholas was first mentioned outside of Byzantium sometime between 755 and 770 when his name was inscribed in a stone register of relics in Sant'Angelo in Pescheria at Rome. In 818, Rabanus Maurus, archbishop of Fulda wrote verses about Saint Nicholas and sometime around 880, John the Deacon of Naples loosely translated a Byzantine life of Saint Nicholas entitled *Methodios ad Theodorum*.[12] The cult of Saint Nicholas took root early on in Germany because of the marriage in 972 of the Greek princess Theophano to Otto II; in fact, an early Saint Nicholas liturgy was composed in Germany.[13] The spread of the cult of Saint Nicholas was surely aided by Alfanus, archbishop of Salerno from 1058 until his death in 1085. An intimate friend of Abbot Desiderius of Monte Cassino, Alfanus wrote a hymn in praise of the saint in which Nicholas is adjudged the equal of no less than the apostles:

> Rome, the *caput mundi*, always celebrates [as?] the equal of the apostles [him] whose ready assistance one (?) seeks and begs not with many prayers.[14]

The aforegoing disparate events pale, however, in the face of the intensity of the interest in the cult of Saint Nicholas after the translation of his relics to Bari in 1087, an event confirmed by Urban II when he visited that city in 1089.[15] The relics were escorted on their journey from Myra to Bari by the Normans who had captured the latter city, an important Apulian port, in 1071.[16] Although not the primary agents, the Normans were certainly influential in spreading the cult of Nicholas throughout Europe.[17] Shortly after the translation of the relics, pilgrims visited from Pisa, Amalfi, Ancona, and Durazzo; Bari's proximity to the port of Brindisi, a common point of departure to the East, must have made the relics of the popular saint particularly accessible. By 1101, little more than a decade after the translation to Bari, there was a hospice in the city for the swelling tide of pilgrims visiting the site.[18] It is estimated that from the translation of the relics in 1087 until the thirteenth century, there were approximately seventy-four churches dedicated to the saint in south Italy, fifty-six in Rome and central Italy, and fifty in Venice and north Italy.[19]

Farther north, the first mention of the church of Saint Nicholas at Montjoie, in what are now the French Alps, appears in two documents dated 1125,[20] and in Germany, shortly after the translation of the relics of the saint to Bari, commercial roads in northeast Germany were flanked by churches dedicated to Saint Nicholas, the patron saint of merchants, among other causes.[21] The efficacy of Saint Nicholas as the patron saint of sailors must have been known to Tuscan pilgrims and crusaders, for a church dedicated to him for the use of Pisan residents is noted in 1192 in

Constantinople.[22] Nicholas of Clairvaux, Saint Bernard's secretary, aptly summarized the esteemed position held by Saint Nicholas:

> The miracles of him whom the whole world and those who live in it praise, are dispersed throughout the whole breadth of the world.[23]

That Saint Nicholas was firmly embedded in twelfth-century culture is also evidenced by his regular appearance in popular literature. For example, Wace (fl. 1170) wrote a *Life of Saint Nicholas*.[24] But the best-known popular literature is that contained in the *Fleury Playbook*, which contains *inter alia* four plays recounting incidents in the life of Saint Nicholas: the *Tres Filiae*, the *Iconia Sancti Nicolai*, the *Tres Clerici*, and *Filius Getronis*.[25] The last is the subject of the facade lintel of San Salvatore in Mustiola at Lucca. There is also evidence, albeit postdating the lintels, that plays concerning Saint Nicholas were performed in Lucca as late as the sixteenth century; and, Christopher Hohler has suggested that the proper office of Saint Nicholas was perhaps composed in Italy, while Sandro Sticca has urged a reassessment of the importance of Italy during the early years of the liturgical drama.[26]

The novel choice of subject matter for both lintels requires examination of textual sources, especially because of the dearth of coeval comparanda in the visual arts. Although the popularity of Saint Nicholas in the West during the twelfth century is not in dispute, the two scenes depicted at San Salvatore in Mustiola at Lucca are not only rarely illustrated in any medium, but also appear together only in texts that postdate the lintels.

A number of texts recount the myriad events in the busy life of Saint Nicholas beginning with his early years in Greece.[27] Indeed, Saint Nicholas is actually a composite of two saints: the fourth-century bishop of Myra, and the abbot of Sion (a town near Myra) who died in 564. The former is known primarily because of the events retold in the sixth-century *Praxis de Stratelatis*. More is known of Nicholas of Sion whose life, the *Vita Nicolai Sionitae*, was written shortly after his death.[28] At an uncertain later date, but unquestionably before the tenth century, the two saints were merged and the miracles performed by Nicholas, Abbot of Sion served to flesh out the rather sparse account of the life of Nicholas, Bishop of Myra. John the Deacon, whose aforementioned loose translation of the *Methodius ad Theodorum* is the primary source for later Western versions, tells us in his prologue that his work contains not only that text, but also a paraphrase of the *Praxis de Stratilatis* and material drawn from later writers. The life of Saint Nicholas thus emerges in a series of complex texts compiled over a period of centuries. Of the two subjects chosen for the lintels of San Salvatore in Lucca, both appear together in only two texts: the Greek *Encomium Neophyti* written ca. 1200,[29] and the Latin *Legenda Aurea* dated ca. 1260.[30] It is likely that these legends were known in twelfth-century Tuscany and southern Liguria, for Jacobus of Voragine, the Dominican compiler of the *Legenda Aurea* was born at Varazze (or Viareggio) on the Ligurian coast just west of Genoa.[31] Their inclusion in the *Legenda Aurea* suggests their currency and, if indeed, the volume was meant for the use of Dominican preachers, the legends' diffusion would have been even more rapid during the latter part of the thirteenth century.[32] The episodes appear moreover in later paintings and frescoes in Tuscany.[33]

While the context for and the interest in Saint Nicholas is easily delineated, it does not explain why San Salvatore in Mustiola at Lucca and the cathedral at Barga were chosen to bear the images of Saint Nicholas and, by extension, why such scenes would have been appropriate in late twelfth-century western Tuscany. The church of San Salvatore at Lucca is, by any standards, a rather small and undistinguished church; its importance in the Middle Ages rests upon the fact the it was made a dependence of San Frediano in Lucca by Innocent II on April 21, 1140.[34] San Frediano, in turn, was not only called upon to reform the Lateran canons in Rome, but also was given charge of Sant'Andrea, the cathedral at Carrara.[35] It is, then, reasonable to surmise that San Salvatore could be embellished with sculpture by Biduinus because it was ruled by the wealthy and powerful canons of San Frediano, who at approximately the same time commissioned a "baptismal font" for their own church.[36] Understandably, Barga, ruled by Lucca throughout the Middle Ages, would want to emulate the more powerful city and most likely commissioned a pupil of Biduinus to make a similar lintel at a later date, so that a like statement could be made.

Because the *Bathing of Saint Nicholas* on the south flank of San Salvatore at Lucca is so unusual and lacks coeval comparanda, its intended meaning can only be speculated upon. I suspect that the scene was used to aggrandize the image of Saint Nicholas because the depiction of the episode is so clearly derived from the *Bathing of the Christ Child* so often attached to *Nativity* scenes. Here, at Lucca, Nicholas not only reminds the viewer of the infant Christ, but also his powers are emphasized because he, unlike Christ, stood without support in his bath a mere few hours after his birth. The iconic nature of the image placed against a blank background emphasizes its importance. The clergy and lookouts in the flanking towers may refer obliquely to the barricades used to protect the port of Pisa and thus to the city's activities abroad.

The right lintel of the west facade of San Salvatore at Lucca, depicting the *Son of Getron*, is a more obvious example of the depiction of an event that clearly evokes the situation in regard to those perceived as infidels in the Holy Land, for the lintel depicts the rescue of a pure young man from the land and person of a pagan and his return to the bosom of his family. This sort of scene surely would have soothed the concerned Lucchese who had permitted or encouraged their sons to embark upon crusade or pilgrimage.[37] The emotional intensity of the conflict between Christians and Moslems is exemplified by the harsh words Adeodatus uses in the *Filius Getronis* to describe Apollo, Marmorinus's pagan god: "He is deceitful and bad; he is stupid, blind, deaf and dumb. . . ."[38]

Adeodatus's rescue from the hands of the Moslem Marmorinus also had further resonance for the citizens of late twelfth-century Tuscany because the episode speaks to specific regulations concerning the association between Christians and Moslems. One of the edicts of the Third Lateran Council, held in 1179, bore the title *De Iudeis et Sarracenis*. Therein, it was stated that Christians could not be servants in the houses of Moslems or Jews. The edict was of such ongoing concern that Bernardus Balbi, the provost of Pavia, brought together seven extracts in the chapter entitled "De Iudeis et Sarracenis" of his *Compilatio prima*, written between 1188 and 1192.[39] The sculptor of the south lintel of the facade of San Salvatore at Mustiola thus embraced a scene known through liturgical drama but uncommon in the visual repertory and cloaked it in a contemporaneous meaning that surely made sense to Lucchese concerned about the fate of their sons on pilgrimage and crusade in far-off lands. The Tuscan participation in both spiritual and commercial activities in the Holy Land is palpable, although too often overlooked.[40] Indeed the *Annals* completed in 1307 by the Dominican historian Tholomeus of Lucca note that in 1180 "there was a great struggle across the sea between the Christians and the Moslems, and the Christians won."[41] Such euphoria was short-lived. The disastrous defeat at Hattin and the fall of Jerusalem were less than a decade away.

1. Pisa, Cathedral

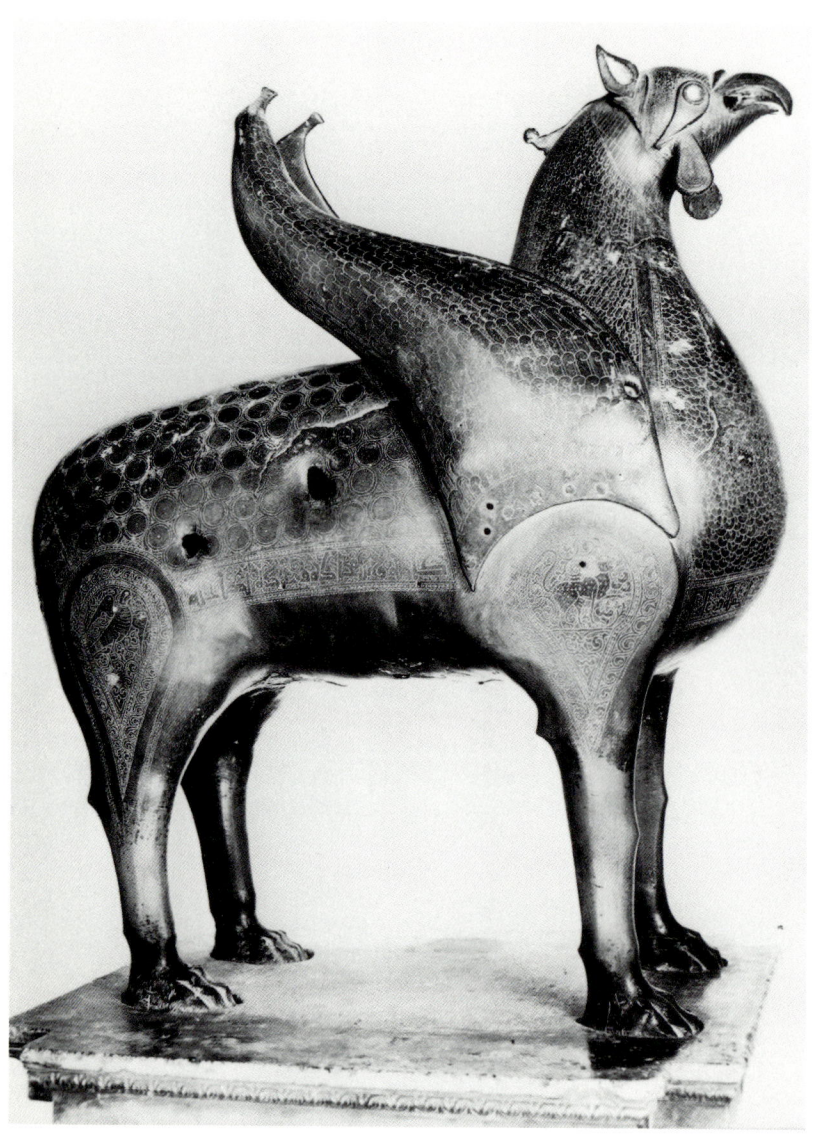

2. Pisa, Museo dell'Opera del Duomo, metal griffin

3. Pistoia, Sant'Andrea, facade

4. Pistoia, Sant'Andrea, center door, lintel, *Magi before Herod* and the *Adoration of the Magi*

5. Cagliari, Cathedral, gospel pulpit, *Annunciation* and *Visitation*

6. Pistoia, Sant'Andrea, center door, left capital, detail, *Visitation*

7. Pistoia, Sant'Andrea, center door, right capital, *Saint Anne and the Annunciation*

8. Parma, Cathedral, facade, right door, right capital, *Visitation*

9. Carrara, Cathedral, nave capital, *Visitation*

10. Lucca, Museo Nazionale di Villa Guinigi, *Annunciation to Zechariah*

11. Groppoli, San Michele, pulpit, *Annunciation* and *Visitation*

12. Pistoia, Cathedral, panel from pulpit, *Visitation*

13. Volterra, Cathedral, pulpit, *Annunciation* and *Visitation*

14. Pistoia, Sant'Andrea, center door, lintel, detail, *Herod*

15. Pistoia, Sant'Andrea, center door, lintel, detail, *Virgin*

16. Pistoia, San Bartolomeo in Pantano, facade

17. Pistoia, San Bartolomeo in Pantano, center door, lintel

18. Pistoia, San Bartolomeo in Pantano, center door, lintel, detail

19. Piacenza, Sant'Ilario, lintel, *Doubting Thomas*

20. Milan, Sant'Ambrogio, sarcophagus, back, *Mission of the Apostles*

21. Pistoia, San Bartolomeo in Pantano, pulpit, *Mission of the Apostles* and *Doubting Thomas*

22. Pistoia, San Giovanni Fuorcivitas, north flank

23. Pistoia, San Giovanni Fuorcivitas, north flank, lintel, *Last Supper*

24. Volterra, Cathedral, pulpit, *Last Supper*

25. San Cassiano a Settimo, facade

26. San Cassiano a Settimo, center portal, lintel, *Raising of Lazarus* and *Entry into Jerusalem*

27. San Cassiano a Settimo, center portal, lintel, detail

28. San Cassiano a Settimo, facade, north lintel

29. San Cassiano a Settimo, facade, south lintel

30. Pisa Cathedral, campanile, detail, animal relief

31. Lucca, Palazzo Mazzarosa, lintel, *Entry into Jerusalem*

32. The Metropolitan Museum of Art, The Cloisters Collection, portal from San Leonardo al Frigido

33. The Metropolitan Museum of Art, The Cloisters Collection, portal from San Leonardo al Frigido, lintel, *Entry into Jerusalem*

34. The Metropolitan Museum of Art, The Cloisters Collection, portal
from San Leonardo al Frigido, left capital

35. Pisa, Cathedral,
capital from campanile

36. Parma, Cathedral, exterior, north apse, *Samson and Delilah*

37. Chartres, Cathedral, facade, south portal,
archivolt, detail, *Grammar*

38. Lucca, San Salvatore in Mustiola, facade and south flank

39. Lucca, San Salvatore in Mustiola, south flank, lintel, *Bath of Saint Nicholas*

40. Lucca, San Salvatore in Mustiola, facade, south lintel, *Son of Getron*

41. Barga, Cathedral, north flank, lintel, *Son of Getron*

42. Pisa, Camposanto, sarcophagus signed by Biduinus

43. Pisa, Camposanto, lion sarcophagus

44. Calci, Sant'Ermalao, baptismal font

45. Pisa, Camposanto, arcaded sarcophagus

46. Pisa, Camposanto, hunting sarcophagus

47. Paris, Louvre, ivory pyxis

48. Pisa, Camposanto, sarcophagus end, pouncing griffin

49. Rome, Museo delle Terme, Early Christian sarcophagus with *Entry into Jerusalem*

50. Charlieu, narthex tympanum, *Marriage at Cana* and *The Sacrifices of the Ancient Law*

51. Jerusalem, Rockefeller Museum, lintel from the Holy Sepulchre, *Raising of Lazarus and Christ and His Disciples Meet Mary Magdalene and Martha*

Chapter Six

The Past

THE CULTURE that spawned the workshop of Guglielmus and his followers, Gruamons, Adeodatus, and Biduinus, looked to the past for affirmation of the present. The Pisans' confidence was engendered and supported by her maritime strength, both commercial and military. The remains of Roman antiquity served the Pisans as more than convenient building blocks, for things Roman were also endowed with political and cultural importance as amply evidenced by the reuse of Roman sarcophagi for three significant personages buried at Pisa's cathedral: Busketus, the first architect of the cathedral; Beatrice, the mother of Matilda of Canossa; and Gregory VIII, who died in Pisa in 1187 after having held the See of Saint Peter for only fifty-seven days.[1] This sort of signification was important to the Pisans, for they viewed themselves as the rightful heirs of the ancient Romans. This notion was clearly expressed in 1087 when the Pisans, with help from the forces of Genoa, Rome, and Amalfi, captured the Moslems of al-Mahdìya and Zawìla in North Africa. On that occasion, a poem was written to celebrate the event; the first four lines trumpet the parallel between medieval Pisa and ancient Rome by likening the Pisans' victory to that of the Romans over Carthage:

> As I embark upon writing the history of the illustrious
> Pisans, I renew [the reader's] memory of the ancient Romans:
> For recently Pisa exhibits the admirable praise which Rome
> received [once upon a time] for conquering Carthage.[2]

Throughout the twelfth century, Pisa continued to nurture her image as the new Rome. The oldest of the three manuscripts of the *Liber Maiorchinus*, a work celebrating Pisa's successful expedition against the Balearic Islands from 1113 to 1115, contains verses inspired by the privileges awarded to Pisa by Frederick Barbarossa on April 6, 1162. Pisa speaks:

> I am customarily called the second Rome, and am rich in privileges
> from Frederick, because of the barbarian peoples whom I defeated
> everywhere.[3]

But the eclectic Pisans apparently saw no dichotomy in thinking of their city as "Roma altera" and incorporating Islamic, as well as Roman, spolia in its buildings. The exteriors of Pisan medieval churches are often decorated with *bacini*, ceramic basins brought back from southern Italy, Sicily, Spain, Morocco, Tunisia, and Egypt.[4] Most impressive, perhaps, is a bronze eleventh-century griffin that was installed atop the cathedral in the late eleventh or early twelfth century and remained in that prominent position until 1828 (fig. 2).[5] At 107 centimeters in height, it must have been clearly visible and well known to Pisans.

Pisa's carefully nurtured self-image must stand as the basis for any understanding of medieval Pisa, for clearly the importance of ancient Rome was imbued in the hearts and souls of all good Pisans. Hence, it is not surprising that Biduinus and his colleagues were well acquainted with ancient Roman art. More specifically, in the work of Biduinus, the affinity with the antique tradition extends beyond a mere medieval adaptation of antique types and is instead embodied in the very roots of his style, for he seems to have been an extraordinarily close student of antiquity. In the Camposanto at Pisa, there is a rather crude strigilated sarcophagus with rounded ends and a small oval clipeus at its center (fig. 42). It is the tomb of Girattus, a Pisan judge, and each end is carved with a worn lion pouncing on another animal that appears to be a small goat. The significance of this sarcophagus does not reside in its coarse style nor in its common format, but rather in the fact that it is signed by Biduinus himself on the upper border: BIDUINUS MAISTER FECIT HANC TU(M)BAM A[. .]NM GIRATTUM.[6] Clearly, then, at some point in his career, most likely at the outset, Biduinus made a copy of an antique sarcophagus in order, no doubt, to educate himself about antique style.[7] Certainly models were plentiful as antique sarcophagi abound in Pisa (fig. 43).

An extraordinary large, unfinished font formerly used for baptism by immersion in the *pieve* dedicated to Sant'Ermalao at Calci also bears ample, albeit somewhat incoherent, witness to the concern with the antique in Romanesque western Tuscany (fig. 44).[8] Carved by an anonymous sculptor from a huge, monolithic block from the nearby quarry at San Giuliano, most likely during the second half of the twelfth century, it is a rectangle measuring 2.2 m × 2.5 m × .9 m.[9] The interior of the huge font has a hollowed-out basin in each corner and steps leading to the bottom. Only the front is carved and, there, the work was left unfinished. This is closely modelled on antique arcaded sarcophagi, a type common in both Roman and Early Christian art and represented among the sarcophagi now in the Camposanto at Pisa (fig. 45).[10]

On the font, an unfinished figure of Christ stands under the central arch of the five arcades. The small figure kneeling in front of him is doubtless a personification of the river Jordan, an image that also appears in the same scene on the pulpit made by Guglielmus for the cathedral at Pisa and now in the cathedral at Cagliari.[11] The four figures flanking Christ, two on each side, stand on four animals, while angels occupy the arcade spandrels. Immediately to the left of Christ, an angel holds his garment; to the right, John the Baptist addresses Christ. The outermost figures on each side are problematical. That at the far left, with clasped hands may be the Virgin, although it must be admitted that she does not usually witness the Baptism. The frontal figure at the far right, clearly a winged angel, holds a smaller, headless, incomplete figure; the intended meaning is not clear, but the so-called figure may indeed be a second garment. This interpretation gains credence by examination of the virtually contemporaneous bronze cathedral doors made by Bonanus probably around 1180 for the Porta San Ranieri of the Pisan cathedral. The panel depicting the Baptism shows two angels standing on hillocks to the left of Christ; each holds a garment.[12] Because of the lack of finish in many areas (e.g., the wings of the angels, the capitals, the columns) and the lack of coherence, the font at Calci may perhaps have been a school piece on which the sculptor or sculptors attempted to emulate antique art. Similarly, but on a lesser scale, a sarcophagus immured in the north transept of San Paolo a Ripa d'Arno at Pisa has been viewed as influential in the development of Pisan Romanesque sculpture.[13]

Biduinus learned his lessons especially well for, in addition to copying an antique Roman sarcophagus, other imitations and adaptations of antique style appear in his work, particularly at San Cassiano a Settimo, where he signed and dated (1180) the lintel depicting the *Entry into Jerusalem* on the center portal.[14] The lintel of the north, or left, portal of that facade is topped by a narrow, dry, medieval-style acanthus border and supported by emulations of antique composite capitals (fig. 28). The lintel itself consists of one long panel framed by two narrow pieces that seem to have been created to extend the lintel to the proper length. At the far left is a tree whose leaves bear the mark of an active drill; at the far right, a horned animal, perhaps a goat, stands on its hindquarters and nibbles at treelike foliage. The long, central section of the lintel begins with a tunic-clad figure playing an oliphant and holding a small animal upside down. The cortege continues with a large bear suckling its cub while she's nipping at a serpent. Another animal with a flowered tail curled around its back stands on the large bear's body. Next, a lion on its hindquarters bites at the rear of a goat, and a ram is poised on the plane in front of the goat. Reading from left to right, this vignette is succeeded by a stag pouncing on a serpent's back, a small boar standing on its hindlegs, another oliphant-blowing figure, and, finally, a doglike animal standing on the back of a cow.

This boisterous assemblage, both animal and human, reveals Biduinus's knowledge of a vast number of animal motifs, a predilection of the school spawned by Guglielmus in Pisa. Two aforementioned, similar animal friezes, one signed by Biduinus and inscribed with the year 1174, are on the first floor of the campanile as well as more extensively on the facade of Pisa's cathedral; even later, animals appear on the interior of that city's baptistery (fig. 30).[15] Many of the motifs can be found on such antique reliefs as those on hunting sarcophagi and those friezes depicting *suovetaurilia*, Roman scenes of sacrifice (fig. 46). Unlike the lintel at San Cassiano a Settimo, however, *suovetaurilia* invariably contain a boar, a ram, and a bull. These well-known scenes, though not enormous in number, appear throughout the Roman empire beginning with the Augustan arch at Susa erected in 9–8 B.C.[16]

But the north lintel at San Cassiano a Settimo is both more than a simple compendium of antique animal motifs and an indication of the catholicity of Biduinus's taste. Many of the animals are distinguished by their imaginative character and their fierceness. These attributes are more similar to works produced in Spain during the Caliphal period (929–1031 A.D.). The ivory pyxis of al-Mughira in the Louvre is a typical example. There, a large medallion contains two lions standing while also attacking bulls (fig. 47).[17] Because of Pisa's wide-ranging trade, such motifs were assuredly well known by Biduinus and others. Similarly, Islamic ivories and textiles influenced some aspects of Romanesque sculpture in Campania, a province also in close contact with the Islamic world.[18]

The south, or right door of the facade of San Cassiano a Settimo has a shorter and simpler lintel than that on the north (fig. 29). Like the north lintel, it is topped by a dry, medieval imitation of an ancient acanthus motif and supported by an equally dry medieval simulation of antique composite capitals. The lintel depicts two fierce, confronting griffins elegantly carved to inhabit the rectangular lintel. The tails of each curve and then at the top extend horizontally to echo the top border of the lintel. The raised hindquarters give way to the winged forequarters, which follow the lintel's lower edge. The griffins' wings and heads then stretch toward the upper border. The taut energy of the griffins contrasts starkly with the rather limp but furry ram standing between them. The dazed animal seems unaware of the griffins, each of whom touch him with their outstretched inner paw. This sorry refugee from a *suovetaurilia* seems curiously out of place, but the griffins themselves reveal Biduinus's keen familiarity with antique representations of the animal, which appear most frequently on sarcophagi and funerary altars as guardians of the dead and symbols of apotheosis.[19] Indeed, the end of an infant's sarcophagus now in the Camposanto at Pisa depicts a winged griffin pouncing on the head of a supine ram (fig. 48).[20] Biduinus was likewise familiar with Islamic griffins; the aforementioned metal griffin once atop Pisa's cathedral may have been seen daily by the young sculptor when he worked on the cathedral's campanile (fig. 2).

The classicizing motifs so prominent at San Cassiano a Settimo are not unique for, in addition to the examples already mentioned at the cathedral, baptistery, and campanile at Pisa, as well as the font in Calci's *pieve*, they appear in many other places in western Tuscany during the Romanesque era. At the aforementioned cathedral at Barga, for example, a small lintel above the center door of the current facade shows two shepherdlike figures, similar to those on the north lintel of San Cassiano a Settimo. But at Barga, they are separated by a rinceau rather than by energetic animals. Two shepherds also appear in a manner similar to that at Barga on the lintel of the flank portal of San Michelotto at Lucca.

The classicizing lintels discussed here, probably carved during a period of about twenty-five years at most, ca. 1165–90, can be broadly divided into two different though related styles. The first, represented by such immediate followers of Guglielmus as Gruamons and Adeodatus, is in part characterized by attention to decorative backgrounds and stocky figures swathed in drapery, as seen at Sant'Andrea, Pistoia. The second, epitomized by Biduinus and his circle favors unadorned backgrounds and more slender figures (e.g., San Salvatore, Lucca).[21] Regardless of the stylistic differences displayed within a relatively narrow spectrum of possible choices, the lintels share conventions that both unite them and differentiate them from other Romanesque sculpture. The lintels still *in situ* are not parts of elaborate facade programs that bear highly complex meanings. Nor are the Tuscan lintels topped by figurative tympana and archivolts. So far as we know, in only two cases, Sant'Andrea at Pistoia and San Leonardo al Frigido, are the lintels supported by figurative capitals. Thus the Tuscan norm differs from the usual perception of Romanesque sculpture, a perception that was defined by French historiography.[22] In France, lintels are but one part of a multifarious program that usually embraces the entire portal, if not the entire facade.

Indeed, one is struck by the profoundly horizontal emphasis of Tuscan Romanesque sculpture, a horizontality accentuated by both the shapes of the blocks and, often, the choice of subject matter, as seen in the processional nature of the three depictions of the *Entry into Jerusalem*, in the combined image of the *Doubting Thomas* and the *Mission of the Apostles*, and in the left to right reading of the *Son of Getron*. The format and organization of the lintels are comparable to antique sarcophagi, be they Roman or Early Christian.[23] Hence it is not surprising that the lintels illustrating the *Entry into Jerusalem* have been rightly compared to Early Christian sarcophagi depicting the same subject (fig. 49).[24]

The types of commissions undertaken by Biduinus urge speculation about the location and composition of his workshop. Romanesque sculpture in western Tuscany does not exist in the context of large-scale projects so familiar in medieval France. Rather, Biduinus's largest extant project was at San Cassiano a Settimo for which he carved three lintels and probably two interior capitals, the first on the right side of the nave, counting from the facade, and the second on the left side. In other cases, he and his older contemporaries, Gruamons and Adeodatus, carved one or two lintels, as at San Salvatore, Lucca, or a lintel and a pair of capitals, as at Sant'Andrea, Pistoia. The nature of the projects in twelfth-century western Tuscany suggests that there was no overwhelming reason for the sculptors to work at the site. Indeed, visual evidence intimates that the sculpture was not made at a given site, but elsewhere; often the sculpture does not fit its architectural setting, a result that could have been achieved had the sculptor been present and measured closely. At Sant'Andrea, Pistoia, for example, the two capitals had to be made smaller so as to fit their setting. A vertical third of the figure of Saint Anne on the right capital has been removed, while somewhat less has been shaved from the corresponding figure on the left capital (figs. 4, 6, and 7). Moreover, both capitals are significantly wider then the door jambs they top and the capitals project slightly beyond the edges of the lintel. Similarly, the lintel of the south portal at San Cassiano a Settimo, that depicting the confronting griffins, is too short for its doorway and had to be expanded on both the left and the right with filler (fig. 29).

That extraordinarily large pieces of stone could be moved and did not inherently have to be carved on site is well known.[25] In this context, the notion is exemplified by the aforementioned font at Calci, for it is 2.55 m wide and 2.25 m deep (fig. 44). While inland transportation is assuredly difficult although possible, shipping on water was easier and more desirable. Evidence from shipwrecks indicates that a vast array of materials from architectural parts to sarcophagi were transported long distances; the pieces were in various states from roughed out to completely finished.[26] In medieval western Tuscany, the Arno, flowing from Florence to Pisa, and the Serchio and its tributary the Auser, in the region of Lucca, could serve well for such transportation. San Cassiano a Settimo is near the Arno, while Barga, north of Lucca is near the Serchio. Even smaller streams, like the Frigido, which runs next to San Leonardo al Frigido, could be used. And the port of Genoa is just a few miles north of Carrara. Indeed, an early quattrocento description of Pisa notes:

> In the middle of the city, there flows a real river called the Arno, on which ships loaded with merchandise come and go to the sea; the merchandise is spread and sent throughout Tuscany and to many places.[27]

When no natural waterway was available, canals were sometimes built. Maragone notes in his *Annales Pisani* for the year 1157 that the wise counsel Coccus made a canal from Monte Pisano to the church of San Zeno at Pisa on which to transport barges of stone for the new city walls.[28]

Clearly, then, there is no reason that the lintels and capitals could not be transported from a workshop at a certain location, unknown to us at present, to their final destination. The nature of some of the commissions also suggest what might be termed a "mail-order business." In all three lintels depicting the *Entry into Jerusalem* the patron saint of the church they decorate (or once decorated) is carved at the left side of the lintel. One can imagine an order being placed and the workshop then personalizing the stock subject. The situation in western Tuscany would thus be similar to that in the Pyrenees where marble altar tables were made at a central location, or to that in England where baptismal fonts and other objects made of stone from Tournai were greatly favored.[29]

There is no concrete evidence that reveals the location of the workshop of Biduinus or that of his slightly older contemporaries. Lucca is, however, a distinct possibility, for although there is every stylistic indication that Biduinus, Gruamons, and Adeodatus were trained in the workshop of Guglielmus in Pisa, there are only two signed works of Biduinus's juvenilia there; the small reliefs on the campanile and the sarcophagus in the Camposanto. Gruamons and Adeodatus left no signed works in Pisa. The interruption of work on both the cathedral and the campanile at Pisa at various times in the second half of the twelfth century would have left little employment for so many sculptors, for Pisa's Romanesque churches rarely display figurative decoration. The workshop may possibly have been in Lucca, for that city has more Romanesque churches than Pisa and a somewhat greater taste for sculpture. The city is also centrally located and was extraordinarily wealthy as a result of its overland trade in textiles and its banking prowess. But regardless of the workshops' exact location, the sculptors worked in a rather narrow geographic area.

That Romanesque sculptors in western Tuscany studied antiquity with such tenacity is ironic, for Pisa was a rather modest city in antiquity, and Lucca was perhaps most famed for her Roman arena.[30] While one can identify some *spolia*,[31] such as the lintel of San Frediano at Pisa, there do not seem to be any carefully matched Roman columns or sets of capitals seen so often in medieval Rome.[32] Indeed, Pisa, better documented than Lucca in regard to building materials, is known to have imported *spolia*, some of which is not especially distinguished. Typical examples of this genre are an inscription from Ostia immured on the exterior of the cathedral and a capital on the interior of San Piero a Grado from the "Auditorium" of Maecenas on the Esquiline.[33] Numerous partial inscriptions offer evidence that the Pisans also used Roman remains as building blocks for their cathedral.[34] In other cases, the *spolia* were larger and might be viewed as trophies. As Abbot Suger of Saint-Denis wanted columns from Rome, and as Abbot Desiderius had columns and bases shipped from Rome to Monte Cassino on the Garigliano River,[35] so too, Bonus, abbot of San Michele at Pisa, the abbey he founded about 1048, noted:

> I built . . . the church . . . and I went to Rome for the columns of this same church and I purchased [them] and [arranged] that they come in a ship by sea at my own expense.[36]

Abbot Bonus also imported columns from Luni and Elba.[37] He and others found it necessary to import building materials over long distances because the quarry at Monte Pisani was not opened until 1156,[38] an opening perhaps necessitated by the building of Pisa's third circle of walls between 1155 and 1161.[39] Both Pisa and Lucca quarried at Monte Pisano, the former at San Giuliano and the latter at Santa Maria del Giudice.[40] Moreover, the famed quarry at Carrara, closed during the earlier Middle Ages, reopened gradually only during the last two decades of the twelfth century and the early years of the thirteenth century.[41]

The disparate formats of Italian and French Romanesque portals resulted in differing attitudes toward the programmatic aspects of Romanesque art. This point may be elucidated by contrasting a tympanum at Charlieu, depicting sacrificial animals, with Biduinus's frieze of carved animals on the lintel of the north portal of the facade at San Cassiano a Settimo (figs. 50 and 28). At Charlieu, a narthex portal dating from the second quarter of the twelfth century has a lintel that imitates, but does not copy directly, a *suovetaurilia* once on the south portal of Notre-Dame de Beaujeau and now in the Musée de la Civilisation Gallo-romaine in Lyon.[42] At Charlieu, the *Marriage at Cana* appears in the lintel and the *Transfiguration* in the archivolt. The portal is thereby unified by the themes of sacrifice, offering, and transformation. Emile Mâle has noted that Peter the Venerable's *Tractatus contra Petrobrusianos*, which contrasts Jewish and Christian sacrifice, is pertinent to the lintel at Charlieu:

> With the flesh of their blood, the ox, the calf, ram. lamb, nanny goat and billy goat filled the altars of the Jews; only the lamb of God, who takes away the sin of the world, is placed on the altars of the Christians.[43]

Peter argues that a variety of animals fills Jewish altars, but only the Lamb of God appears on Christian altars. The portal at Charlieu thus makes a complex iconographic statement that references the history of Christianity and differentiates it from Judaism. At San Cassiano a Settimo, Biduinus uses some of the same imagery in a much more straightforward way that perhaps sought to indicate the links with the past rather than the differences from it. In twelfth-century western Tuscany, absorption in the past is a key element in the understanding of the present.

Chapter Seven

The Present

WHEN PISA, and by extension other cities in western Tuscany, sought comparison with ancient Rome, the intention was not one of servile imitation but, rather, a comparison of equals. In this sense, the image that Pisa desired differed from that fostered by the Gregorian reform. In the latter, aspects of the late antique church were revived in an attempt to return the church to its former spiritual splendor. In the case of Pisa, however, her military victories are compared to the triumph of Rome over Carthage, a military event of great import. Spiritual revival is not the issue.

Pisa's casting of itself in the image of ancient Rome was not mere idle bragging because, in truth, she controlled the Mediterranean basin in much the same way ancient Rome had at the height of its power. Pisa's domination did not result from the Crusades, but from such earlier conquests as those at Reggio (1005), Sardinia (1015–16), Bona in north Africa (1034), and Palermo (1063). Indeed it was partly because of these triumphs over the Moslems that Urban II raised Pisa to an archbishopric in 1092.[1] In 1099, when 120 Pisan ships participated in the liberation of Jerusalem from the infidels,[2] the city was merely continuing activities for which it was already renowned. In addition to its territories in the East, Pisa also had colonies in France at the mouth of the Rhône and its tributaries: Saint-Gilles-du-Gard, Fréjus, Narbonne, and especially Montpellier. And, after Frederick Barbarossa defeated Milan in 1162, he gave to Pisa, an ally whose sea power he needed, the Italian littoral from Civitavecchia to Portovénere as well as inland territories.[3]

The Italians themselves did not always become citizens of the territories they occupied; virtually autonomous, profit-making entities, they were most closely linked to their area of origin. One of Bernard of Clairvaux's comments appearing in a letter about the second Crusade, in which he links mercantile and spiritual interests, seems especially applicable to the inhabitants of western Tuscany:

> If you are a prudent merchant, if you are a man fond of acquiring this world's goods, I am showing you certain great markets; make sure not to

let the chance pass you by. Take the sign of the cross and you will obtain in equal measure remission of all the sins which you have confessed with a contrite heart. If the cloth itself is sold, it does not fetch much; if it is worn on a faithful shoulder it is certain to be worth the kingdom of God.[4]

Having established themseves firmly in the Holy Land, the Pisans played little part in the second Crusade, perhaps because they were so preoccupied by their rivalry with both Genoa and Lucca. After the defeat at Hattin and the loss of Jerusalem, the prime cause of the third Crusade, the Pisans did, however, distinguish themselves in the reconquest of Tyre and Acre, significant port cities that were much more pivotal economically than Jerusalem.[5] Indeed, Acre became the primary Pisan center. Pisa, then, can be said to have had a long history in the Levant. That history, while principally related to trade and commerce, also resulted in great familiarity with the Moslems, the "Agareni" of Pisan medieval documents. The conflict between commerce and faith was clearly observable in the Third Lateran Council when Alexander III sought to excommunicate merchants from all the Italian maritime cities who traded with the Moslems across the sea.[6]

The Pisans' successful battles against the Moslems had repercussions in the city itself, for the spoils garnered helped pay for a new cathedral. Begun in 1063 in celebration of the victory over Palermo, a date earlier than that of most of the major Romanesque cathedrals in northern Europe, Pisa's cathedral was the first element of an extensive complex that was ultimately to include the campanile, the baptistery, and the Camposanto or burial ground.[7] Dedicated to the Virgin of the Assumption and consecrated by Gelasius II on September 26, 1118,[8] the cathedral may be viewed as an assertation of Pisa's dominance in the Mediterranean. Two prominent inscriptions on the facade allude to Pisa's triumphs.[9] One notes battles that took place against the Moslems between 1005 and 1034, while the other notes the Pisans' victory over Palermo in 1063. Pisans were thus reminded daily of the tangible connections among crusade, wealth, and piety.

The Pisans may not have been particularly active in Jerusalem, the spiritual center of the Holy Land, although one early patriarch, Daimbert, was Pisan, but they were certainly not unaware of the symbolism of the architecture of that revered city. In its church of the Holy Sepulchre,[10] begun about 1150, Pisa joined the countless other locales in western Europe that possessed imitations of the Holy Sepulchre, be they entire buildings or smaller structures contained within a particular church.[11] Similar in plan and virtually contemporaneous is the chapel of Sant'Agata built by the canons of San Paolo a Ripa d'Arno behind their church.[12] Of even greater importance because of its prominent location is the baptistery of Pisa, directly opposite the facade of the cathedral. An inscription on the first interior pilaster at the left notes that it was begun in 1152 and supervised by Diotsalvi, the architect also responsible for the aforementioned church of the Holy Sepulchre at Pisa. Employing the principles masterfully laid out by Richard Krautheimer, Max Seidel has argued that Pisa's baptistery is, too, modelled on the Anastasis.[13] Finally, another parallel between Jerusalem and Pisa may have existed in that the latter once had a Porta Aurea, or Golden Gate, as did Jerusalem. Pisa's city gate, no longer extant, bore an inscription celebrating the triumphs in the Balearic Islands (1113–15); the inscription is now above the entrance to the church of the Madonna dei Galletti in Lungarno Pacinotti.[14]

Clearly, then, notions of military might, triumph and trade were central to Pisa in the eleventh and twelfth centuries as they were to such neighboring cities as Lucca, which, because it lacked a seaport and could depend only on the Serchio River, eventually dominated inland trade in north Italy and France. In any case, the prevailing mood would seem to have been more secular, especially commercial, than sacred. This outlook is manifested in other ways. For instance, Bernardo Maragone, the already cited chronicler of Pisa's history, was not a cleric but a layman.[15] Similarly, Raynerius, Pisa's patron saint never took clerical orders.[16] Born in 1117, he was a wild youth whose family had made its fortune in maritime trade; converted to sanctity in 1136, he never received formal training in the priesthood. Raynerius left for the Holy Land in 1140 and remained there as an ascetic and a pilgrim for thirteen years, during which time it is noted that he spent the night in prayer beside Christ's tomb in the Holy Sepulchre.[17] After performing many miracles in both the Holy Land and in and around Pisa, Raynerius died in 1160 and was buried in the Pisan cathedral with great ceremony. Thereafter, he performed a great number of posthumous miracles. André Vauchez has associated this phenomenon of lay saints with the early development of communal government, especially in Tuscany and Lombardy, and differentiates the phenomenon from that of sainted kings.[18]

A relatively high degree of literacy, as well as the need to record, commemorate, and explain, is also suggested by the vast number of inscriptions that appear on medieval monuments in western Tuscany.[19] Some inscriptions merely identify the sculptor (e.g., Biduinus, Gruamons). These authorial inscriptions do not adhere to a consistent form, even within the oeuvre of a particular sculptor. Biduinus, for example, is merely noted as the sculptor of the lintels now in the Palazzo Mazzarosa and on the south flank of San Salvatore, Lucca. On the center lintel of the facade of San Cassiano a Settimo, however, Biduinus's authorship is noted in highly flattering terms: "Biduinus did in learned fashion this work you see."[20] Other inscriptions simply provide convenient labels, as on the lower lintel of San Bartolomeo in Pantano at Pistoia, where each of the apostles is identified by name.[21] Somewhat more elaborate are those inscriptions that cite directly from the Bible in order to identify a particular scene. Typical are the two inscriptions quoted from Luke 1:13 on the left capital of Sant'Andrea, Pistoia: "Do not be afraid Zechariah for your prayer is heard," and "Elizabeth your wife [will bear a son]."[22]

Romanesque portals in western Tuscany occasionally bear lengthier inscriptions that are more interpretive than narrative. On the lintel of San Giovanni Fuorcivitas at Pistoia, for example, the inscription does not describe the *Last Supper* but rather explains that the institution of the eucharist symbolizes the end of the old order and the beginning of the new order:

> While He is eating, Christ gives the disciples the words of greeting.
> While He is eating, He gives the new law and ends the old.[23]

The nine narrative lintels dicussed here are not only the sum total of the extant narrative lintels in western Tuscany, but they also reflect and embody the culture of that area.[24] Those most obviously relevant are the three lintels depicting the *Entry into Jerusalem* from San Leonardo al Frigido, from Sant'Angelo in Campo just outside Lucca, and that still *in situ* at San Cassiano a Settimo. The subject, rare in the monumental sculpture of Romanesque Italy, must have had important resonance for the citizens of western Tuscany where commercial and pilgrims' voyages to the Holy Land were not only the norm but were ongoing throughout the entire era. It is not necessary to associate the three lintels with a specific crusading event as Adolph Katzenellenbogen attempted in the case of the tympanum at Vézelay.[25] The scene is quite simply emblematic not only of the continuous and continuing voyages to the Holy Land, but also of the repeated petitions for aid and entreaties for assistance that dominated the era. R. C. Smail has noted that the number of solicitations far exceeded the number of crusades and that such appeals were especially common in the second half of the twelfth century. In fact, in the forty years between the second and third Crusades, they were made twice in every decade.[26] Clearly, then, missions to the Holy Land, for whatever purpose, were virtually a daily topic of concern. Assisted by the presence of their particular patron saint at the end of the three processions, Tuscan citizens could re-enact Christ's triumphal entry into Jerusalem and view it as a metaphor for their own activities even though commerce and warfare seem generally to have triumphed over piety, as far as the city was concerned. Collective and personal memories are thus fused together.[27]

Similarly, the two lintels at San Salvatore in Mustiola in Lucca and the single lintel at the cathedral in Barga that illustrate events from the life of Saint Nicholas reverberate locally on various levels. The Lucchese lintels, earlier than that at Barga, were carved about one hundred years after the saint's relics, escorted by the Normans, arrived in Bari in 1087. The translation of Nicholas's relics were regarded in part as a ploy to bolster Bari's prominence in its attempt to relocate the episcopal see from nearby Canosa. The significance of the relics was realized early on by the Venetians who, at about the time of the first Crusade, claimed to have translated the saint's relics to Venice. The Genoese also tried to claim the relics, thereby suggesting their value in regard to the self-definition and self-image of the three cities.[28] The pervasive interest in Saint Nicholas's cult and relics is but one aspect of the mercantile power struggles. Nicholas was a likely saint for all these rival seafaring cities, for he performed many miracles at sea and was the patron saint of tradesmen, *inter alia.*

The Lucchese and Barga lintels depicting the story of Adeodatus, the son of Getron and Euphrosina, who was captured by the infidel Marmorinus and made a servant at the latter's court, is also reflective of contemporary concerns in western Tuscany. Those going to the East for whatever motives risked being seized as was Adeodatus. His capture and his eventual rescue and return to his parents must have been a story dear to the heart of Tuscan parents who feared for their sons. The notion that their sons would be forced to live among the heathen was no empty worry.[29]

The seemingly straightforward religious subject matter of the three lintels in Pistoia had important contemporaneous relevance, as described fully earlier in this essay. The *Journey of the Magi* and the *Adoration of the Magi* on the lintel of Sant'Andrea, it will be recalled, seem to allude to Frederick Barbarossa's acquisition of the Magi's treasured relics in the conquest of Milan, while the *Last Supper* at San Giovanni Fuorcivitas suggests the duties of those cloistered there in regard to pilgrims. At San

Bartolomeo in Pantano, the rare joint image of the *Mission of the Apostles* and the *Doubting Thomas* is clearly concerned with issues of faith relevant to both pilgrimage and crusade.

All nine lintels thus have multivalent meanings that are both historical and contemporary in the context of western Tuscany in the latter half of the twelfth century. They are part of a culture which, I propose, consciously or unconsciously blurred the boundaries between sacred and secular, between today and yesterday, between the object and the viewer. Exemplary of this attitude is the vow taken by crusaders that was developed in the twelfth century, for it was an outgrowth of the ceremony during which pilgrims received the staff and the scrip. The language is telling, for the crusader's mission is compared to the voyage of a pilgrim: "Accept this staff and support for the travel and labor of the route. . . ."[30]

This sort of mutual symbiosis and interpenetration is pertinent to another often discussed issue in medieval studies, that is, the relationship among images, liturgy, and drama. Emile Mâle's well-known argument concerning the influence of liturgical drama on Romanesque iconography was refined by Otto Pächt, who sought to identify more closely the extent of that influence.[31] Such scholars of medieval drama as Sandro Sticca, Robert Edwards, and Patrick Collins have propounded the relevance of the visual arts for medieval theater.[32] Because painters and carvers were employed to make theatrical sets and props for pageants, cross-fertilization was both natural and inevitable.[33] Indeed, Innocent III perceived the importance of dramatic performances when, in 1207, he decreed that such activities were acceptable if undertaken primarily for devotional purposes and did not undermine the faith of the populace.[34] There are, I think, three ways in which the issue may be approached in regard to the Tuscan lintels: clear evidence of the influence of drama on images provided by figures or scenes that do not appear elsewhere in the visual arts but do appear in medieval drama, a shared way of visual thinking seen in the organization of narratives, and the notion of the audience's reception of the lintels and its members' local participation in the events illustrated.[35]

In the first instance, the lintel of Sant'Andrea at Pistoia is telling (fig. 4). The *Adoration of the Magi* on the right part of the lintel is, it will be recalled, a standard image, while the *Magi before Herod* is unusual because of the presence of the Nuntius who kneels facing the despot. The Nuntius, a unicum in medieval visual culture, appears in the liturgical drama concerning the Magi in the *Fleury Playbook*. There, he announces the arrival of the Magi and serves dramatically as a transition between the preceding and succeeding scene.

In a similar manner, the panel depicting the *Visitation* from the pulpit of the cathedral at Pistoia seems to be related directly to liturgical drama for it too contains a supernumerary figure lacking a parallel in visual art (fig. 12). I refer, of course, to the figure of the deacon who clearly has no place in a *Visitation* scene. The *Annunciation* play, which also includes the *Visitation*, lacks an early extant text from the twelfth century or even from the thirteenth.[36] Rather, the play is known from two fourteenth-century manuscripts housed in northeast Italy: a processional in Cividale (Museo Archeologico, CII, fols. 69v–71r) and an *ordo* in Padua (Biblioteca Capitolare, C.56, fols. 35v–38r). The latter is especially useful because of its extensive rubrics. We are told, for example, that prior to the beginning of the drama, standing in the sacristy are Mary, Elizabeth, Joseph, and Joachim. The last mentioned is probably a scribal error; Zechariah is meant, for Joachim, as the Virgin's earthly father, would have had no relationship to the events depicted.[37] Joseph's presence is also noteworthy. They are dressed in their costumes and accompanied by a deacon and a subdeacon who carry the silver-bound gospel and epistle books; Gabriel is absent because he is described as being vested in the baptistery while awaiting his miraculous entrance.[38] On the Pistoia panel, the deacon stands at the far left of the scene as if prepared to lead the costumed characters from the sacristy.

Also related to medieval theater is the lintel of San Bartolomeo in Pantano also at Pistoia (fig. 17). As noted earlier, the combination of the *Doubting Thomas* and the *Mission of the Apostles* has no textual basis in any of the gospels nor do the two scenes appear together elsewhere. Yet as Karl Young has pointed out, the stage directions for the *Peregrinus* play clearly link the two scenes.[39] Moreover, the staging of the play may have occasionally taken place in a church.[40] The lintel of San Bartolomeo in Pantano thus captures for eternity on the exterior of the church that which was performed occasionally inside the church. Given the puissance of the aforegoing associations, it is all the more unfortunate that little is known of medieval drama in Pistoia or, for that matter, throughout Italy where secure documentation really begins with the *lauda*.

The second way in which the Romanesque sculpture in western Tuscany shares concerns with medieval theater is in the notion of arrangement and organization. The lintels depicting the *Son of Getron* at San Salvatore in Mustiola at Lucca and at the cathedral of Barga are apposite examples (figs. 40 and 41). The telling details lie in the scenes at the left and right. In the former, Saint Nicholas is shown serving at Marmorinus's court. The king sits enthroned at the narrow end of the table at the left, while the queen and three other figures sit behind the table whose cloth is composed of three sets of catenary folds. At the right, in the scene depicting the feast in the house of Adeodatus's parents, the exact same arrangement is used, save that there are only three figures behind the table. With no difficulty, one can easily envision a stage set made to serve for the two incidents thereby enabling the audience to contrast the meaning of the two banquets.[41] Here, then, is a case in which parallel modes of visual organization suggest a mutual interdependence.

The capitals supporting the lintel of Sant'Andrea in Pistoia are also similarly balanced. As will be recalled, the left capital depicts the Annunciation to Zechariah on its front and the Visitation on its right, or inner, face; the right capital depicts the Annunciation on its front and Saint Anne on its left, or inner, face. In the broadest sense, the capitals of Sant'Andrea at Pistoia might be viewed as pendants, the *Annunciations* on the front of each capital and the females meeting (the *Visitation*) and observing (Saint Anne) on the inner faces of the capitals. The almost symmetrical arrangement may echo the way in which the drama of the *Annunciation* and *Visitation* was staged, for a platform was provided for Mary and a separate platform was provided for Zechariah and Elizabeth.[42]

Reception and participation are fully evidenced in the three lintels depicting the *Entry into Jerusalem*. The general association of the scene with the era of pilgrimage and crusade is too evident to bear repetition. It would nonetheless be a mistake to assume that the depiction of this event merely illustrates one of the four gospel accounts (Matthew 21:1–11; Mark 11:7–10; Luke 19:35–40; John 12:12–18) and is endowed with an updated, relevant meaning. Rather, the singing apostles holding palms or such liturgical objects as censers enact an event familiar to medieval worshippers: the procession that takes place on Palm Sunday.[43] The material is drawn from the liturgy itself rather than from the liturgical drama because the latter focussed on the resurrection of Christ rather than on the events leading up to it.[44]

The three lintels depicting the *Entry into Jerusalem* all have, it will be recalled, the patron saint of the particular church following the apostles at the end of the procession to Jerusalem (figs. 26, 31, and 33).[45] Parishioners were thus enabled to participate through mimetic activity in

Christ's entry into Jerusalem in the same way that the patron saint of each of the churches having a lintel depicting the *Entry into Jerusalem* did. Each of the saints both represented the populace in the procession and firmly grounded that procession in a local context. Surely, to the citizens of each town, the image seen on the respective church's lintel also served as a reminder of the Palm Sunday processions that took place locally each year. Documented from early on and replete with local variants, they nonetheless all contain elements of movement through and about the town in an attempt to reenact Christ's journey in the Holy Land.[46] The participatory ceremony thus had compound meaning associated with both private and public commitment. In sum, the presence of the appropriate patron saint as well as the depiction of a procession well known to all cast the observer as an engaged participant in the solemn procession that opened Holy Week throughout Christendom. The universality of crusade and pilgrimage is bound together with specificity of place. This sort of liturgical anamnesis, shared by the inhabitants of a particular locale, was both a personal and a communal memory, for it has both individual and group resonances, private and public associations.[47] Liturgy and theater interact, as historical time fuses with actual time to become ritual time.[48] The historical becomes personal.[49]

In western Tuscany, Romanesque sculpture may have found its stylistic roots in the past, but its subject matter was firmly grounded in present realities. Not only did its iconography eschew eschatology, but it was also more accessible for it was neither densely theological nor framed in an elaborate construct known only to the highly educated. Instead, the Romanesque lintels of western Tuscany speak largely of contemporaneous themes that could be both understood by local viewers and perceived as emblematic of local concerns. Indeed, the entire series of lintels, seemingly paratactic in an iconographic sense, are in reality intimately related, for the medieval Tuscan concern with contemporaneous matters did not encourage the often abstract theological speculation common in France and throughout northern Europe. The Tuscans were citizens of the commercial world, not of the Cluniac or university world. For them, the directness of the here and now was more relevant than the next life. The accessibility of the western Tuscan images, their communality and commonality, and their invitation to the viewer to participate all suggest that they partake of a culture that is more or less universally understood within its ambient, a vernacular culture, if you will. The sacred and the secular were intertwined in a manner both unprecedented and highly successful. One is reminded of Boncompagno of Signa's comment concerning memory. In his *Rhetorica Novissima* written at Bologna in 1235, he defines memory as:

> a glorious and admirable gift of nature by which we recall things past, we embrace present things, and we contemplate future things through their likeness to past things.[50]

AFTERWORD

The literature of art history, whether written by Italians or *forestieri*, has not been kind to Italian Romanesque sculpture. Sebastiano Ciampi, writing in 1810, refers to "Other monuments of such barbarous style."[1] Attitudes had not changed by the middle of the nineteenth century when Charles C. Perkins alluded to the "rude national style."[2] Nor did matters improve in the early years of this century when David A. E. Lindsay noted of Tuscan Romanesque sculpture that:

> Knowledge of the structure of the human form is absent, and not withstanding an occasional proof of a developed sense of decoration, it is not easy to ascribe merit to this group of artists.[3]

Indeed, the aforegoing criticism is but a later expression of the sort of attitude expressed by Vasari in his *Vite*, a work that came to be fundamental to the education of gentlemen.[4] Two issues are relevant. The first concerns Vasari's interest in art that looked like the natural world or seemed lifelike. Clearly, judging by this criterion, Italian Romanesque sculpture could not measure up when compared to Renaissance works. In the Italian context, Nicola Pisano's pulpit for the cathedral at Pisa, signed in 1259, is usually seen as a proto-Renaissance monument in which the sculptor clearly understood antique precedents. The inference is that prior to the mid-thirteenth century, the study or imitation of antiquity was not germane. Even the august Erwin Panofsky, in his magisterial *Renaissance and Renascences in Western Art*, failed to see the continuities in medieval Italy and instead looked to northern Europe for an interest in antiquity before the era of the Renaissance.[5]

The second pertains to the organization of the *Vite* as a series of biographies. While Vasari himself did not write individual biographies of Italian Romanesque sculptors, his methodology persists because so much of Italian Romanesque sculpture is signed—Wiligelmus, Gruamons, Adeodatus, Nicholaus, Biduinus, Antelami to name merely the major figures. Because Vasari's methods are so thoroughly engrained in the Italian consciousness, there has been a tendency to emphasize attribution problems whose pertinence to the biographical approach is unquestionable. Iconographical issues are too often overlooked.

Thus, Italian Romanesque art in all media has suffered from comparative neglect. Much commentary is concerned with what it is not, rather than with what it is. The situation is different in France. Because the French considered the medieval era to be a positive epoch in their collective history, they began to study the art of that era seriously in the early years of the nineteenth century, despite the devastations of the Revolution. The French sought to investigate the Middle Ages in a framework other than that provided by antiquity and the Renaissance eras which historiographically had been the specific purview of Italy. French medieval art thus came to be seen as innovative, a mantle that Italians certainly never sought to claim for the Middle Ages. Even Viollet-le-Duc, travelling south in 1836–37, eschewed most of the medieval monuments of north Italy in his haste to get to Pompeii, Herculaneum, and Sicily.[6]

Thus, French monuments have tended to define one's expectations of medieval art—aesthetically, chronologically, stylistically, and iconographically—in the same way that French scholarship framed and formed the study of the Crusades. Yet the monuments discussed in this extended essay have little to do with French Romanesque art. Instead, the Italian Romanesque monuments while coeval with many French early Gothic monuments, are not concerned with such common French themes as eschatology or the cult of the Virgin, and adhere closely to the style of Roman antiquity in both their format and their carving.

Rather than return to fruitless arguments concerning the primacy of France, Spain, or Italy fomented by such scholars as Kingsley Porter and Paul Deschamps, questions tailored to individual circumstances must be asked.[7] Thus, in Italy, one needs to look at communal government rather than feudalism, at civic life and the identification with one's town or territory, at secular culture dominated by commerce rather than at theological or philosophical speculation, and at the manipulation of the past rather than at the innovations of the present. The parameters need to be redefined so that Mediterranean Romanesque may be understood as one of the many coexisting styles prevalent during this fertile era. The hermeneutics of monolithic methodology, nationalistic or chauvinistic, do not suffice here. Instead, the understanding of twelfth-century portal sculpture within the matrix of pilgrimage and crusade affords insights into the unique interplay between Tuscan civic and world views.

EXCURSUS: TUSCANY AND THE HOLY SEPULCHRE, JERUSALEM

The preponderance of sculpted lintels in western Tuscany depicting the *Entry into Jerusalem* is noteworthy. The prominence of the theme has elicited comparisons between the three Tuscan lintels and the figurative lintel of the Holy Sepulchre in Jerusalem (figs. 26, 31, 33, and 51). Indeed, it has been suggested that a Tuscan carved the latter.[1] The issue is vexed because stylistic analysis is rendered difficult by the application of a latex-like substance to the Holy Sepulchre lintels in an effort to conserve them. Additionally, the chronology of the Holy Sepulchre lintels is problematic. They are carved on separate panels that could have been added at some time after the consecration in 1149, for other work on the church continued after that date.

Supporting the relationship between Tuscany and Jerusalem is the overall organization of the portals. In both cases, the lintel is the primary element and a sculpted tympanum is lacking. Against the relationship is the observation that the Holy Sepulchre's figurative lintel has little in common stylistically or iconographically with the Tuscan lintels. Rather, all partake of a general classicism that is germane to Mediterranean Romanesque art, be it in Tuscany, Campania, or southeastern France. If, for example, the Holy Sepulchre lintel is viewed with the lintel at San Cassiano a Settimo, several clear differences emerge.[2] On the former, the drapery is much softer and lacks the densely packed repetitive folds seen at San Cassiano a Settimo. At the Holy Sepulchre, the drapery folds are deeper and less regular. The figures on the San Cassiano lintel are more exaggerated than those on the Holy Sepulchre lintel; parts of the bodies are more emphasized and heads jut forward. Moreover, the iconography of the respective versions of the *Raising of Lazarus* differ in all aspects. Although the three Tuscan lintels depicting the *Entry into Jerusalem* differ stylistically among themselves, none is closely comparable to the Holy Sepulchre lintel.

The chronology of the relationship between the Tuscan lintels and the Holy Sepulchre lintel seems especially contorted. If the latter was in place by the consecration in 1149, its sculptor would then be seen as appearing in Tuscany some thirty years later. If, on the contrary, the Holy Sepulchre's lintel was carved at some time after the consecration, it could be coeval with the Tuscan lintels. If, as I argue here, there is little stylistic relationship between the two, the point is moot.

NOTES

1. G. Rossetti, "Pisa: assetto urbano e infrastruttura portuale," in *Città portuali del mediterraneo. Storia e archeologia. Atti del Convegno internazionale di Genova 1985*, ed. E. Poleggi (Genoa, 1989), 263–86. For a map of the course of the Arno from Pisa to Fucecchio, see P. Cipollaro and C. Notarianni, *L'Arno* (Florence, 1974), 63.

2. T. Szabò, "Les routes toscanes du XIe au XIV siècle," in *L'homme et la route en Europe occidentale au moyen âge et aux temps modernes, deuxièmes journées internationales d'histoire, 20–22 settembre 1980* (Auch, 1982), 269.

3. On Tuscan roads in general, see T. Szabò, *Comuni e politica stradale in Toscana e in Italia nel Medioevo*, Biblioteca di storia urbana medievale, 6 (Bologna, 1992).

4. See Raymond Chevallier, *Roman Roads*, trans. N. H. Field (1976; rev. ed., London, 1989).

5. For the various names given to the Via Francigena, see E. Repetti, "Via Francigena," *Dizionario geografico, fisico, storico della Toscana*, vol. 5 (1843; reprint, Rome, 1969), 715–16. The literature on the Via Francigena is vast and growing. Convenient compendia, especially concerning the route in Tuscany, and citations of earlier literature may be found in the works of Renato Stopani: *La Via Francigena in Toscana. Storia di una strada medievale*, Collana di studi storico-territoriali. Aspetti e vicende dell'insediamento umano in Toscana, 11 (Florence, 1984); *La Via Francigena nel senese, storia e territorio* (Florence, 1985); *Storia e cultura della strada in Valdelsa nel medioevo* (Poggibonsi and S. Gimignano, 1986); *Le grandi vie di pellegrinaggio del medioevo. Le strade per Roma* (Florence, 1986); *La Via Francigena. Una strada europea nell'Italia del Medioevo* (Florence, 1988); with G. Muzzi and T. Szabò, *La Valdelsa, La Via Francigena e gli itinerari per Roma e Compostella*, Quaderni del Centro Studi Romei, 2 (Florence, 1988); *Le vie di pellegrinaggio del Medioevo. Gli itinerari per Roma, Gerusalemme, Compostella: con una antologia di fonti*, Vie della storia (Florence, [1991]). For the Via Francigena in the Emilia-Romagna, see A. C. Quintavalle, *La strada Romea* [Milan: 1974]; Quintavalle, *Vie dei pellegrini nell'Emilia medievale* (Milan, 1977); Quintavalle, et al., *Romanico medio-opadano. Strada, città, ecclesia* (Parma, 1983).

6. For an excellent study of the Lombard era in Italy, see Chris Wickham, *Early Medieval Italy. Central Power and Local Society 400–1000* (1981; reprint, Ann Arbor, Mich., 1989).

7. For the Via Francigena in Rome, see Isa Belli Barsali, "Contributo alla topografia medioevale di Roma. 1. La Via Francigena presso la città leonina," *Studi romani* 21 (1973), 451–68.

8. On hospices in general, see V. Pfaff, "Hospitalaria, scholaria, pecunaria und die Päpste des späten XII Jahrhunderts," *Historische Jahrbuch* 97–98 (1978): 463–97; Amintore Fanfani, "Note sull'industria alberghiera italiana nel medioevo," *Archivio storico italiano* 22 (1934): 259–72. On the relationship between economic issues and pilgrimages, see E. Cohen, "Roads and Pilgrimage: A Study in Economic Interaction," *Studi medievali* 3d ser., 21/1 (1980): 321–41.

9. On Lucca, see E. B. Garrison, "Early Lucchese Manuscripts (to ca. 1150)," *Studies in the History of Mediaeval Italian Painting* (Florence, 1957), vol. 3, 221–23; *Lucca e la Tuscia nell'alto medioevo. Atti del V Congresso internazionale di studi sull'alto medioevo, 1971* (Spoleto, 1973); D. Corsi, *La pace di Lucca con Pisa e Firenze negli anni 1181 e 1184*, Accademia lucchese di scienze, lettere e arti, Studi e Testi, 12 (Lucca, 1980); V. Tirelli, "Lucca nella seconda metà del secolo XII. Società e istituzioni," *I ceti dirigenti dell'età comunale nei secoli XII e XIII* (Pisa, 1982), 157–231; Raoul Manselli, "La Repubblica di Lucca," in *Comuni e signorie nell'Italia nordorientale e centrale: Lazio, Umbria e Marche, Lucca*, Storia d'Italia VII², ed. Giuseppe Galasso (Turin, 1987), 610–731.

On the history of Pistoia, see the first chapter of David Herlihy, *Medieval and Renaissance Pistoia. The Social History of an Italian Town, 1200–1430* (New Haven, 1967); Natale Rauty, *Storia di Pistoia*, vol. 1, *Dall'alto medioevo all'età precomunale* (Florence, 1988).

For the history of Pisa, see especially Gino Benvenuti, *Storia della repubblica di Pisa*, 4th ed. (Pisa, 1982); C. Violante, *Economia, società, istituzioni a Pisa nel medioevo. Saggi e ricerche* (Bari, 1980); G. Cachiagi, *Pisa*, 4 vols. (Pisa, 1970); David Herlihy, *Pisa in the Early Renaissance. A Study of Urban Growth*, Yale Historical Publications, Miscellany 68 (New Haven, 1958); N. Caturegli, ed., *Regestum Pisanum* (Rome, 1938). William Heywood, *A History of Pisa. Eleventh and Twelfth Centuries* (Cambridge, 1921).

10. Quoted in Herlihy, *Pisa in the Early Renaissance*, 21. The text is from the *Inferno* XXXIII, 30: " . . . per che i Pisan veder Lucca non ponno."

11. On the importance of this mountain range, see Chris Wickham, *The Mountains and the City. The Tuscan Appennines in the Early Middle Ages* (Oxford, 1988). See also A. Palmieri, "Le strade medievali fra Bologna e la Toscana," *Atti e memorie della Regia deputazione di storia patria per le provincie di Romagna*, 4th ser., 8 (1918): 25–47; N. Rauty, "Il castello di Batoni e l'antico itinerario per Modena attraverso l'Appennino pistoiese," *Bullettino storico pistoiese* 74, ser. 3, 7 (1972): 65–86; Thomas Szabò, "Strassenbau und Strassensicherheit in Territorium von Pistoia (12.–14. Jh.). Untersuchungen zur Verkehrspolitik einer mittelalterlichen Kommune," *Quellen und Forschungen aus italienischen Archiven und Bibliotheken* 57 (1977): 88–137, trans.: "Strada e sicurezza nel territorio pistoiese (secoli XII–XIV). Ricerche sulla politica viaria di un comune medi-

oevale," trans. M. Ronzani, in Thomas Szabò, *Comuni e politica stradale*, 195–234.

12. On *pievi*, see E. Nasalli Rocca, "Pievi ed ospedali," *Atti del primo congresso italiano di storia ospitaliera. Reggio Emilia 14–17 giugno 1956* (Reggio Emilia, 1957), 493–507; and C. Violante, "Che cos'erano le pievi? Primo tentativo di studio comparato," *Critica storica* 26, nos. 2–3 (1989): 429–38.

13. For Barbarossa's relationship with Italy, see Isa Lori Sanfilippo, ed., *Federico I Barbarossa e l'Italia nell'ottocentesimo anniversario della sua morte. Atti del convegno. Roma, 24–26 maggio 1990* (= *Bullettino dell'Istituto storico italiano per il medio evo e archivio Muratoriano* 96 [Rome, 1990]). Also invaluable is F. Opll, *Das Itinerar Kaiser Friedrich Barbarossas (1152-1190)* (Vienna, 1978).

14. See, for example, Corsi, *La pace di Lucca con Pisa e Firenze negli anni 1181 e 1184*.

15. M. Amari and C. Schiaparelli, eds., *L'Italia descritta nel Libro del Re Ruggero compilato da Edrisi*, Atti della Reale Accademia dei Lincei 274 (1876–77) (Rome, 1883), 84–86; Benjamin ben-Jonah of Tudela, *The Itinerary of Rabbi Benjamin of Tudela*, trans. and ed. A. Asher, vol. 2 (New York, 1841), 31–38.

16. " . . . peregrinis stacio bene nota carinis." Guntheri Poetae Ligurinus, Erwin Assmann, ed., MGH SS Rerum Germanicarum, LXIII (Hannover, 1987), 244, line 239. Maria Wenglinsky graciously collaborated on the translation of many of the Latin texts and inscriptions. Unless otherwise noted, the translations are ours.

17. Jens T. Wollesen, *Die Fresken von San Piero a Grado bei Pisa* (Bad Oeynhausen, 1977), 7. During the sanctification of the altar of the church, some drops of blood fell from Clement's nose onto the altar, where they may still be seen today.

18. See S. Andreucci, "La strada romea et peregrina in territorio lucchese," *La Provincia di Lucca* 11, no. 3 (July–September 1971): 73–82.

19. For a summary annotated list of the earlier literature on the sculpture, see Dorothy F. Glass, *Italian Romanesque Sculpture: An Annotated Bibliography* (Boston, 1983), 143–46, nos. 349–66. See also H. Schwarzmaier, *Lucca und das Reich bis zum Ende des 11. Jahrhunderts. Studien zur Sozialstruktur einer Herzogstadt in der Toskana*, Bibliothek des Deutschen Historischen Instituts in Rom, 41 (Tübingen, 1972); pages 335–73 appear in translation as *Movimenti religiosi e sociali a Lucca nel periodo tardo-longobardo e Carolingio (Contributo alla leggenda del Volto Santo)*, Accademia Lucchese di Scienze, Lettere e Arti, Studi e Testi, 7 (Lucca, 1973); Clara Baracchini and Maria Teresa Filieri, eds., *Il Volto Santo. Storia e culto. Catalogo della mostra* (Lucca, 1982), and *Lucca, Il Volto Santo e la civiltà medioevale. Atti, Convegno internazionale di studi. Lucca, Palazzo Pubblico 21–23 ottobre 1982* (Lucca, 1984). For a related Tuscan monument dating to the late twelfth century, see Anna Maria Maetzke, ed., *Il Volto Santo di Sansepolcro. Un grande capolavoro medievale rivelato dal restauro* (Milan, 1994).

20. On the history of the hospice at Altopascio, see Enrico Coturri, "L'ospedale di S. Jacopo di Altopascio in Toscana lungo la via Francesca," in *Pistoia e il Cammino di Santiago. Una dimensione europea nella Toscana medioevale. Atti del Convegno internazionale di studi, Pistoia, 28-29-30 settembre 1984*, ed. L. Gai (Naples, 1987), 331–42; F. McArdle, *Altopascio. A Study in Tuscan Rural Society, 1587–1784* (Cambridge, 1978); L. Bertelli, "L'ordine dei cavalieri di Altopascio," *Giornale storico della Lunigiana e del territorio lucense*, n.s. 16 (1965): 39–45; Bertelli, "Gli ospitalieri di Altopascio in Italia e in Europa," in *Atti del primo congresso europeo di storia ospitaliera, 6–12 giugno 1960* (Reggio Emilia, 1962), 151–67; Bertelli, "L'ospizio e il paese di Altopascio (dalle origini all'anno 1239)," in *Atti del primo congresso italiano di storia ospitaliera. Reggio Emilia 14–17 giugno 1956* (Reggio Emilia, 1957), 60–72; D. Biagotti, "La Magione dei Cavalieri di Altopascio," *Atti della R. Accademia lucchese di scienze, lettere ed arti* n.s. 5 (1942): 247–65; E. Emerton, "Altopascio—A Forgotten Order," *American Historical Review* 29 (1923–24): 1–23; F. Muciaccia, "I cavalieri dell'Altopascio (con documenti inediti)," *Studi storici* 6 (1897): 33–92; 7 (1898): 215–32; 8 (1899): 347–97.

21. On the Via Cassia in Pistoia proper, see N. Rauty, "La via consolare Cassia attraverso Pistoia," *Bullettino storico pistoiese* 68 (3d ser., 1) (1966): 3–14.

22. On Atto, in addition to the general histories of Pistoia, see *ActaSS Mai*, vol. 5, 180–200. Quinto Santoli, "Pistoia ai tempi di S. Atto," *Bullettino storico pistoiese* 55 (1953): 57–75; Benvenuto Matteucci, "Attone (Atto), vescovo di Pistoia," in *BS* 2, cols. 573–76; Alessandro Pratesi, "Attone," *DBI* 4, cols. 566–67; Edward B. Garrison, "Twelfth Century Initial Styles of Central Italy: Indices for the Dating of Manuscripts, Part II. Materials (Continued). The Late Geometrical Style in the Third Quarter of the Twelfth Century (Continued). 8. The Pistoiese Region," *Studies in the History of Mediaeval Italian Painting* (Florence, 1957), vol. 3, 33–34; Atto's putative birth in Spain is now doubted; see Pratesi, "Attone."

23. On Rainerius, see R. A. Fletcher, *Saint James's Catapult. The Life and Times of Diego Gelmírez of Santiago de Compostela* (Oxford, 1984), 324. I am indebted to Professor Alison Stones for sharing with me her soon-to-be-published information concerning Rainerius's stay in Paris and his connections with Cardinal Matthew of Albano.

24. The authenticity and distribution of the body parts of Saint James is debated: John of Würzburg saw the head in the Holy Land in the Cathedral of Saint James of the Armenians, in about 1170, while the the saint's hand was in England during the same era. On this and related issues, see R.B.C. Huygens, ed., *Peregrinationes Tres. Saewulf. Iohannes Wirziburgensis. Theodericus*, Corpus Christianorum, Continuatio Mediaevalis, CXXXIX (Turnhout, 1994), 132, lines 1319–33, translated in John Wilkinson with Joyce Hill and W. F. Ryan, *Jerusalem Pilgrimage 1099–1185*, Works Issued by the Hakluyt Society, 2d ser., no. 167 (London, 1988), 267; Roberto Plotino and Justo Fernández Alonso, "Giacomo il

Maggiore," in *BS* 6, cols. 363–88; J. A. Lefrançois, "James (Son of Zebedee), St.," *New Catholic Encyclopedia*, vol. 7 (New York, 1967), 809; Brian Kemp, "The Miracles of the Hand of St. James," *Berkshire Archaeological Journal* 65 (1970): 1–19; Karl Leyser, "Frederick Barbarossa, Henry II and the Hand of St. James," *English Historical Review* 90 (1975): 481–506; Sabatino Ferrali, *L'apostolo S. Jacopo il Maggiore e il culto a Pistoia* (Pistoia, 1979); Klaus Herbers, *Die Jakobuskult des 12. Jahrhunderts und der 'Libri Sancti Jacobi'*, Historische Forschungen 7 (Wiesbaden, 1984).

25. *ActaSS Iulii*, vol. 6, 25–28, 59–68, esp. 60. The authenticity of the piece of Saint James's head resident in Pistoia thankfully does not rest on the bull concerning the re-invention of the relics issued by Pope Leo XIII on November 1, 1884, a few years after the excavations at Santiago de Compostela, even though he does reiterate Pistoia's claims therein; see Joseph Pennachi and Victor Piazzesi, eds., *Acta Santae Sedis* 17 (1884; reprint, New York, 1968), 262–69. Rather, Pistoia's stake in a piece of Santiago's acclaimed relic is more secure and of older lineage. As Lucia Gai has noted in two extensive studies, *L'Altare argenteo di San Iacopo nel Duomo di Pistoia, Contributi alla storia dell'oreficeria gotica e rinascimentale italiana* (Turin, 1984) and "Testimonianze jacobee e riferimenti compostellani nella storia di Pistoia dei secoli XII–XIII," in *Pistoia e il Cammino di Santiago. Una dimensione europea nella Toscana medioevale. Atti del Convegno internazionale di studi, Pistoia, 28–29–30 settembre 1984*, ed. Lucia Gai (Naples, 1987), 119–230, an inventory of the *Opera di San Iacopo* undertaken in 1261, the second such inventory, includes "duos libros de legenda sancti Iacobi." Formerly *Opera di San Jacopo* 25 and now *Documenti vari* 1 in the Archivio di Stato at Pistoia, the now damaged and fragmentary manuscript did not appear in the first inventory taken in 1244. This manuscript is catalogued in Lucia Gai et al., *L'Apostolo San Jacopo in documenti dell'Archivio di Stato di Pistoia* (Pistoia, 1984), 37–41. Gai thus hypothesizes that the manuscript was made at some point between the first and second inventories, a view confirmed by the paleographical evidence. The first sixteen folios contain the *Passio minor* from Compostela and thus follow the text of the *Codex Calixtinus*. The manuscript also includes an account of the translation of the relic from Compostela to Pistoia as written by one Clericus Cantarinus of Pisa, who was a chancellor in that city from 1140 until 1147; see Ottavio Banti, "'Cantarinus, Pisanae Urbis Cancellarius' (ca. 1140–1147). Fu lo strumento della preminenza politica di un vescovo in regime consolare?" *Bollettino storico pisano* 40–41 (1971–72): 23–29. Cantarinus is known to have been part of the circle of Archbishop Baldwin of Pisa, a reformer on intimate terms with Bernard of Clairvaux and Innocent II. Although Cantarinus's twelfth-century account is now lost, Pistoia's *Documenti vari* 1 of the thirteenth century contains his text (fols. 10v–16). That manuscript also contains copies of four letters concerning the relic and its translation written by Archbishop Gélmirez of Santiago de Compostela to Bishop Atto of Pisa. Such circumstantial evidence may suggest that *Documenti vari* 1 is a copy of a twelfth-century

manuscript; indeed, an early copy of the *Liber Sancti Iacobi* may perhaps have existed at Pistoia. Professor Alison Stones makes this suggestion in the as yet unpublished material referred to in note 23, *supra*.

26. On the chapel, see Gai, *L'altare argenteo*, and N. Rauty, *L'antico palazzo dei vescovi a Pistoia*, vol. 1, *Storia e restauro*, Arte e Archeologia, Studi e Documenti, 19 (Florence, 1981).

27. Paul F. Kehr, *Italia Pontificia*, vol. 3, *Etruria* (1908; reprint, Berlin, 1961), 128, nos. 1 and 2. Ferrali, *L'apostolo S. Jacopo*, 23, notes that Eugene III does not list Pisa because Baldwin, archbishop of Pisa, died in October 1145 and the pope did not ratify Baldwin's successor, Villanus, until June 1, 1146.

28. Gai, *L'altare argenteo*.

29. Rauty, *L'antico palazzo*, 112–13.

30. On Eugenius III, see recently H. Zimmermann, "Eugenio III, papa," *DBI* 43, 490–96. On Bernard of Clairvaux, see P. Zerbi, "I rapporti di S. Bernardo di Chiaravalle con i vescovi e le diocesi d'Italia," in *Vescovi e diocesi nel Medioevo (Sec. IX-XIII). Atti del II Convegno di storia della chiesa in Italia (Roma, 5-9 sett. 1961)*, Italia sacra, 5 (Padua, 1964), 219–34.

31. F. Liotta, ed., *Miscellanea Rolando Bandinelli, Papa Alessandro III* (Siena, 1986); P. Brezzi, "Alessandro III, papa," *DBI* 2, 183–89.

32. R. Pescaglini Monti, "Le dipendenze polironiane in diocesi di Lucca," in *L'Italia nel quadro dell'espansione europea del monachesimo cluniacense*, Atti del Convegno internazionale di storia medievale, Pescia 26–28 novembre 1981, Italia Benedettina VIII (Cesena, 1985), 143.

33. L. Carratori and B. Hamilton, "Daiberto," *DBI* 31, 679–84.

34. M. L. Favreau-Lilie, *Die Italiener im Heiligen Land vom ersten Kreuzzug bis zum Tode Heinrichs von Champagne (1098-1197)* (Amsterdam, 1989); P. Pierotti, *Pisa e Accon. L'insediamento nella città crociata. Il porto. Il fondaco*, Ecostoria, 3 (Pisa, 1987); G. Airaldi and B. Z. Kedar, eds., *I comuni italiani nel regno crociato di Gerusalemme*, Collana storica di fonti e studi (Genoa, 1986); R. J. Lilie, *Handel und Politik zwischen dem byzantinischen Reich und den italienischen Kommunen Venedig, Pisa und Genua in der Epoche der Komnenen und der Angeloi (1081-1204)* (Amsterdam, 1984); C. Otten-Froux, "Les pisans en Orient de la première croisade a 1406," 2 vols., Ph.D. diss. (Paris, 1981); J. Prawer, "The Italians in the Latin Kingdom," *Crusader Institutions* (Oxford, 1980), 217–49; Prawer, *The Crusaders' Kingdom. European Colonialism in the Middle Ages* (New York and Washington, 1972); V. Slessarev, " 'Ecclesia mercatorum' and the Rise of Merchant Colonies," *Business History Review* 41 (1967): 177–97; G. Rossi Sabatini, *L'espansione di Pisa nel Mediterraneo fino alla Meliora*, Studi di lettere, storia e filosofia pubblicati dalla R. Scuole Normale Superiore di Pisa, 6 (Florence, 1935).

35. Peter Classen, *Burgundio von Pisa. Richter-Gesandter-Übersetzer*, Sitzungsberichte der Heidelberger Akademie der Wissenschaften, Philosophisch-

historische Klasse (Heidelberg, 1974); Filippo Liotta, "Burgundione da Pisa," *DBI* 15, 423–38; Antoine Dondaine, "Hugues Ethérien et Léon Toscan," *Archives d'histoire doctrinale et littéraire du moyen âge* 27 (1952): 67–134; Charles H. Haskins, *Studies in the History of Mediaeval Science*, 2d ed. (Cambridge, Mass., 1927), 213–18.

36. For the development of the city of Pisa, see the recent work by Emilio Tolaini, *Pisa*, La città nella storia d'Italia (Bari, 1992); *Il duomo e la civiltà pisana del suo tempo* (Pisa, 1986).

37. For the cathedral, see E. Carli, *Il duomo di Pisa* (Florence, 1989); U. Boeck, "Der Pisaner Dom zwischen 1089 und 1120. Beobachtungen zu Bautechnik und Bauhausführung der ersten Baustufe," *Architectura* 11 (1981): 1–30; C. Smith, "The Date and Authorship of the Pisa Duomo Facade," *Gesta* 19/2 (1980): 185–92; P. Sanpaolesi, *Il duomo di Pisa e l'architettura romanica toscana delle origini*, Cultura e storia pisana, 4 (Pisa, 1975). Adriano Peroni, *Der Dom von Pisa*, 3 vols., Mirabilia Italiae, 3 (Munich, 1995) appeared too late to be consulted.

For the campanile, see P. Sanpaolesi, *Il campanile di Pisa* (Pisa, 1956).

For the baptistery, see Monica Chiellini Nari, *Le sculture nel Battistero di Pisa. Temi e immagini dal medioevo: i rilievi del deambulatorio* (Ospedaletto, 1989); C. Smith, *The Baptistery at Pisa*, Outstanding Dissertations in the Fine Arts (New York and London, 1978); C. Sheppard, "The East Portal of the Baptistery and the West Portal of the Cathedral of Pisa. A Question of Dates," *Gazette des beaux-arts* 52 (1958): 5–22.

For the Camposanto, see I. Belli Barsali, "Sui recenti studi di topografia, urbanistica e architettura medioevale pisana," *Bollettino storico pisano* 46 (1977): 537–48.

38. C. Klapisch-Zuber, *Les maîtres du marbre, Carrare 1300-1600* (Paris, 1969), 34.

39. On the dome, see Christine Smith, "East or West in 11th-Century Pisan Culture: The Dome of the Cathedral and Its Western Counterparts," *Journal of the Society of Architectural Historians* 43 (1984): 195–208.

40. Marvin Trachtenberg, "Gothic/Italian 'Gothic': Toward a Redefinition," *Journal of the Society of Architectural Historians* 50 (1991): 22–37, esp. 33.

41. Giovanna Tedeschi Grisanti, "Dalle Terme di Caracalla. Capitelli reimpiegati nel Duomo di Pisa," *Atti della Accademia Nazionale dei Lincei, Rendiconti*, ser. 9, 1 (1990): 161–85.

42. Jerrilynn Dodds, ed., *Al-Andalus. The Art of Islamic Spain* (New York, 1992), 216–18; Giovanni Curatola, ed., *Eredità dell'Islam. Arte islamica in Italia. Palazzo Ducale. 30 ottobre 1993–30 aprile 1994* [Milan, 1993], 126–31.

43. William Melczer, *La porta di Bonanno nel duomo di Pisa. Teologia ed immagine* (Ospedaletto, 1988); Albert Boeckler, *Die Bronzetüren des Bonanus von Pisa und des Barisanus von Trani*, Die frühmittelalterlichen Bronzetüren, 4 (Berlin, 1953).

44. Stefan Burger, "L'architettura romanica in Lucchesia ed i suoi rapporti con Pisa," *Annali della scuola normale superiore di Pisa*, 2d ser. 23 (1954): 121–28.

45. For the pulpit now in Cagliari, in addition to the general literature on Italian Romanesque sculpture, see primarily Enrico Brunelli, "Appunti sulla storia dell'arte in Sardegna: Gli amboni del duomo di Cagliari," *L'Arte* 4 (1901): 59–67; Dionigi Scano, "A proposito del pulpito pisano dell'antica cattedrale di Cagliari," *L'Arte* 4 (1901): 204–7; Scano, *L'antico pulpito del duomo di Pisa scolpito da Guglielmo d'Innsbruck* (Cagliari, 1905); Scano, *Storia dell'arte in Sardegna dal XI al XIV secolo*, esp. 277–94. Biblioteca storica sarda, 1 (Cagliari and Sassari, 1907); Igino Benvenuto Supino, *Arte pisana* (Florence, 1904), 107–9; Reinhard Zech, "Meister Wilhelm von Innsbruck und die pisaner Kanzel im Dome zu Cagliari," inaugural diss., Albertus-Universität zu Königsberg Pr., 1935; Martin Weinberger, "Nicola Pisano and the Tradition of Tuscan Pulpits," *Gazette des beaux-arts*, 6th ser., 55 (1960): 129–46; Heydasch-Lehmann, 88–122; Clara Baracchini and Maria Teresa Filieri, "I pulpiti," in *Niveo de Marmore. L'uso artistico del marmo di Carrara dall'XI al XV secolo*, ed. Enrico Castelnuovo (Genoa, 1992), 120–25.

46. On the shipping of stone in antiquity and the Middle Ages, see chapter 6 of this volume.

47. Because of the importance of the pulpit, it is all the more unfortunate that those charged with the care of the cathedral at Cagliari resolutely forbid the taking of photographs. To my knowledge, there are no complete views of each of the pulpits. Published photographs of individual panels are often taken from plaster casts stored in Pisa. For blurry photographs of the fronts of both pulpits as now constituted, see Weinberger, "Nicola Pisano and the Tradition of Tuscan pulpits," 134, fig. 3; 135, fig. 4.

48. On the work of Adeodatus and Gruamons, see chapters 2 and 3 of this volume.

On the career of Biduinus, see chapters 4 and 5 of this volume.

CHAPTER 2

1. On Sant'Andrea, see Sebastiano Ciampi, *Notizie inedite della sagrestia pistoiese de'belli arredi del campo santo pisano e di altre opere di disegno del secolo XII. al XV* (Florence, 1810), 24–26; Francesco Tolomei, *Guida di Pistoia per gli amanti delle belle arti con notizie degli architetti, scultori, e pittori pistoiesi* (1821; reprint Sala Bolognese, 1975), 141ff.; Schmarsow, 36–38; Giuseppe Tigri, *Nuova guida di Pistoia e dei suoi dintorni* (Pistoia, 1896), 26, 28–29; Odoardo H. Giglioli, *Pistoia nelle sue opere d'arte* (Florence, 1904), 21–23; Venturi, 940–43; Gaetano Beani, *La pieve di S. Andrea apostolo in Pistoia. Memoria storica* (Pistoia, 1907); A. Kingsley Porter, *Romanesque Sculpture of the Pilgrimage Roads* (Boston, 1923), vol. 1, 160 n. 2; Biehl, 51; Salmi, 88–89; Crichton, 101–2; Roberto Salvini, "La scultura romanica pistoiese," *Il romanico pistoiese nei suoi*

rapporti con l'arte romanica dell'occidente. Atti del I Convegno internazionale di studi medioevali di storia e d'arte (Pistoia-Montecatini Terme, 27 settembre–3 ottobre 1964 (Pistoia, 1966), 171–73; *Il patrimonio artistico di Pistoia e del suo territorio, Catalogo storico descrittivo* (Pistoia, 1967–70), 171–72; Mario Bruschi, "Note d'archivio per la storia della pieve di S. Andrea," *Bullettino storico pistoiese* 3d ser., 19 (1984): 93–106; Giuliana Bonacchi Gazzarrini, "Schede storiche," in Giovanni Michelucci and Aurelio Amendola, *Pistoia. Leggere una città* (Pistoia, 1988), 156–57; Heydasch-Lehmann, 128–31.

2. Alfredo Barbacci, "Il restauro della facciata del Sant'Andrea di Pistoia," *Bollettino d'arte* 3d ser. 29 (1935): 506–9; Giulio Valiano, "I restauri alla Pieve di S. Andrea," *Bullettino storico pistoiese* 34 (1932): 29–31.

3. The statue in the tympanum is post-medieval.

4. TUNC ERANT OPERARII VILLANUS ET PATHUS FILIUS TIGNOSI / A.D. MCLXVI. See, most recently, Pilo Turi, "Corpus Iscriptionum Pistoriensium," *Bullettino storico pistoiese* 77 (1975): 131. Pèleo Bacci, "Gruamonte ed altri maestri di pietra che lavorarono alle facciate di S. Giovanni Forcivitas in Pistoia. Note e documenti (secoli XII–XIV)," *Rivista d'arte* 3 (1905): 57–58, notes that the inscription was added toward the end of the sixteenth century, but misreads the date as 1196. Salmi, 99 n. 22, concurs with Bacci about the date of the inscription itself but observes, correctly in my view, that Bacci took 1166 for 1196. Although the carved inscription is a later addition, the information contained therein has not been questioned. The inscription, perhaps replacing an effaced painted version, may have been added at the time of the rededication in 1587.

5. FECIT HOC OP(us) GRUAMONS MAGIST(er) BON(us) ET AD(e)ODAT(us) FRATER EIUS. Turi, "Corpus Iscriptionum Pistoriensium," 131. See also Monica Vannucci, "La firma dell'artista nel medioevo: testimonianze significative nei monumenti religiosi toscani dei secoli XI–XIII", *Bollettino storico pisano* 56 (1987): 132.

On the brothers, see I. Belli Barsali, "Adeodato," *DBI* 1, 273–74.

6. VENIUNT ECCE MAGI SIDUS REGALE SECUTI FALLERIS HERODES QUOD XR(istu)M P(er)DERE VOLES MELCHIOR CASPAR BALTASAR MAGOS STELLA MONET PUERO TRIA MUNERA DON[ANT]. Turi, "Corpus Iscriptionum Pistoriensium," 131.

7. Front: NE TIMEA(s) ZACHARIAS QUUM EXA[UDITA ESSET] ORA[TIO TUA]. Inner face: [ELI]SABET UXOR TUA [PARIET FILIUM]. Turi, "Corpus Iscriptionum Pistoriensium," 132.

8. [SANCT]A ANNA, on the inner face, and on the front, [AVE M]ARIA GRATIA PLENA TECUM / MAGISTER ENRIGUS ME FECIT. Turi, "Corpus Iscriptionum Pistoriensium," 132.

9. At Cagliari, the panel of the *Annunciation* and *Visitation* bears the inscription POST GABRIEL AVE ELISABETH FESTINAT, while that on the *Adoration of the Magi* reads INTRANTES ORANT PUERUM CUI MUNERA DONANT. See Brunelli, "Appunti sulla storia dell'arte in Sardegna: Gli amboni del duomo di Cagliari," 62, 66.

10. The portal is a pastiche; it is not known whether the capitals were part of the original conception. For an extended discussion of the portal, see chapter 4.

11. G. Kaster, "Zacharias, Vater Johannes, des Täufers," *LCI* 8, cols. 634–36.

12. On the *Visitation*, see M. Lechner, "Heimsuchung Mariens," *LCI* 2, cols. 229–35; Schiller 1, 55–56.

13. On the *Annunciation*, see J. H. Emminghaus, "Verkündigung an Maria," *LCI* 4, cols. 422–37; Schiller I, 33–52.

14. The inmost sides of the inner faces of both capitals, that is, the sides closest to the door, have been so much reduced in width that parts of the figures have disappeared.

15. In this sense, it is significant that the Index of Christian Art lists the figure of St. Anne on the Pistoia capital as a portrait rather than as a participant in a scene.

16. *PL* 15, cols. 1554, 1558–59. In Lucca, there are two central Italian, possibly Tuscan manuscripts from the second quarter of the twelfth century that contain the relevant material: Lucca, Bibl. Governativa, 1379 (St. Ambrose on Luke); and Lucca, Bibl. Capit. 47. Garrison does not give the dates at which the manuscripts entered their respective collections. See Edward B. Garrison, "Checklist of Tuscan Transitional Manuscripts, Second Quarter of the Twelfth Century," *Studies in the History of Mediaeval Italian Painting*, vol. 1, 176.

17. Joseph is also present at the *Annunciation* on a relief from Charlieu dated ca. 1100 as well as on the Royal Portal at Chartres Cathedral. See Joan Evans, *Cluniac Art of the Romanesque Period* (Cambridge, 1950), 96 and pl. 167a, and Adelheid Heimann, "The Capital Frieze and Pilasters of the Portail Royal, Chartres," *Journal of the Warburg and Courtauld Institutes* 31 (1968): 73–102, esp. 78–79. The *Annunciation to Zechariah* and the *Annunciation to the Virgin* appear together on a capital in the choir of Notre-Dame du Port at Clermont Ferrand. See Bernhard Rupprecht, *Romanische Skulptur in Frankreich*, 2d ed. (Munich, 1984), 101–3, pl. 127; Zygmunt Swiechowski, *Sculpture romane d'Auvergne*, Le Bibliophile en Auvergne, 16 (Clermont-Ferrand, 1973), 126 and figs. 108–11.

18. Arturo Carlo Quintavalle, *La cattedrale di Parma e il romanico europeo* (Parma, 1974), fig. 278. On pp. 158–60, the author discusses the relationship between the sculpture at the cathedral at Parma and that at Carrara. He suggests that the *Visitation* capital at Parma as well as the Isaac capital, on the facade at Carrara and the *Visitation* capital (the first at the right in the nave at Carrara) are by the same hand, the "Maestro dei Mesi." A view of the Carrara *Visitation* capital from a different angle may be found in Franco Buselli, *S. Andrea Apostolo. Duomo a Carrara* (Genoa, 1972), 77, fig. 104.

19. On the cathedral of Carrara, see Mario Salmi, "Il duomo di Carrara," *L'Arte* 29 (1926): 124–35; Adolfo Angeli, "Carrara nel medioevo," *Atti della società ligure di storia patria* 54, fasc. 2 (1929): 5–29; Luigi Lavagnini, "Il duomo di Carrara," *Atti e memorie della Deputazione di storia patria per le antiche*

provincie modenesi 10th ser., 5 (1970): 147–65; Antonella Marchetti Pollina, "La chiesa di S. Andrea di Carrara negli antichi documenti lucchesi," *Atti e memorie della Deputazione di storia patria per le antiche provincie modenesi* 10th ser., 5 (1970): 173–81; Buselli, *S. Andrea Apostolo*.

20. The figure is not labelled and the inscription reads POST GABRIEL AVE ELISABETH FESTINAT ADIRE. He must be Joseph because he stands next to the *Annunciation*.

21. On this form of the *Annunciation*, see Don Denny, "The Annunciation from the Right from Early Christian Times to the Sixteenth Century," Outstanding Dissertations in the Fine Arts (New York and London, 1977). Denny does not discuss the pulpit in Cagliari. He observes (22) that the *Annunciation* from the right occurs with notable frequency on bronze doors of the eleventh and twelfth centuries (e.g., Monreale and Pisa). See Albert Boeckler, *Die Bronzetüren des Bonanus von Pisa und des Barisanus von Trani*, Die frühmittelalterlichen Bronzetüren, 4 (Berlin, 1953), pls. 6 and 69. These doors at Pisa and Monreale are by Bonanus of Pisa and date from ca. 1180. Denny (22–23) opines that there is no particular explanation for the reversed *Annunciation* in these monuments.

22. "S[ANCTUS] GABRIEL S[ANCTUS] ZACHARIA S[ANCTA] ELISABET." L. Bertolini Campetti et al., *Museo di Villa Guinigi, Lucca. La villa e le collezioni* (Lucca, 1968), 83–84 and fig. 30. Prior to being placed in the museum, the panel occupied various parts of the Altopascio complex; its original function is not known. Measuring 65 cm × 67 cm × 13 cm, it is rather small for a pulpit panel. On Altopascio, see especially Mario Salmi, "Sant'Jacopo all'Altopascio e il Duomo di Pisa," *Dedalo* 6 (1925–26): 483–515; Salmi dates the facade a few years after 1166, associates it with the style of Gruamons, notes that the relief was in the third chapel at the left, and suggests that that the relief functioned like the capitals at Sant'Andrea, Pistoia. Guglielmo Lera, "La chiesa dei cavalieri di Altopascio e le sue opere d'arte," *Giornale storico della Lunigiana e del territorio lucense* n.s. 16 (1965): 56–64 (for World War II damage); Giuseppe Dal Canto, "La vecchia chiesa curata di S. Giacomo di Altopascio nell'inventario del 1740," *La Provincia di Lucca* 11, no. 4 (October 1971): 61–70; Guido Tigler, "Una statua romanica ad Altopascio (per il problema della scultura monumentale nel Medioevo)," *Arte medievale* 2d ser., 4, no. 2 (1990): 123–33 (useful for restorations); Castelnuovo, ed., *Niveo de Marmore*, 141–42.

23. On San Michele at Groppoli, see Salmi, 100 n. 28; Fabio Redi, *La Pieve di S. Michele in Groppoli*, Quaderni pistoiesi di storia dell'arte, 4 (Pistoia, 1976), esp. 23–48.

24. On this and related panels, see Gaetano Beani, *La cattedrale pistoiese. L'altare di S. Jacopo e la sacrestia de'belli arredi. Appunti storici documentati* (Pistoia, 1903). Carlo Calzecchi, "Sculture romaniche del duomo di Pistoia, rinvenute durante recenti lavori," *Arti* 2 (1939): 104–6; Castelnuovo, ed., *Niveo de Marmore*, 140–41. The latter entry, written by Clara Baracchini and Maria Teresa Filieri, dates the panel to the second half of the twelfth century and, following

Sanpaolesi, associates it with the work of Guglielmus himself. To my eye, it is both more monumental and less rigid and should hence be assigned a date closer to 1200.

25. On the stylistic differences between the surviving panels of the Pistoia pulpit, see Weinberger, "Nicola Pisano and the Tradition of Tuscan Pulpits," 146 n. 15.

26. INFANS EXULTAT STERILEM DUM VIRGO SALUTAT. See Luke 1:40–41.

27. There is surprisingly little literature on Volterra. See Enzo Carli, *Volterra nel Medioevo e nel Rinascimento* (Pisa, 1978), esp. 37–40. Porter, *Romanesque Sculpture*, vol. 1, 201, assigned the pulpit to the later career of the sculptor who carved the capitals at Brive.

28. See chapter 7 of this volume for observations concerning this sort of exploration.

29. The star could perhaps have been painted. I thank Jaroslav Folda for this suggestion. William Tydeman, *The Theater in the Middle Ages. Western European Stage Conditions, c. 800–1576* (Cambridge, 1978), 168, notes that at Valenciennes in 1547, the star was obscured by means of a cloud suspended from heaven while the Magi spoke with Herod.

30. The identification of the two figures is not secure. See most recently, Heydasch-Lehmann, 84. For an illustration, see Castelnuovo, ed., *Niveo de marmore*, 121, figs. 22 and 23.

31. Attendants often stand behind Herod's throne. Occasionally a sword-bearer sits in front of Herod. See, for example, Cambridge, Emmanuel College MS. 252, folio 8r, a twelfth-century manuscript. The image is reproduced in Miriam Anne Skey, "The Iconography of Herod in the Fleury Playbook and in the Visual Arts," in *The Fleury Playbook. Essays and Studies*, eds. T. P. Campbell and C. Davidson, Early Drama, Art and Music Monograph Series 7 (Kalamazoo, Mich., 1985), pl. 5. On the manuscript, see M. R. James, *Catalogue of the Western Manuscripts in the Library of Emmanuel College* (Cambridge, 1904), 150–52. I am indebted to Adelaide Bennett Hagens for calling this folio to my attention.

32. K.A.M. Hartmann, "Ueber das altspanische Dreikönigsspiel," Ph.D. diss. (University of Leipzig, 1879), 5 n. 1. For a useful compendium of texts concerning the Magi, see Winifred Sturdevant, *The 'Misterio de los Reyes Magos'. Its Position in the Development of the Mediaeval Legend of the Three Kings*, Johns Hopkins Studies in Romance Literatures and Languages, 10 (Baltimore, 1927), 6–45. For northern European plays concerning the Magi, see Norbert King, *Mittelalterliche Dreikönigsspiele*, 2 vols. (Freiburg, 1979).

33. H. Kehrer, *Die Heiligen Drei Könige in Litteratur und Kunst* (Leipzig, 1908–9), vol. 2, 146; Hofmann, *Die Heiligen Drei Könige*, 155.

34. Collins, *Repertory*, 119. The late twelfth or early thirteenth century *Fleury Playbook* is generally believed to have originated at the Abbey of Saint Benoît de Fleury at Saint-Benoît-sur-Loire. Like Jacobus de Voragine's somewhat later *Legenda aurea* (ca. 1260), it is a compilation of texts that were no doubt widely

diffused. See C. Clifford Flanigan, "The Fleury Playbook, the Traditions of Medieval Latin Drama, and Modern Scholarship," in *The Fleury 'Playbook'. Essays and Studies*, eds. T. P. Campbell and C. Davidson, Early Drama, Art, and Music Monograph Series 7 (Kalamazoo, Mich., 1985), 1–25.

35. On this gesture and its significance, see Gerhart B. Ladner, "The Gestures of Prayer in Papal Iconography of the Thirteenth and Fourteenth Centuries," in *Didascaliae. Studies in Honor of Anselm M. Albareda Prefect of the Vatican Library, Presented by a Group of American Scholars*, ed. Sesto Prete (New York, 1961), 245–75, and reprinted in his *Images and Ideas in the Middle Ages. Selected Studies in History and Art*, vol. 1, Storia e Letteratura, Raccolta di Studi e Testi, 155 (Rome, 1983), 209–37, esp. 220–22. I cite page numbers from the reprint. Jacques Le Goff, "The Symbolic Ritual of Vassalage," *Time, Work, and Culture in the Middle Ages* (Chicago and London, 1982), 237–87. It is known that the gesture was current in Pistoia in the mid-thirteenth century. When new priests assigned to San Giovanni Fuorcivitas were invested, part of the ceremony consisted of paying homage to the priest of the cathedral at Prato by putting his hands either on a book or in the hands of the priest from Prato. See Renzo Fantappiè, "La chiesa di S. Giovanni Forcivitas e i suoi rapporti con la propositura di Prato," *Bullettino storico pistoiese* 3d ser. 6 (1971): 79–124. On p. 118, document no. 17, dated August 23–24, 1243, states: "Et ipse presbiter Benemellius ad recipiendam ab eis dictam confirmationem surgens et, . . . iuntis ambabus manibus suis misit eas in manibus eorumdem domini Iandonati et domini presbiteri Boncristiani et sic ab eis, dantibus ipsam confirmationem pro parte Pratensis Eclesie, recepit."

36. Schiller 1, 95; *PL* 38, cols. 1026 ff.

37. Salmi, *Romanesque Sculpture in Tuscany*, 89. For a contemporaneous local example, see Maria Cecilia Mazzi, ed., *Museo civico di Pistoia: catalogo delle collezioni*, Catalogo del Museo Civico, 3 (Florence, 1982), 94–95.

38. For the former, see Ludwig Schreiner, *Die Frühgotische Plastik südwestfrankreichs. Studien zum Style Plantagenet zwischen 1170 und 1240 mit besonderer Berücksichtigung der Schluszsteinzyklen* (Cologne and Graz, 1963), pl. XVI, fig. 54. For the latter, see Miriam Skey, "Herod's Demon-Crown," *Journal of the Warburg and Courtauld Institutes* 40 (1977): 274–76. The changing image of Herod in this era is treated in an interesting article by Skey, "The Iconography."

39. Salmi, 89, suggests that the figure is in the act of benediction and that the form is based on an Etruscan urn. He cites no specific comparisons and I have been unable to find any. Heydasch-Lehmann, 128–29, notes that small figures also appear on the Cagliari pulpit on the throne of Joseph in the *Nativity* and on the throne of the Virgin in the *Adoration of the Magi*.

40. Heydasch-Lehmann, 84.

41. Gai, "Testamonianze jacobee," 192, notes the aptness of the scene for the Pistoian lintel. See also, for example, Marie-Madeleine Gauthier, *Les Routes de la*

Foi. Reliques et reliquiaires de Jérusalem à Compostelle (Fribourg, 1983), 62–66; Gary Vikan, "Pilgrims in Magi's Clothing: The Impact of Mimesis on Early Byzantine Pilgrimage Art," in *The Blessings of Pilgrimage*, ed. Robert Ousterhout, Illinois Byzantine Studies I (Urbana and Chicago, 1990), 98–107.

42. As, for example, on a mid-twelfth-century ivory. See Hanns Swarzenski, *Monuments of Romanesque Art. The Art of Church Treasures in North-Western Europe*, 2d ed. (Chicago and London, 1967), pl. 125, fig. 286.

43. Gordini and Raggi, "Magi," col. 518.

44. Patrick J. Geary, "I Magi e Milano," *Il millennio Ambrosiano: La città del vescovo dai Carolingi al Barbarossa*, ed. Carlo Bertelli (Milan, 1988), 274–87, esp. 277–82.

45. Hofmann, *Die Heiligen Drei Könige*, 73–95.

46. Rolf Lauer, "Dreikönigenschrein," *Ornamenta Ecclesiae. Kunst und Künstler der Romanik in Köln. Katalog zur Ausstellung des Schnütgen-Museums in der Josef-Haubrich-Kunsthalle*, vol. 2 (Cologne, 1985), 216–25.

47. Peter Munz, "Frederick Barbarossa and the 'Holy Empire,'" *Journal of Religious History* 3 (1964–65): 20–37, esp. 32.

48. Geary, "I Magi e Milano," *passim*.

49. Willibald Sauerländer, "Les chapiteaux de la cathédrale Saint-Jean à Besançon," ed. René Tournier, *Franche-Comté romane, Bresse romane*, La nuit des temps (La Pierre-qui-vire, 1979), 215–30, 52; René Tournier, "La cathédrale Saint-Jean," *Franche-Comté* 207–14. In the cited publication, Professor Sauerländer did not agree with Tournier concerning the significance of the capitals. During a conversation on October 21, 1992, Professor Sauerländer noted that he had previously been too harsh and would now probably accept the significance of the relics' passage. I am grateful to him for his interest and kindness.

50. Rainald of Dassel's itinerary is discussed by Jakob Torsy in "Achthundert Jahre Dreikönigenverehrung in Köln," *Kölner Domblatt* 23–24 (1964): 16–17.

51. Tournier, "La cathédrale Saint-Jean," 211.

52. Peter Partner notes that the particular interests of each city and region determined allegiances during the conflicts between Alexander III (1159–81) and Barbarossa. See *The Lands of St. Peter. The Papal State in the Middle Ages and the Early Renaissance* (Berkeley and Los Angeles, 1972), 207.

53. Garrison, "Twelfth Century Initial Styles of Central Italy," 34. The bishop's name is also given as Traziano.

54. Gai, "Testimonianze jacobee," 196; Rauty, *L'antico palazzo dei vescovi*, 101.

CHAPTER 3

1. On San Bartolomeo in Pantano, see: G. Borelli, *Fondazione e progressi della venerabile abbazia di S. Bartolomeo in Pistoia* (Pistoia, 1754); Ciampi, *Notizie inedite della sagrestia pistoiese*, 27; Tolomei, *Guida di Pistoia*, 70ff.; Schmarsow,

39–40; Tigri, *Nuova guida di Pistoia*, 33–37; Giglioli, *Pistoia nelle sue opere d'arte*, 3–4; Venturi, 943–44; Gaetano Beani, *S. Bartolomeo Ap. La chiesa e l'abbazia in Pistoia* (Pistoia, 1907); Porter, *Romanesque Sculpture*, vol. 1, 160 n. 2; Biehl, 54; Salmi, 89–90; Emiliano Lucchesi, *I monaci Benedettini e Vallombrosani nella diocesi di Pistoia e Prato, Note storiche* (Florence, 1941), 51–75; Crichton, 102; Pilo Turi, "I restauri della chiesa di S. Bartolomeo in Pantano ed il pergamo di Guido da Como," *Bullettino storico pistoiese* n.s. 3 (1961): 317–26; Salvini, "La scultura romanica pistoiese," 173; *Il patrimonio artistico di Pistoia*, 140–42; Mario Bruschi, *Il complesso abbaziale di S. Bartolomeo in Pistoia* (Pistoia, 1981); Italo Moretti and Renato Stopani, *La Toscana*, Italia romanica, vol. 4, Già e non ancora, arte, vol. 19 (Milan, 1982), 230–36; Bonacchi Gazzarrini, "Schede storiche," 157–58; Heydasch-Lehmann, 132–33.

2. Beani, *S. Bartolomeo Ap.*, 19.

3. RODOLFIN(U)S OP(erarius) ANNI D(omi)NI MCLXVII. Salmi, 100 n. 26, states that although the date was added late in the sixteenth century, it is nonetheless correct. For the inscription, see Turi, "Corpus Iscriptionum Pistoriensium," 134 no. 11.

4. See, for example, Salmi, 89–90.

5. [SIMON] MATHEUS PHILIPP(us) MATHIAS BA[RTHOLOMEUS] [THOMAS] [IESUS] IOH(anne)S PETRUS ANDREAS TATD(eu)S JACOB(us) JACOB(us). Turi, "Corpus Iscriptionum Pistoriensium," 133–34.

6. For the election of Matthias, see Acts 1:21–26.

7. PAX EGO SU(m) VOB(is) Q(u)O SIT FIRMIS(s)IMA DO B(is) / CERNITE D(is)CRETE Q(ui)A S(um) D(eus) ECCE VIDETE / ME Q(u)OQ(ue) PALPATE SICUT DEBETIS AMATE / EXPLOS(is) MORB(is) P(er) CLIMATA QUATUO(r) ORB(is) / FONTE SACRO LOTU(m) MUNDU(m) C(on)VERTITE TOTUM. Turi, "Corpus Iscriptionum Pistoriensium," 133.

8. "Ecce videte me q(u)oq(ue) palpate."

9. On the *Incredulity of Thomas*, see Evelyn Sandberg-Vavalà, *La croce dipinta italiana e l'iconografia della passione* (Verona, 1929), 361–67, 490–91; "Thomaszweifel" in *LCI* 4, cols. 301–3; Gert von der Osten, "Zur Ikonographie des ungläubigen Thomas angesichts eines Gemäldes von Delacroix," *Wallraf-Richartz Jahrbuch* 27 (1965): 371–88; Schiller 3, 108–14. Sabine Schunk-Heller, *Die Darstellung des ungläubigen Thomas in der italienischen Kunst bis um 1500 unter Berücksichtigung der lukanischen Ostentatio Vulnerum*, Beiträge zur Kunstwissenschaft, vol. 59 (Munich, 1995), appeared too late to be consulted. On the Nazareth capitals, see Jaroslav Folda, *The Nazareth Capitals and the Crusader Shrine of the Annunciation*, The College Art Association of America, Monographs, 42 (University Park and London, 1986), 36. On the ampullae, see André Grabar, *Ampoules de terre sainte (Monza-Bobbio)* (Paris, 1958), 25–26 and pl. XV, 37 and pl. XLII(2).

10. Michael Brandt and Arne Eggebrecht, eds., *Bernward von Hildesheim und das Zeitalter der Ottonen. Katalog der Ausstellung. Hildesheim 1993* (Hildesheim, 1993), vol. 2, ill. IV–35 on 191 and text on 192–93.

11. See Otto K. Werckmeister, "The Emmaus and Thomas Pillar of the Cloister of Silos," *El Romanico en Silos. IX Centenario de la Consagracion de la Iglesia y Claustro. 1088–1988* (Silos, 1990), 149–61.

12. Venturi, 180 and 182, fig. 161; Arthur Kingsley Porter, *Lombard Architecture*, vol. 1 (New Haven, 1917), 423 and 423 n. 7; Géza de Francovich, *Benedetto Antelami. Architetto e scultore e l'arte del suo tempo*, vol. 1 (Milan, 1952), 28 and 28–29 n. 38; Pietro Berzolla and Armando Siboni, *Guida all'architettura romanica nel piacentino* (Piacenza, 1966), 48–50; Sergio Stocchi, *Emilie romane. Plaine du Po*, La nuit des temps, vol. 62 (La Pierre-qui-vire, 1984), 77–78; Ersilio Fausto Fiorentini, *Le chiese di Piacenza* (Piacenza, 1985), 235–37.

13. René Jullian, *L'éveil de la sculpture italienne. La sculpture romane dans l'Italie du nord* (Paris, 1945), vol. 1, 130; vol. 2, pl. LV(1).

14. PAL\PATE ET VI\DETE Q[UI]A E\GO IP\SE S\UM. Porter, *Lombard Architecture*, vol. 1, 423 and 423 n. 7, identifies the inscription as Luke 24:39. Curiously, he identifies the scene as the *Supper at Emmaus* when, actually, the passage cited follows that scene and refers to the *Mission of the Apostles*.

15. PAX VOBIS CUNCTIS EGO SUM NOLITE TIMERE VULNERA SED LATERIM. . . . The inscription is problematical. De Francovich, *Benedetto Antelami*, 28–29 n. 38, omits the last three legible words of the inscription. De Francovich erroneously cites p. 223 of Porter's *Lombard Architecture*, vol. 1; 423 is the correct page.

16. For a map showing the Via Cassia running through the center of Pistoia, see Rauty, *Storia di Pistoia*, 18, fig. 7.

17. "Pax vobis, ego sum! Nolite timere." See Collins, *Repertory*, 82–83.

18. Giglioli, *Pistoia*, 21, notes that Romanesque sculpture is derived from Early Christian sarcophagi and Byzantine ivories. In the context of the historiography of Italian medieval art, the observation is precocious.

19. On these sarcophagi, see especially Adolf Katzenellenbogen, "The Sarcophagus in S. Ambrogio and St. Ambrose," *Art Bulletin* 29 (1947): 249–59; Katzenellenbogen, "The Separation of the Apostles," *Gazette des beaux-arts* 6th ser., 35 (1949): 81–98. Illustrations may be found in Giuseppe Wilpert, *I sarcofagi cristiani antichi* (Rome, 1929), 3 vols. plus Atlas. For the *Mission of the Apostles*, see Adolf Katzenellenbogen, "The Central Tympanum at Vézelay. Its Encyclopedic Meaning and Its Relation to the First Crusade," *Art Bulletin* 26 (1944): 141–51.

20. For the iconography of the *Mission of the Apostles*, especially in the East, see David Talbot Rice, *The Church of Haghia Sophia at Trebizond* (Edinburgh, 1968), 172–77. Charles T. Little, "The Magdeburg Ivory Group: A Tenth Century New Testament Narrative Cycle," Ph.D. diss. (New York University, 1977), 74–77, notes the variety of scenes used to depict *Christ Charging the Apostles*.

21. *Jacopo Grimaldi. Descrizione della basilica antica di S. Pietro in Vaticano. Codice Barberini Latino 2733*, ed. Reto Niggl, Codices e Vaticanis Selecti 32 (Vatican City, 1972), 353–54, fols. 307v–308v. The latter folio contains a col-

ored drawing of the apse. See also Christopher Walter, "Papal Political Imagery in the Medieval Lateran Palace," *Cahiers archéologiques* 20 (1970), 155–76.

22. See primarily Maria Teresa Olivari, "Le opere autografe di Guido Bigarelli da Como," *Arte lombarda* 10, pt. 2 (1965): 33–44; Olivari, "Ancora su Guido Bigarelli," *Arte lombarda* 11, pt. 2 (1966): 31–38; Giulia Brunetti, "Indagini e problemi intorno al pulpito di Guido da Como in S. Bartolommeo a Pistoia," in *Il romanico pistoiese nei suoi rapporti con l'arte romanica dell'occidente. Atti del I Convegno internazionale di studi medioevali di storia e d'arte (Pistoia-Montecatini Terme, 27 sett.–3 ott. 1964* (Pistoia, 1966), 371–77; Clara Baracchini and Maria Teresa Filieri, "I pulpiti," in *Niveo de Marmore*, ed. Enrico Castelnuovo, 120–25.

23. PA(n)DIT(ur) H(ic) AN(te) (con)SPECTUM DISCIPULO(rum) THOMA DISTANTE Q(ui) NULLI CREDIT EO(rum). Turi, "Corpus Iscriptionum Pistoriensium," 135.

24. DISCIP(u)LIS EDIT SE X(ristus) ET O(m)NIA CREDIT THOMAS CUM TANGIT Q(ui)B(us) OS ERRANTIB(us) ANGIT. Turi, "Corpus Iscriptionum Pistoriensium," 135.

25. On the *Appearance of Christ to the Apostles*, see W. Medding, "Erscheinung Christi" in *LCI* 1, cols. 671–72; and, Ingrid Haug, "Erscheinungen Christi (E. vor den Jüngern)" in *RDK* 5/2, cols. 1327–50.

26. Purely descriptive words (THOMAS QUID QUERIS IAM TACTO VULNERE CREDIS) also accompany the scene at San Marco, Venice. See Otto Demus, *The Mosaics of San Marco in Venice*. I. *The Tenth and Eleventh Centuries* (Chicago, 1984), vol. 1, 208–9; vol. 2, pl. 351. The scroll held by Thomas reads: DOMI|NUS MEUS ET DEUS MEUS. See Schiller 2, 349.

27. Young, *Drama of the Medieval Church*, vol. 1, 433–36. The most developed version of the *Peregrinus* is the Norman text used in Sicily during the twelfth century and now Madrid, Biblioteca Nacional, MS C 132, fols. 105v–108r. See Young, *Drama of the Medieval Church*, vol. 1, 478–80.

28. The translation is by Adolph Katzenellenbogen, "The Sarcophagus in S. Ambrogio and St. Ambrose," 250–51. "Ex quo perspicuum est exstructa per apostolos spirituali Jerusalem, id est Ecclesia, . . . revelari bracchium Domini cunctis gentibus et videre salutare ejus omnes fines terrae." *PL* 24, col. 520.

29. Katzenellenbogen, "The Central Tympanum at Vézelay," 149. He quotes the translation from August C. Krey, *The First Crusade. The Accounts of Eye-Witnesses and Participants* (1921; reprint, Gloucester, Mass., 1958), 261. For the original Latin, see Raimundi de Aguilers, *Historia Francorum qui Ceperunt Iherusalem* in *Recueil des historiens des croisades, Historiens occidentaux*, vol. 3 (Paris, 1866), 300: "In hac autem die ejecti apostoli ab Iherosolymis per universum mundum dispersi sunt. In hac eadem die, apostolorum filii Deo et patribus urbem et patriam vindicaverunt."

30. On San Giovanni Fuorcivitas, see Ciampi, *Notizie inedite*, 26–27; Tolomei, *Guida di Pistoia*, 97–99; Schmarsow, 36; Tigri, *Nuova guida di Pistoia*, 66–69; Giglioli, *Pistoia*, 22; Venturi, 944; Bacci, "Gruamonte ed altri maestri," 57–76;

Bacci, "La chiesa di S. Giovanni 'Forcivitas' di Pistoia e i suoi ultimi restauri," *Bollettino d'arte* 1, fasc. 11 (1907): 23–30; Porter, *Romanesque Sculpture*, vol. 1, 160 n. 2; Biehl, 50; Salmi, 89, 99 n. 25; Crichton, 102; Roberto Salvini, "La scultura romanica pistoiese," 173; Albino Secchi, "Restauro ai monumenti romanici pistoiesi," in *Il romanico pistoiese*, 107–9; *Il patrimonio artistico di Pistoia*, 118–20; Fantappiè, "La chiesa di San Giovanni Fuorcivitas," 79–124; Bonacchi Gazzarrini, "Schede storiche," 155–56; Moretti and Stopani, *La Toscana*, 255–59; Heydasch-Lehmann, 126–28.

31. GRU-AM-ONS- MAG-ISTER- BON-US FE-C(it) HO-C OP-US.

32. Turi, "Corpus Iscriptionum Pistoriensium," 136; Vannucci, "La firma dell'artista," 133. The latter does not indicate the letters on individual pieces of marble.

33. On the Last Supper, see Laura Hibbard Loomis, "The Table of the Last Supper in Religious and Secular Iconography," *Art Studies* 5 (1927): 71–88; E. Lucchesi Palli and L. Hoffscholte, "Abendmahl," in *LCI* 1, cols. 10–18; Schiller 2, 25–41; Ludwig Hödl, "Abendmahl, Abendmahlstreit," in *Lexikon des Mittelalters*, vol. 1 (Munich and Zurich, 1980), cols. 22–27.

34. Heydasch-Lehmann, 128, urges a date of 1162.

35. Fantappiè, "La chiesa di San Giovanni Fuorcivitas," 85. Bacci, "La chiesa di San Giovanni 'Fuorcivitas'," 29, dates the cloister to the late twelfth century but adduces no evidence.

36. Fantappiè, "La chiesa di S. Giovanni Fuorcivitas," 85, 93–95.

37. CENANS DISCIPULIS CHRISTUS DAT VERBA SAL[UTIS CENANS NO]VAM TRIBUIT LEG(em) VETEREM QUOQUE FINIT. The inscription is virtually illegible and is known primarily from the older literature. See Turi, "Corpus Iscriptionum Pistoriensium," 136.

38. Creighton E. Gilbert, "Last Suppers and their Refectories," in *The Pursuit of Holiness in Late Medieval and Renaissance Religion*, eds. C. Trinkhaus and H. A. Oberman, Studies in Medieval and Reformation Thought 10 (Leiden, 1974), 371–402.

39. The sole possible exception is an eleventh- or twelfth-century relief from an unidentified location in San Bassiano at Lodi Vecchio and now in the cathedral at Lodi. Unlike the San Giovanni Fuorcivitas relief, all the figures sit on the same side of the table. See Venturi, vol. 3, 131, fig. 111; Beatrice Canestro Chiovenda, *L'ambone dell'isola di San Giulio*, Monografie e studi d'arte antica e moderna 10 (Rome, 1955), pl. 35.

40. On the cathedral at Modena, see *inter alia*, Arturo Carlo Quintavalle, *La cattedrale di Modena: problemi di romanico emiliano*, 2 vols. (Modena, 1964–65). On the *pontile* specifically, see Erika Doberer, "Il ciclo della passione sul pontile di Modena," in *Romanico padano, Romanico europeo. Convegno internazionale di studi. Modena-Parma 26 ottobre–1 novembre 1977* (Parma, 1982), 391–98; Willibald Sauerländer, "La cultura figurativa emiliana in età romanica," in *Nicholaus e l'arte del suo tempo. Atti del seminario tenutosi a Ferrara dal 21 al 24 settembre 1981*, ed. A. M. Romanini (Ferrara, 1985), vol. 1, 51–92.

41. The Volterra pulpit is little studied. See Enzo Carli, *Volterra nel Medioevo e nel Rinascimento* (Pisa, 1978), 37–40. For the symbolism of the fish on the table, see Liselotte Wehrhahn-Stauch, "Christliche Fischsymbolik von den Anfängen bis zum hohen Mittelalter," *Zeitschrift für Kunstgeschichte* 35 (1972): 1–68, esp. 34.

42. The *Last Supper* on the bronze doors of San Zeno at Verona depicts Judas on the opposite side of the table. See Albert Boeckler, *Die Bronzetür von San Zeno*, Die frühmittelalterlichen Bronzetüren, 3 (Marburg, 1931), pl. III/16.

43. IUDE CUM CENAT PRO SIGNO MANDERE SE DAT. Brunelli, "Appunti sulla storia dell'arte in Sardegna: Gli amboni del duomo di Cagliari," 64. For an illustration, see Heydasch-Lehmann, 237, fig. 58.

44. On the French examples, see Richard Hamann, *Die Abteikirche von St. Gilles und ihre künstlerische Nachfolge* (Berlin, 1955), 333–57.

45. For the relationship between this sort of portal organization and contemporaneous commentaries concerning the nature of the eucharist, see Adolf Katzenellenbogen, *The Sculptural Program of Chartres Cathedral. Christ-Mary-Ecclesia* (Baltimore, 1959), 12–15. The arrangement of the Last Supper on the *pontile* at Modena is similar to that on the Provençal lintels, save that the apostles are more rigid and restrained. On the relationship between the *pontile* at Modena and Romanesque sculpture in Provence, see especially Sauerländer, "La cultura figurativa," 51–92.

46. Léon Pressouyre, "St. Bernard to St. Francis: Monastic Ideals and Iconographic Programs in the Cloister," *Gesta* 12 (1973): 71–92. Moreover, Ilene H. Forsyth, "The 'Vita Apostolica' and Romanesque Sculpture: Some Preliminary Observations," *Gesta* 25 (1986): 77, notes the frequent depiction of the apostles in distinctive collegiate groups during the twelfth century, while Kathleen Nolan, "Narrative in the Capital Frieze of Notre-Dame at Etampes," *Art Bulletin* 71 (1989): 181–82, discusses the active participation of the apostles as a reference to the *vita apostolica*. She also notes the special charge given to canons to celebrate mass. It may be relevant that the other pulpit *Last Suppers* discussed here, those at Cagliari, Pistoia, and Volterra, were all made for cathedrals while San Giovanni Fuorcivitas at Pistoia was a monastery. Specifically in regard to S. Bénigne at Dijon, see Willibald Sauerländer, *Gothic Sculpture in France, 1140–1270* (New York, 1972), 391, notes that the subject was favored for entrances to monastic churches in Burgundy and southern France, perhaps as a response to regional heretical movements.

47. Carra Ferguson O'Meara, *The Iconography of the Façade of Saint-Gilles-du-Gard*, Outstanding Dissertations in the Fine Arts (New York and London, 1977), 28, 142.

48. Creighton Gilbert has noted that during the Renaissance, this sort of non-sacramental *Last Supper* commonly appeared in refectories while the eucharistic type of *Last Supper* was reserved for altars and chapels. Gilbert, "Last Suppers," 395.

49. See chapter 1, pp. 5–6.

50. Rauty, *L'antico palazzo dei vescovi*, 285, document no. 17.

51. Rauty, *L'antico palazzo dei vescovi*, 286, document no. 19, and 287, document no. 22. On the use of brick in Tuscany, see Piero Sanpaolesi, "Alcuni edifici romanici in cotto in Toscana," *Atti del II Convegno nazionale di storia dell'architettura. Assisi, 1–4 ottobre 1937* (Rome, 1939), 127–38.

52. Paolo Caucci von Saucken, "La Via Francigena e gli itinerari italiani a Compostella," in *Europäische Wege der Santiago Pilgerfahrt*, ed. Robert Plotz, Jakobus Studien, 2 (Tübingen, 1990), 119. See also Caucci von Saucken, "Le chemin italien de Saint-Jacques," *Saint-Jacques de Compostelle* (Turnhout, 1985), 63–75 ; Caucci von Saucken, "The 'Via Francigena' and the Italian Routes to Santiago," in *The Santiago de Compostela Pilgrim Routes*, Council of Europe, Architectural Heritage Reports and Studies, 16 (Strasbourg, 1989), 59–63; Jole Scudieri Ruggieri, "Il pellegrinaggio compostellano e l'Italia," *Cultura neolatina* 30 (1970): 185–98.

CHAPTER 4

1. Biduinus has not received extensive monographic attention. For summaries of his career, see I. Belli Barsali, "Biduino," in *DBI* 10, 365–67; E. Castelnuovo, "Maestranza pisana di Biduino, capitello figurato," in *Da Biduino ad Algardi. Pittura e scultura a confronto*, ed. G. Romano (Turin, 1990), 11–15; V. Ascani, "Biduino," in *Enciclopedia dell'arte medievale* 3 (Rome, 1992), 502–6.

2. On the site, see Gabriella Garzella, "Cascina. L'organizzazione civile ed ecclesiastica e l'insediamento," in *Cascina*, vol. 2, *Cascina dall'antichità al medioevo* (Ospedaletto, 1986), 86–95. For the sculpture, see, in addition to previously cited general works, Maria Laura Cristiani Testi, "Biduino e la chiesa dei S.S. Casciano e Giovanni," *Cascina*, vol. 4, *L'arte medievale a Cascina e nel suo territorio* (Ospedaletto, 1987), 93–121.

3. On the *Entry into Jerusalem*, see E. Baldwin Smith, *Early Christian Iconography and a School of Ivory Carvers in Provence*, Princeton Monographs in Art and Archaeology, 6 (Princeton, 1918), 121–28; Walter W. S. Cook, "The Earliest Painted Panels of Catalonia (V)," *Art Bulletin* 10 (1927): 153–204, esp. 167–78; Erich Dinkler, *Der Einzug in Jerusalem. Ikonographische Untersuchungen im Anschlusz an ein bisher unbekanntes Sarkophagfragment*, Arbeitsgemeinschaft für Forschung des Landes Nordrhein-Westfalen, Geisteswissenschaften, 167 (Opladen, 1970); E. Lucchesi-Palli, "Einzug in Jerusalem," in *LCI* 1, cols. 593–7; Schiller 2, 18–23.

4. HOC OPUS QUOD CERNIS BIDUINUS DOCTE PEREGIT.

5. UNDECIES CENTUM ET OCTAGINTA POST ANNI TEMPORE QUO DEUS EST FLUXERUNT DE VIRGINE NATUS.

6. Garzella, "Cascina," 87.

7. The taste for lavishly carved animals continued in Pisa at least into the early thirteenth century as can be seen on some of the interior capitals of the

city's baptistery. Chiellini Nari, *Le sculture nel Battistero di Pisa*, esp. figs. 40–53.

8. On the iconography of the Raising of Lazarus, see Richard Hamann, "Das Lazarusgrab in Autun," *Marburger Jahrbuch für Kunstwissenschaft* 8–9 (1936): 182–328, esp. 291–305; H. Meurer, "Lazarus von Bethanien," in *LCI* 3, cols. 33–38; Schiller I, 181–86.

9. On the identification of the Pharisees, see Collins, *The Production of Medieval Church Music-Drama*, 161–62. Simon is listed among the cast of the Fleury *Raising of Lazarus*.

10. Schiller I, 181. The literature on Palm Sunday rites is vast. See especially: A. de Santi, "La Domenica delle Palme nella storia liturgica," *La civiltà cattolica* 57, no. 1339 (1906): 3–18; no. 1340 (1906): 159–77; Adolph Franz, *Die kirchlichen Benediktionen im Mittelalter* (1909; reprint, Graz, 1960), vol. 1, 470–507; O. Braun, "Der Palmsonntag in Jerusalem zur Zeit der Kreuzzüge, *Historisch-politische Blätter für das katholische Deutschland* 171 (1923): 497–512; George Malherbe, "La dramatisation médiévale de la procession des Rameaux," *Bulletin paroissial liturgique* (1933): 99–108; A. Baumstark, "La solennité des palmes dans l'ancienne et la nouvelle Rome," *Irenikon* 13 (1936): 3–24; Noële Maurice-Denis Boulet, "Le dimanche des rameaux," *La Maison-Dieu* 41 (1955): 16–33; H.A.P. Schmidt, *Hebdomada Sancta*, vol. 1 (Rome, 1956), 270–72; H. J. Gräf, *Palmenweihe und Palmenprozession in der lateinischen Liturgie* (Steyl, 1959); D. Balboni, "Il rito della benedizione delle palme (Vat. lat. 4770)," *Collectanea Vaticana in honorem Anselmi M. Card. Albareda*, Studi e Testi, 219 (Rome, 1962), 55–74.

11. C. Vogel and R. Elze, eds., *Le pontifical romano-germanique du dixième siècle*, Studi e Testi 227 (Vatican City, 1963), vol. 2, 40–51. The tenth-century pontifical is the same as *Ordo L*; for the Palm Sunday ritual, see M. Andrieu, ed., *Les ordines Romani du haut moyen age*, Spicilegium sacrum Lovaniense, Etudes et documents, fasc. 29, vol. 5 (Louvain, 1961), 162–83.

12. C. Vogel, *Medieval Latin Liturgy: An Introduction to the Sources*, rev. and trans. by W. G. Storey and N. K. Rasmussen (Washington, D.C., 1986), 230–31. Originally published as *Introduction aux sources de l'histoire du culte chrétien au moyen âge* (Spoleto, 1981). On the distinctive characteristics of the Lucchese liturgy, see Giovanni Mercati, "Usi liturgici non romani in Toscana?," *Rassegna gregoriana* 2 (1903), cols. 23–26. Mercati's suggestion was later developed by Martino Giusti: "L'Ordo officiorum' della cattedrale di Lucca, *Miscellanea Giovanni Mercati*, vol. II: *Letteratura medioevale*, Studi e Testi, 122 (Vatican City, 1946), 523–66, and "L'antica liturgia lucchese," *Lucca, Il Volto Santo e la civiltà medioevale. Atti. Convegno internazionale di studi. Lucca, Palazzo Pubblico, 21–23 ottobre 1982* (Lucca, 1984), 21–44. For further observations on the Palm Sunday rite in central Italy, see Gräf, *Palmenweihe und Palmenprozession*, 57–69.

13. "Contulit et mores festivos et stationes, Quod non est Tuscis omnibus

ecclesiis." Rangerius of Lucca, *Vita metrica s. Anselmi Lucensis episcopi*, G. Schwartz et al., eds., MGH SS 30/2, lines 707–8.

14. "O filii et filiae, Rex caelestis, Rex gloriae, Morte surrexit hodie. Alleluia!" Collins, *Medieval Church Music-Dramas*, 195.

15. Kathleen M. Ashley, "The Fleury 'Raising of Lazarus' and Twelfth-Century Currents of Thought," in *The Fleury Playbook. Essays and Studies*, Thomas P. Campbell and Clifford Davidson, eds., Early Drama, Art, and Music Monograph Series, 7 (Kalamazoo, Mich., 1985), 100–19.

16. Sant'Angelo in Campo is about three kilometers from Lucca on the road leading to the Ponte S. Pietro on the Serchio River. See Emanuele Repetti, *Dizionario geografico fisico storico della Toscana*, vol. 1 (Florence, 1833), 86. In the mid-nineteenth century, the lintel was on the exterior of the chapel at the Villa Mazzarosa. See Antonio Mazzarosa, *Guida di Lucca e dei luoghi più importanti del ducato* (Lucca, 1843), 164–65. I have been unable to ascertain exactly when the lintel was moved to the Palazzo Mazzarosa in Lucca proper.

17. HOC OPUS [PER]EGIT MAGISTER BIDUINUS. On the various readings of the inscription and the damage to it, see F. Kobler, "Das Pisaner Affenkapitell in Berlin-Glienicke," in *Munuscula Discipulorum. Kunsthistorische Studien Hans Kauffmann zum 70. Geburtstag 1966*, eds. T. Buddensieg and M. Winner (Berlin, 1968), 162 n. 18.

18. Ridolfi, *Lucca*, 86. For the image of Saint Michael, see *inter alia*, Max de Fraipont, "Les origines occidentales du type de saint Michel debout sur le dragon," *Revue belge d'archéologie et d'histoire de l'art* 7 (1937): 289–301.

19. Boeckler, *Die Bronzetüren des Bonanus von Pisa und des Barisanus von Trani*; J. White, "The Bronze Doors of Bonanus and the Development of Dramatic Narrative," *Art History* 11 (1988): 158–94. The question of the chronological relationship between Biduinus's work and Bonanus's doors made for the cathedral at Pisa is moot, for Bonanus's doors in the Porta di San Ranieri of the cathedral are undated. The doors he made for the main portal of Pisa's cathedral bore an inscription giving the year as 1180; these doors were destroyed by fire in 1595.

20. A. Caleca, *La dotta mano. Il Battistero di Pisa* (Bergamo, 1991), 39–70.

21. For a more detailed map showing the location of San Leonardo al Frigido, see P. Giorgieri, *Carrara*, La città nella storia d'Italia (Rome and Bari, 1992), 28.

22. "Fluvius deinde re et nomine Frigidus, aquis arenisque perlucidus, secus Massam amaenissimam terram descendit in pelagus." G. Sforza, "Massa di Lunigiana nella prima metà del secolo XVIII," *Atti e memorie della R. Deputazione di storia patria per le provincie modenesi*, ser. 5, 5 (1907), 93 n. 2; Massimo Bertozzi, *Massa* (Genoa, 1985), 7 and 7 n. 2.

23. "Nizza della nostra Toscana." Noted by Sforza, "Massa di Lunigiana," 99.

24. Benedict of Peterborough, *Ex Gestis Henrici II et Ricardi I*, MGH SS XXVII, 131.

25. F. P. Magoun, Jr., "The Pilgrim Diary of Nikulas of Munkathvera: the Road to Rome," *Mediaeval Studies* 6 (1944): 350.

26. Geo Pistarino, "Diocesi, pievi e parrocchie nella Liguria medievale (secoli XII–XV)," in *Pievi e parrocchie nella Liguria medievale (sec. XII–XV). Atti del VI convegno di storia della chiesa in Italia (Firenze, 21–25 sett. 1981)* (Rome, 1984), vol. 2, 646.

27. The portal has been published most extensively by Carmen Gómez-Moreno, "The Doorway of San Leonardo al Frigido and the Problem of Master Biduino," *Metropolitan Museum of Art Bulletin* 23 (June 1965): 349–61. See also G. A. Matteoni, *Guida delle chiese di Massa Lunense* (Massa, 1879), 94–96; U. Giampaoli, "Una scultura di maestro Biduino nella chiesa di S. Leonardo al Frigido," *Giornale storico della Lunigiana* 13 (1923): 113–21; Salmi, "Sant'Jacopo di Altopascio e il Duomo di Pisa," 499; Salmi, *L'architettura romanica in Toscana* (Milan, 1927), pl. 216; Salmi, *Romanesque Sculpture in Tuscany* (Florence, 1928), 91–92; L. Pfanner, *Le origini di Massa, la 'Taberna Frigida' e la chiesa con l'ospedale di S. Leonardo al Frigido* (Massa, 1954); Pfanner, "I lavori della Sopraintendenza ai Monumenti e Gallerie di Pisa agli edifici monumentali della Lunigiana e Garfagnana," *Giornale storico della Lunigiana*, n.s. 7 (1956): 50–52; Belli Barsali, "Biduino"; Kobler, "Das Pisaner Affenkapitell in Berlin-Glienicke"; A. Borg, "Observations on the Historiated Lintel of the Holy Sepulchre, Jerusalem," *Journal of the Warburg and Courtauld Institutes* 32 (1969): 25–40; Borg, "The Holy Sepulchre Lintel," *Journal of the Warburg and Courtauld Institutes* 35 (1972): 389–90; L. Castelnuovo-Tedesco, "Romanesque Sculpture in North American Collections. XXII. The Metropolitan Museum of Art. Part II: Italy (1)," *Gesta* 24/1 (1985): 71–73; Heydasch-Lehmann, 157–61. Maria Adelaide Marcucci, *Guida storica ed artistica delle chiese di Massa*, [Massa, 1987] is meant to commemorate the one-hundredth anniversary of the publication of Matteoni's guide. For financial reasons, not all the churches discussed by Matteoni are included; San Leonardo al Frigido is among those omitted. A comprehensive bibliography on the site can be found in Maria Grazia Armanini, "Resti scheletrici umani rinvenuti in località S. Leonardo al Frigido," *Giornale storico della Lunigiana e del territorio lucense* n.s. 37 (1986): 75–81.

28. The year 1870 is given in "Mostra di arte italiana," *Sele arte* 13, fasc. 75 (1965): 25. No source is given for the information. The correct date of the removal is probably at least a decade later, that is, 1880, for Matteoni describes it as *in situ* in his *Guida*, 95, published in 1879. For a photograph of the portal installed at the Villa Monticello, see *Dedalo* 6 (1925–26): 499; there, only the lintel and capitals are visible.

29. Gómez-Moreno, "Doorway."

30. Colombo Angeletti, *S. Leonardo. Abate di Noblat* (Rome, 1966). See also B. Cignitti and C. Colafranceschi, "Leonardo da Nobiliacum," in *BS* 7, cols. 1198–1208; J. Dünninger, "Leonhard von Noblac," *LCI* 7, cols. 394–98. On his later cult in Tuscany, see M. Seidel, "Ikonographie und Historiographie: 'Conver-

satio Angelorum in Silvis'. Eremiten-Bilder von Simone Martini und Pietro Lorenzetti," *Städel Jahrbuch* 10 (1985): 113–26. On his cult is eastern Italy, see Berengario Gerola, "Il culto di S. Leonardo ed i suoi ex-voto nei XIII comuni," *Il Folklore italiano. Archivio trimestrale per la raccolta e lo studio delle tradizioni popolari italiane* 5 (1930): 99–125. For Saint Leonard's cult in the eastern Alps, see Leopold Kretzenbacher, "Die Ketten um die Leonhardkirchen im Ostalpenraume. Kulthistorische Beiträge zur Frage der Gürtung von Kultobjekten in der religiösen Volkskultur Europas," in *Kultur und Volk. Beiträge zur Volkskunde aus Österreich, Bayern und der Schweiz. Festschrift für Gustav Gugitz zum achtzigsten Geburtstag*, ed. Leopold Schmidt (Vienna, 1954), 165–202.

31. Similarly, a pilgrim's medal now in the Musée Cluny at Paris shows the saint freeing a prisoner. See Yves Bottineau, *Les Chemins de Saint-Jacques* (Paris, 1964), 84. Bottineau does not date the medal. For this and other examples, see Colette Lamy-Lassalle, "Enseignes de pèlerinages de Saint Léonard," *Bulletin de la société nationale des antiquaires de France* (1990): 157–67.

Demus, *The Mosaics of San Marco*, vol. 2, *Text*, 26, likewise suggests the relevance of Saint Leonard for the Crusaders. Saint Leonard also appears holding both manacles and a cross on an icon from Saint Catherine's on Mount Sinai made for a Western patron sometime between ca. 1170 and ca. 1187. On this icon, see most recently, Jaroslav Folda, *The Art of the Crusaders in the Holy Land, 1098–1187* (Cambridge and New York, 1995), 461–62 and pl. 10:19. See also Kurt Weitzmann, "Icon Painting in the Crusader Kingdom", *Dumbarton Oaks Papers* 20 (1966): 54–55 and fig. 8.

32. On the cathedral at Parma, see Quintavalle, *La cattedrale di Parma*. For a color illustration of the capital, see R. Tassi, *Il duomo di Parma*, I. *Il tempo romanico* (Milan, 1966), 41, pl. 22. Iconographically, the left doorpost of San Leonardo al Frigido is similar to two panels from the pulpit at Castellarquato in the Emilia-Romagna, though the style differs. See A. C. Quintavalle, "Castellarquato e Moissac; un pontile e un ambone post-wiligelmici," *Romanico padano, civiltà d'occidente*, Raccolta pisana di saggi e studi, 25, ed. Carlo L. Ragghianti (Florence: 1969), pls. 169 and 175.

33. See above, chapter 2, pp. 13–15.

34. The ape capital currently *in situ* is a poor copy. See Sanpaolesi, *Il campanile di Pisa*, 47. There is also an ape capital in the matroneum of the cathedral at Pisa; see Joselita Serra, "Un capitello del duomo di Pisa," *Commentari* 12 (1961): 245–46.

35. Friedrich Kobler, "Das Pisaner Affenkapitell." The capital, now badly damaged, has recently been published by Gerd-H. Zuchold, *Der "Klosterhof" des Prinzen Karl von Preussen im Park von Schloss Glienicke in Berlin*, vol. 2, *Katalog der von Prinz Karl von Preussen im "Klosterhof" aufbewahrten Kunstwerke* (Berlin, 1993), 19 and pl. 7a. On the campanile sculpture, see also M. L. Cristiani Testi, "Sculture nel campanile pisano," *Critica d'arte* 41, fasc. 147

(1976): 14–30; Castelnuovo, "Maestranza pisana di Biduino, capitello figurato," 11–15.

36. H. W. Janson, *Apes and Ape Lore in the Middle Ages and the Renaissance* (London, 1952), 30, 37, 47. The *Bestiary* notes the similarity between monkeys and the devil. See T. H. White, *The Bestiary. A Book of Beasts* (New York, 1954), 34–35.

37. William Coffman McDermott, *The Ape in Antiquity*, Johns Hopkins University Studies in Archaeology, 27, ed. David M. Robinson (Baltimore, 1938), 110.

38. McDermott, *The Ape in Antiquity*, 110.

39. Janson, *Apes and Ape Lore*, 47.

40. For illustrations of apes and monkeys as companions of *jongleurs*, see Chiara Settis Frugoni, "La rappresentazione dei giullari nelle chiese fino al XII sec.," in *Il contributo dei Giullari alla drammaturgia italiana delle origini. Atti del II convegno di studio. Viterbo, 17–19 giugno 1977* (Città di Castello, 1978), 113–34, esp. figs. 25–26.

41. For St. Cassian of Imola, see H. Delehaye, *Les passions des martyrs et les genres littéraires* (Brussels, 1921), 407–11; F. Lanzoni, "Le leggende di San Cassiano d'Imola," *Didaskelion* n.s. 3, fasc. 2 (1925; reprint, Amsterdam, 1969), 1–44; Lanzoni, *Le diocesi d'Italia dalle origini al principio del secolo VII (AN. 604)*, Studi e Testi, 35 (Vatican City, 1927), 773–74; G. D. Gordini, "Cassiano di Imola," in *BS* 3, cols. 909–11; Magdalen Bless-Grabher, *Cassian von Imola: die Legende eines Lehrers und Märtyrers und ihre Entwicklung von der Spätantike bis zur Neuzeit*, Geist und Werk der Zeiten, 56 (Bern, 1978), esp. 93–96; A.-M. Palmer, *Prudentius on the Martyrs* (Oxford, 1989), 242–43, 263, 273, 275.

42. This issue is dicussed more fully in chapter 7.

Chapter 5

1. On San Salvatore in Mustiola, see Tommaso Felice Trenta, *Guida del forestiere per la città e il contado di Lucca* (Lucca, 1820), 116–19; Giorgio Giorgi, *S. Salvatore in Mustiola*, Le Chiese di Lucca, 4 (Lucca, 1981); Isa Belli Barsali, *Lucca. Guida alla città*, 2d ed. (Lucca, 1988), 248–49; Luca Ricca, Simonetta Simonetti and Gerardo Nolledi, *450 Anniversario della fondazione della Compagnia del S.S. Nome di Gesù* (Lucca, 1990).

2. On the lintels, see Venturi, 948–49; Biehl, 71–72; Salmi, 92–93, 101 n. 42; Toesca, 742ff.; Crichton, 103; Heydasch-Lehmann, 168–70.

3. On Biduinus, see chapter 4, n. 1.

4. BIDVUINO ME FECIT HOC OP(us). Vannucci, "La firma dell'artista," 127.

5. S(ANCTUS) NICA OLAUS P(RES)B(I)T(ER).

6. The literature on Barga is sparse. See Arnaldo Bonaventura, *I Bagni di Lucca, Coreglia e Barga*, Italia artistica, ser. I, 75 (Bergamo, 1914); Alfredo Della Pace, *Il duomo di Barga e le terre robbiane di Barga* (Barga, 1927), 16; Luigi

Perà, *Il duomo di Barga*, I monumenti italiani. Reale Accademia d'Italia, ser. 1, fasc. 11 (Rome, 1937); Perà, *Il duomo di Barga e i suoi ampliamenti* (Pisa, 1938). See the last mentioned, 26 n. 2, for the peregrinations of the lintel. It was placed in its current position during the restoration begun in 1926.

7. On this incident, see Virginia Wylie Egbert, "St. Nicholas. The Fasting Child," *Art Bulletin* 46 (1964): 68–70; Léon Pressouyre, "Nouvelle identification d'une statue-colonne de Saint-Maur-des-Fossés," *Bulletin monumental* 122 (1964): 393–94.

8. On the use of this principle in scenes from the life of St. Nicholas, see Nancy Patterson Ševčenko, *The Life of St. Nicholas in Byzantine Art*, Centro Studi Bizantini, Bari, Monografie I (Turin, 1983). In addition to the bibliography on the Bathing of the Christ Child cited by Ševčenko, see Vincent Juhel, "Le bain de l'Enfant-Jésus. Des origines à la fin du douzième siècle," *Cahiers archéologiques* 39 (1991): 111–32.

9. The towers are similar to those appearing later (1290) on a Genoese marble plaque commemorating that city's capture of the port of Pisa. See, most recently, Castelnuovo, ed., *Niveo de marmore*, 199, fig. 43.

10. On the Péccioli altarpiece, see Edward B. Garrison, *Italian Romanesque Panel Painting. An Illustrated Index* (Florence, 1949), 152, no. 398; Hellmut Hager, *Die Anfänge des italienischen Altarbildes. Untersuchungen zur Entstehungsgeschichte des toskanischen Hochaltarretabels* (Munich, 1962), 95 and pl. 135.

11. The classic work by Karl Meisen, although predominantly concerned with northern Europe is nonetheless valuable. See his *Nikolauskult und Nikolausbrauch im Abendlande. Eine kultgeographisch-volkskundliche Untersuchung*, Forschungen zur Volkskunde, 9–12 (1931; reprint, Mainz, 1981), Quellen und Abhandlungen zur mittelrheinischen Kirchengeschichte, 41. Also useful are: Karlheinz Blaschke, "Nikolaipatrozinium und städtische Frühgeschichte," *Zeitschrift der Savigny-Stiftung für Rechtsgeschichte* 84, Kanonistische Abteilung 53 (1967): 273–337; Niccolò Del Re and Maria Chiara Celletti, "Nicola (Nicolò)," in *BS* 9, cols. 923–48; L. Petzold, "Nikolaus von Myra (von Bari)," in *LCI* 8, cols. 45–58; Charles W. Jones, *The Saint Nicholas Liturgy and Its Literary Relationships (Ninth to Twelfth Centuries)*, University of California English Studies, 27 (Berkeley and Los Angeles, 1963); Jones, *Saint Nicholas of Myra, Bari and Manhattan. Biography of a Legend* (Chicago, 1978); Edward G. Clare, *St. Nicholas, His Legends and Iconography* (Florence, 1985); Patrick J. Geary, *Furta Sacra. Thefts of Relics in the Central Middle Ages*, rev. ed. (Princeton, 1990), 94–103. For the cult of Saint Nicholas in the area around Lucca, see Augusto C. Ambrosi, "Il culto di S. Nicolao in Garfagnana e in Lunigiana", *Archivio storico per le province parmensi* 4th ser. 19 (1967), 35–53.

For Saint Nicholas in Byzantine art, see Ševčenko, *Life*. On the translation of the relics and the development of the cult, see especially: Antonio Gambacorta, "Culto e pellegrinaggi a San Nicola di Bari fino alla prima Crociata," in *Pel-*

legrinaggi e culto dei santi in Europa fino alla 1ª Crociata, 8–11 ottobre 1961, Convegni del centro di studi sulla spiritualità medievale, 4 (Todi, 1963), 485–502; A. Pertusi, "Ai confini tra religione e politica. La contesa per le reliquie di San Nicola tra Bari, Venezia e Genova," *Quaderni medievali* 5 (June 1978):, 6–56; Vera von Falkenhausen, "Bari bizantina: profilo di un capoluogo di provincia (secoli IX–XI)," *Spazio, società, potere nell'Italia dei comuni,* ed. Gabriella Rossetti (Naples, 1986), esp. 220–27; Gerardo Cioffari, "L'origine del culto di S. Nicola in Puglia," *Nicholaus* 11 (1983): 145–53; Cioffari, *S. Nicola nella critica storica* (Bari, 1987); Cioffari, "La vita," in *San Nicola di Bari e la sua basilica. Culto, arte, tradizione,* ed. Giorgio Otranto (Milan, 1987), 20–36.

12. Jones, *Saint Nicholas,* 47, 94. A Latin text may be found in Angelo Mai, *Spicilegium Romanum* (Rome, 1840), vol. 4, 323–39. For an Italian translation of John the Deacon's *Vita,* see Pasquale Corsi, *La traslazione di San Nicola: le fonti,* Centro Studi Nicolaiani, Studi e Testi, 8 (Bari, 1987); for his translation, Corsi uses the reprint of B. Mombritius, *Sanctuarium seu Vitae Sanctorum* 2 (Paris, 1910), 305–9 (= folios 168r–170r of the original edition). On John the Deacon, see F. Savio, "Giovanni Diacono, biografo dei vescovi napoletani," *Atti della Reale accademia delle scienze di Torino* 50 (1914): 974–88; D. Mallardo, "Giovanni diacono napoletano," *Rivista di storia della chiesa in Italia* 2 (1948): 317–37.

13. Jones, *Saint Nicholas,* 108; Jones, *Liturgy, passim.*

14. "Mundi Roma caput suis / aequalem celebrat semper apostolis, / cuius crebra iuvamina / non multis precibus quaerit et impetrat." See Anselmo Lentini, "La leggenda di S. Nicola di Mira in un'ode di Alfano cassinese," *Medioevo Letterario Cassinese. Scritti vari,* ed. Faustino Avagliano, Miscellanea Cassinese, 57 (Montecassino, 1988), 247–58; the poem quoted here appears on 250, lines 61–64. See also Lentini and Fausto Avagliano, *I carmi di Alfano I, Archivescovo di Salerno,* Miscellanea Cassinese, 38 (Monte Cassino, 1974). Additional medieval hymns about Saint Nicholas may be found in Guido Maria Dreves, *Liturgische Hymnen des Mittelalters aus Handschriften und Wiegendrucken,* Analecta Hymnica Medii Aevi, 22 (Leipzig, 1895), 205–12, nos. 348–58; the hymn of Alfanus of Salerno is no. 348 therein.

15. *PL* 141, cols. 59–60. For Urban II as a promoter of the cult of Saint Nicholas, see C. H. Brakel, "Die vom Reformpapsttum geförderten Heiligenkulte," *Studi gregoriani* 9 (Rome, 1972), esp. 294–97, 301–2, 305.

16. Otto E. Albrecht, *Four Latin Plays of St. Nicholas from the 12th Century Fleury Play-book* (Philadelphia, 1935), 14–15.

17. Jones, *Liturgy,* 26.

18. Von Falkenhausen, "Bari bizantina," 226.

19. Clare, *Saint Nicholas,* 55. Meisen, 174, citing a Sacramentary written for the cathedral at Ivrea between 1075 and 1090, suggests that the feast of Saint Nicholas was observed earlier in north Italy than in central Italy.

20. W.A.B. Coolidge, *Swiss Travel and Swiss Guide-books* (London, 1889), 4.

21. Blaschke, "Nikolaipatrozinium."

22. Clare, *St. Nicholas*, 17–18.

23. "Cujus miracula per totam mundi latitudinem diffunduntur; quem laudat orbis terrae, et qui habitant in eo." *PL* 184, col. 1055. Also quoted by Albrecht (*Four Latin Plays of Saint Nicholas*, 16) who cites Meisen, *Nikolauskult und Nikolausbrauch*, 297, for the attribution of the sermon.

24. Mary Sinclair Crawford, *Life of St. Nicholas*, Publications of the University of Pennsylvania Series in Romanic Languages and Literatures, 12 (Philadelphia, 1923); Einar Ronsjö, ed., *La vie de Saint Nicolas par Wace. Poème religieux du XIIe siècle publié d'après tous les manuscrits*, Etudes romanes de Lund, 5 (Lund and Copenhagen, 1945).

25. On the *Fleury Playbook*, see especially: Albrecht, *Four Latin Plays of St. Nicholas*; Collins, *The Production of Medieval Church Music-Drama*; Campbell and Davidson, eds., *The Fleury Playbook. Essays and Studies*; C. W. Brockett, "'Persona in Cantilena': St. Nicholas in Music in Medieval Drama," *The Saint Play in Medieval Europe*, ed. C. Davidson, Early Drama, Art and Music Monograph Series, 8 (Kalamazoo, Mich., 1986), 11–29; Young, *Drama*, vol. 2, 307–60. The lintels would seem to give lie to Ambrosi's comment ("Il culto di S. Nicolao," 51) that the intensity of the cult diminished in the area around Lucca.

26. Laura Tarroni, *La festa di S. Nicola nelle istituzioni scolastiche medioevali* (Bari, 1988), 42–43; Christopher Hohler, "The Proper Office of St. Nicholas and Related Matters with Reference to a Recent Book," *Medium Aevum* 36 (1967): 40–48, a review of Jones, *The Liturgy*; H. Silvestre also published an extensive review in *Revue d'histoire ecclésiastique* 60/1 (1965): 138–46; Sandro Sticca, "Italian Theater of the Middle Ages: from the 'Quem quaeritis' to the 'Lauda'," *Forum Italicum* 14 (1980): 275–310; Sticca, "Italy: Liturgy and Christocentric Spirituality," *The Theater of Medieval Europe. New Research in Early Drama*, ed. Eckehard Simon (Cambridge, 1991), 169–88.

27. Here, the lucid explanation of Ševčenko is most helpful. See her *Life of St. Nicholas*, 18ff.

28. For this life, see Ihor Ševčenko and Nancy Patterson Ševčenko, *The Life of Saint Nicholas of Sion*, The Archbishop Iakovos Library of Ecclesiastical and Historical Sources, 10 (Brookline, Mass., 1984). The Greek texts were published by Gustav Anrich, *Hagios Nikolaos. Der Heilige Nikolaos in der griechischen Kirche*, 2 vols. (Berlin, 1913–17).

29. *Bibliotheca hagiographica graeca* 1364; Anrich, *Hagios Nikolaos*, vol. 1, 392–417, esp. 393, 409–10; Ševčenko, *The Life*, 66–69, 143–48. In the Greek legends, the lad rescued from the pagans is named Basil rather than Adeodatus. On the Greek legend, see also A. P. Kazhdan, "Saint Nicholas, Saint George and the Cretans' Attacks," *Byzantion* 54 (1984): 176–82.

30. William Granger Ryan, trans., *The Golden Legend. Readings on the Saints* (Princeton, 1993), vol. 1, 21–27.

31. Ryan, *The Golden Legend*, vol. 1, xiii; for an interesting, recent characterization of the *Golden Legend*, see Evelyn Birge Vitz, "From the Oral to the Written in Medieval and Renaissance Saints' Lives," *Images of Sainthood in Medieval Europe*, eds. Renate Blumenfeld-Kosinski and Timea Szell (Ithaca and London, 1991), 97–114, esp. 101ff.

32. Ryan, *Golden Legend*, vol. 1, xvii–xviii.

33. Kaftal, *Iconography*, 755–67. See note 10 also.

34. Paul F. Kehr, *Italia Pontificia*, vol. 3, *Etruria* (1908; reprint, Berlin, 1961), 411.

35. Kehr, *Etruria*, 432, no. 97; Enrico Coturri, "La canonica di S. Frediano di Lucca dalla prima istituzione (metà del sec. XI) alla unione alla congregazione riformata di Fregionaria (1517)," *Actum Luce* 3 (1974): 47–80; E. B. Garrison, "Three Manuscripts for Lucchese Canons of S. Frediano in Rome," *Journal of the Warburg and Courtauld Institutes* 38 (1975): 1–52; Marchetti Pollina, "La chiesa di S. Andrea di Carrara negli antichi documenti lucchesi," 173–78; W. Gehrt, *Die Verbände der Regularkanonikerstifte S. Frediano in Lucca, S. Maria in Reno bei Bologna, S. Maria in Porto bei Ravenna und die 'cura animarum' im 12. Jahrhundert* (Frankfurt am Main, 1984), 8–78; P. Gy, "L'influence des chanoines de Lucques sur la liturgie du Latran," *Revue des sciences religieuses* 58 (1984): 31–41.

36. Heydasch-Lehmann, *passim*.

37. In a similar vein, Emile Bertaux suggested that the frescoed depiction of the *Filius Getronis* in Santa Annunziata at Minuto, near Amalfi on the Campanian coast, was a constant reminder of Moslem incursions. *L'Art dans l'Italie méridionale* (1903; reprint, Paris, 1968), 282.

38. "Mendax et malus est; stultus, caecus, surdus et mutus est. . . ." Young, *The Drama of the Medieval Church*, vol. 2, 353.

39. On this issue, see Peter Herde, "Christians and Saracens at the Time of the Crusades," *Studia Gratiana* 12 (1967): 359–76, *passim*. See chapter XXVI of the acts of the Third Lateran Council: "Ne Christiani habitent cum Judaeis vel Saracenis." See G. D. Mansi, *Sacrorum Conciliorum*, vol. 22 (Venice, 1778), col. 231.

40. Raoul Manselli, "Lucca e Lucchesi nei loro rapporti con la prima crociata," *Italia e Italiani alla prima crociata* (Rome, 1983), 125–35; Franco Cardini, "La società lucchese e la prima crociata," *Actum Luce* 8 (1979): 7–30; Cardini, "Toscani verso Gerusalemme," *'De Finibus Tuscie'. Il medioevo in Toscana*, Politica e storia 8 (Florence, 1989), 76–102.

41. "Magnus fuit conflictus ultra mare inter Christianos et Saracenos, et prevaluerunt Christiani." Bernhard Schmeidler, ed., *Die Annalen des Tholomeus von Lucca in doppelter Fassung nebst Teilen der Gesta Florentinorum und Gesta Lucanorum*, MGH Scriptores Rerum Germanicarum, n.s. 8 (Berlin, 1930), 75. On the same page and for the same year, Tolomeo notes "Magna pars Ytalie crucesignata est ad recuperationem Terre Sancte, sed precipue in Tuscia Florentini, Lucani

et Pisani." (A large part of Italy was marked with the cross for [the purpose of] the retaking of the Holy Land; but especially the Florentines, Lucchese, and Pisans.) Schmeidler believes this information to be false.

CHAPTER 6

1. Fulvia Donati and Maria Cecilia Parra, "Pisa e il reimpiego 'laico': La nobilità di sangue e d'ingegno, e la potenza economica," in *Colloquio sul reimpiego dei sarcofagi romani nel medioevo. Pisa 5.–12. September* (sic) *1983*, eds. Bernard Andreae and Salvatore Settis, Marburger Winckelmann-Programm, 1983 (Marburg, 1984), 103–19; Maria Cecilia Parra, "Rimeditando sul reimpiego: Modena and Pisa viste in parallelo," *Annali della Scuola normale superiore di Pisa. Classe di lettere e filosofia*, 3d ser. 13 (1983): 453–83. Parra summarizes some of the material in "Pisa e Modena: spunti di ricerca sul reimpiego 'intorno' al Duomo," in *Lanfranco e Wiligelmo. Il duomo di Modena* [Modena, 1984], 355–50. In discussing Pisa's evocation of ancient Roman ideals, Parra, "Rimeditando sul reimpiego," 465, quotes Saint Bernard's phrase "Assumitur Pisa in locum Romae" to bolster her point. As indicated by the rest of the phrase, "et de cunctis urbibus terrae ad apostolicae sedis culmen aligitur," St. Bernard's phrase concerns a comparison with Christian Rome. For the text, see J. Leclercq, O.S.B., and H. Rochais, *Epistolae. I. Corpus Epistolarum 1–180*, S. Bernardi Opera, vol. VII (Rome, 1974), 325.

2. "Inclitorum Pisanorum scripturus istoriam, / antiquorum Romanorum renovo memoriam: / nam extendit modo Pisa laudem admirabilem, / quam recepit olim Roma vincendo Cartaginem."

Giuseppe Scalia, "Il carme pisano sull'impresa contro i Saraceni del 1087," *Studi di filologia romanza offerti a Silvio Pellegrini* (Padua, 1971), 597.

3. "Ego Roma altera iam solebam dici, / que sum privilegiis dives Federici. / propter gentes barbaras quas ubique vici." Giuseppe Scalia, "'Romanitas' pisana tra XI e XII secolo. Le iscrizioni romane del duomo e la statua del console Rodolfo," *Studi medievale* 3rd ser. 13/2 (1972): 804.

4. Graziella Berti and Liana Tongiorgi, *I bacini ceramici medievali delle chiese di Pisa* (Rome, 1981); Graziella Berti and Paola Torre, *Arte islamica in Italia: i bacini delle chiese pisane: 26 maggio–25 settembre 1983, Roma, Palazzo Brancaccio* (Pisa, 1983); *Le Ceramiche medievali delle chiese di Pisa. Contributo per una migliore comprensione delle loro caratteristiche e del loro significato quale documento di storia*, Bollettino storico pisano. Collana storica, 25 (Pisa, 1983); D.S.H. Abulafia, "The Pisan *Bacini* and the Medieval Mediterranean Economy: a Historian's Viewpoint," *Papers in Italian Archaeology*, IV: *The Cambridge Conference*, part iv, *Classical and Medieval Archaeology*, eds. C. Malone and S. Stoddart, B.A.R. International Series, 246 (Oxford, 1985), 287–302.

5. See chapter 1, note 42.

6. Alfredo Stussi, "La tomba di Giratto e le sue epigrafi," *Studi mediolatini e*

volgari 36 (1990) [1992]: 63–71, esp. 64. The sarcophagus was intended for Girattus. The meaning of A[. .]NM has been interpreted variously. See Stussi, 64. On the lower edge of the sarcophagus there is a much-discussed inscription written in the vernacular. A full bibliography appears in Stussi, 70–71. See also Ignazio Baldelli, "Le iscrizioni latine e volgari nelle porte di Bonanno Pisano," in *Le porte di bronzo dall'antichità al secolo XIII*, ed. Salvatorino Salomi (Rome, 1990), vol. 1, 397. The sarcophagus has also been discussed by S. Settis, "Verbreitung und Wiederverwendung antiker Modelle," in *Studien zur Geschichte der Europäischen Skulptur in 12./13. Jahrhundert*, eds. H. Beck and K. Hengevoss-Dürkop (Frankfurt am Main, 1994), vol. 1, 359.

7. Late antique sarcophagi were not only copied or imitated but, on occasion, were reworked into a contemporary form. See Marion Lawrence, "A Gothic Reworking of an Early Christian Sarcophagus," *Art Studies* 7 (1929): 89–103.

8. The presence in Tuscany of numerous freestanding baptisteries as well as fonts for immersion is worthy of further investigation.

9. On the font, see Schmarsow, *S. Martin von Lucca*, 208ff.; Mario Ermalao Martini, *La pieve di Calci, Guida per il visitatore*, 2d ed. (Calci, 1990); Heydasch-Lehmann, 135–37; Maria Laura Cristiani Testi, "'Classico' e 'Romanzo' nell'incompiuto Fonte di Calci," *Critica d'arte* 45, fasc. 172–74 (July–December 1980): 107–32. The last mentioned dates the font, prematurely in my view, to the second quarter of the twelfth century.

10. See, for example, Peter Kranz, *Jahreszeiten-Sarkophage. Entwicklung und Ikonographie des Motivs der Vier Jahreszeiten auf Kaiserzeitlichen Sarkophagen und Sarkophagdeckeln*, Die Antiken Sarkophagreliefs, 54. (Berlin, 1984), 187, no. 11, for a Roman example in the Camposanto at Pisa. For Early Christian arcaded sarcophagi, see Giuseppe Wilpert, *I sarcofagi cristiani antichi*, Monumenti dell'antichità cristiana (Rome, 1929), vol. I, pls. XI(1), XII(4), XII(5).

11. For an illustration, see Castelnuovo, ed., *Niveo de marmore*, 121, fig. 23.

12. Albert Boeckler, *Die Bronzetüren des Bonanus von Pisa und des Barisanus von Trani*, pl. 13; Ursula Mende, *Die Bronzetüren des Mittelalters* (Munich, 1983), fig. 176.

13. Piero Sanpaolesi, "Ispirazioni da un modello di scultura classica in Pisa nel XII e XIII secolo," *Mitteilungen des Kunsthistorischen Institutes in Florenz* 7 (1953): 280–82.

14. For this lintel, see chapter 4. In parallel circumstances, the frieze of the Holy Sepulchre in Jerusalem has been compared to Early Christian sarcophagi of the Bethesda type. See Borg, "The Holy Sepulchre Lintel," 389–90.

15. For the baptistery, see most recently Chiellini Nari, *Temi e immagini dal medioevo: i rilievi del deambulatorio*.

16. For the arch at Susa, see Bianca Maria Felletti Maj, "Il fregio commemorativo dell'arco di Susa," *Pontificia accademia romana di archeología, Rendiconti* 33 (1960–61): 129–53. On *suovetaurilia* in general, see Inez Scott Ryberg, *Rites of the State Religion in Roman Art*, American Academy in Rome, Memoirs 22

(Rome, 1955); Jean Prieur, "Les arcs monumentaux dans les Alpes occidentales: Aoste, Suse, Aix-le-Bains," *Aufstieg und Niedergang der Römischen Welt, Geschichte und Kultur Roms im Spiegel der Neueren Forschung* II, vol. 12:1: *Künste*, ed. Hildegard Temporini (Berlin and New York, 1982), 442–75; Gerhard M. Koeppel, "Die historischen Reliefs der römischen Kaiserzeit. I, Stadtrömische Denkmäler unbekannter Bauzugehörigkeit aus augusteischer und julisch-claudischer Zeit," *Bonner Jahrbuch* 183 (1983): 61–144, esp. 124–29; Koeppel, "Die historischen Reliefs der römischen Kaiserzeit. IV, Stadtrömische Denkmäler unbekannter Bauzugehörigkeit aus hadrianischer bis konstantinischer Zeit," *Bonner Jahrbuch* 186 (1986): 1–90, esp. 2–5.

17. Dodds, ed., *Al-Andalus. The Art of Islamic Spain*, 192–97.

18. Dorothy F. Glass, *Romanesque Sculpture in Campania. Patrons, Programs, and Style* (University Park, Penn., 1991), 59, 82.

19. On the griffin, see Karl Lehmann-Hartleben and Erling C. Olson, *Dionysiac Sarcophagi in Baltimore* (Baltimore, 1942), 30–31; Mary A. Johnstone, "The Griffin, the Coat-of-Arms of Perugia," *Studi etruschi* 2d ser., 30 (1962): 335–52; Anna Marguerite McCann, *Roman Sarcophagi in the Metropolitan Museum of Art* (New York, 1978); Christiane Delplace, *Le griffon de l'archaïsme à l'époque impériale. Etude iconographique et essai d'interprétation symbolique*, Etudes de philologie, d'archéologie et d'histoire anciennes, L'Institut historique belge de Rome, 20 (Brussels and Rome, 1980); Alfred Frazer, *Samothrace. The Propylon of Ptolemy II*, Bollingen Series, LX:10 (Princeton, 1990).

20. The sarcophagus (C 15 int.) is possibly from a house near Santa Caterina at Pisa. See *Camposanto Monumentale di Pisa* (Pisa, 1977), vol. 1, 166 and pl. CXII, fig. 237.

21. C. Baracchini et al., "Architettura e scultura medievali nella diocesi di Lucca: criteri e metodi," in *Romanico padano, romanico Europeo*, ed. A. C. Quintavalle (Parma, 1982), 289–304.

22. Indeed, when French reliefs do not appear to be firmly embedded in an architectural framework, they evoke detailed comment. See, for example, Marilyn Schmitt, " 'Random' Reliefs and 'Primitive' Friezes: Reused Sources of Romanesque Sculpture," *Viator* 11 (1980): 123–45; Nurith Kenaan-Kedar, "The Margins of Society in Marginal Romanesque Sculpture," *Gesta* 31/1 (1992): 15–24; Kenaan-Kedar, *Marginal Sculpture in Medieval France* (Aldershot, 1995). Similarly, employing the expectations of French Romanesque sculpture, A. C. Quintavalle, *La cattedrale di Modena*, has argued that the Genesis reliefs on the facade of the cathedral at Modena were once intended for a *pontile* at the entrance to the crypt. For a summary of the issues and a refutation, see Eric Fernie, "Notes on the Sculpture of Modena Cathedral," *Arte lombarda* 14/2 (1969): 88–93.

23. Antique influence in Tuscany has been previously examined by Carl D. Sheppard: "Romanesque Sculpture in Tuscany: A Problem of Methodology," *Gazette des beaux-arts* 6th ser. 54 (1959): 97–108; "Classicism in Romanesque Sculpture in Tuscany," *Gesta* 15 (1976): 185–92.

24. Gómez Moreno, "The Doorway of San Leonardo al Frigido," 359.

25. For quarrying in antiquity, see the fundamental and still important study by J. B. Ward-Perkins, *Quarrying in Antiquity. Technology, Tradition and Social Change*, Proceedings of the British Academy 57 (= Mortimer Wheeler Archaeological Lecture, British Academy, 1971) (London, 1972). More recent literature is reviewed in a useful study by Hazel Dodge, "Ancient Marble Studies: Recent Research," *Journal of Roman Archaeology* 4 (1991): 28–50. Also pertinent are two studies by Patrizio Pensabene, "Considerazioni sul trasporto di manufatti marmorei in età imperiale a Roma e in altri centri occidentali," *Dialoghi di Archeologia* 6 (1972): 317–62; and "Amministrazione dei marmi e sistema distributivo nel mondo romano," in *Marmi antichi*, ed. Gabriele Borghini, Materiali della cultura artistica, 1 (Rome, 1989), 43–54. For the transportation of stone from the European continent to England, see Richard Gem, "Canterbury and the Cushion Capital: a Commentary on Passages from Goscelin's 'De Miraculis Sancti Augustini'," in *Romanesque and Gothic. Essays for George Zarnecki*, vol. I, 83–101 (Woodbridge, Suffolk, and Wolfeboro, N.H., 1987). I am indebted to Deborah Kahn for the last mentioned reference.

26. G. Kapitän, "Church Wreck off Marzamemi," *Archaeology* 22 (1969): 122–33; Patrizio Pensabene, "A Cargo of Marble Shipwrecked at Punta Scifo near Crotone (Italy)," *International Journal of Nautical Archaeology* 7/2 (May 1978) 105–18.

27. Emilio Tolaini, *Forma Pisarum. Storia urbanistica della città di Pisa. Problemi e ricerche*, 2d ed. (Pisa, 1979), 101. "Per lo mezzo della città li passa un fiume reale che si chiama Arno, per lo quale vanno e vengono navili per mare carichi di mercanzia, la quale mercanzia si spande et manda per tutta Toscana et in molto luoghi."

28. Christiane Klapisch-Zuber, *Les maîtres du marbre. Carrare 1300–1600* (Paris, 1969), 34–35.

29. For the Pyrenees, see Paul Deschamps, "Tables d'autel de marbre exécutées dans le midi de la France au Xe. et au XIe. siècle," in *Mélanges d'histoire du Moyen Age offerts à M. Ferdinand Lot par ses amis et ses élèves* (Paris, 1925), 137–68. For Tournai stone, see Paul Rolland, "L'expansion tournaisienne aux XIe. et XIIe. siècles. Art et commerce de la pierre," *Annales de l'Academie Royale d'Archéologie de Belgique* 72 (1924): 175–217; Elizabeth Schwartzbaum, "Three Tournai Tombslabs in England," *Gesta* 20/1 (1981): 89–97.

30. On Roman Pisa, see Luisa Banti, "Pisae," *Atti della Pontificia accademia romana di archeología*, ser. 3, Memorie 6 (1943):, 67–141; Tolaini, *Forma Pisarum*, 1–62. On Roman Lucca, see Alberto Riparbelli, ed., *Lucca romana* (Lucca, 1982).

31. Fundamental for the study of *spolia* is Arnold Esch, "Spolien. Zur Wiederverwendung antiker Baustücke und Skulpturen im mittelalterlichen Italien," *Archiv für Kulturgeschichte* 51 (1969): 1–64. More recent and also useful is Michael Greenhalgh, *The Survival of Roman Antiquities in the Middle Ages*

(London, 1989); some of the material therein appeared earlier as "'Ipsa ruina docet': l'uso dell'antico nel Medioevo," *Memoria dell'antico nell'arte italiana*, vol. 1. *L'uso dei classici*, ed. Salvatore Settis, Biblioteca di storia dell'arte, n.s. 1 (Turin, 1984), 113–67. For Tuscany particularly, see the now dated study by Paolo Fontana, "I marmi antichi nelle chiese medievali di Toscana," in *Saggi sull'architettura etrusca e romana. Atti del III Convegno nazionale di storia dell'architettura (Roma 9–13 ottobre 1938)* (Rome, 1940), 201–5.

32. Greenhalgh, *The Survival of Roman Antiquities in the Middle Ages*, 136; Ronald Malmstrom, "The Colonnades of High Medieval Churches at Rome," *Gesta* 14 (1975): 37–45; Dale Kinney, "Spolia from the Baths of Caracalla in S. Maria in Trastevere," *Art Bulletin* 68 (1986): 379–97.

33. Doriana Cattalini, "Un capitello da Roma a San Piero a Grado," *Prospettiva*, fasc. 31 (Oct. 1982): 73–77.

34. On these inscriptions, see Scalia, "'Romanitas' pisana," 791–843. Armando Petrucci contrasts the location of the inscriptions at Pisa with the location of those on the cathedral at Salerno. See his "La scrittura tra ideologia e rappresentazione," in *Storia dell'arte italiana*, pt. 3, *Situazione, momenti, indagini*, vol. 2. *Grafica e immagine. I. Scrittura, Miniatura, Disegno*, ed. F. Zeri, Storia dell'arte italiana, 9*. (Turin, 1980), 7–9.

35. On Saint-Denis, see Beat Brenk, "Sugers Spolien," *Arte medievale* 1 (1983): 101–7. On Monte Cassino, see *Chronica Monasterii Casinensis*, ed. H. Hoffmann, MGH SS 34 (Hannover, 1980), 394.

36. " . . . edificavi . . . Ecclesiam . . . Et perrexi ad Romam per columnas ipsius Ecclesie; et comparavi, & feci eas venire in navim per mare de nostro pretio." Cited in Greenhalgh, *The Survival of Roman Antiquities*, 127. See Ludovico Antonio Muratori, *Antiquitates Italicae Medii Aevi* (Milan, 1741), vol. 4, col. 788.

37. Greenhalgh, *The Survival of Roman Antiquities*, 127. See Muratori, *Antiquitates Italicae Medii Aevi* 4, col. 790. "Et est tam perfecta domus . . . cum columnas quas de Insula Ilba & de Luni adduci feci."

38. *Rerum Italicarum Scriptores* VI, 16ff.

39. Tolaini, *Forma Pisarum*, 65.

40. Francesco Rodolico, *Le pietre della città d'Italia* (Florence, 1953), 264–77. For quarries in the area between Pistoia and Florence, see Renate Müller, *Die Entwicklung der Naturwerksteinindustrie im toskanischen Apennin als Funktion städtebaulicher Gestaltung* (Frankfurt am Main, 1975).

41. Klapisch-Zuber, *Les maîtres du marbre*, 52.

42. Daniel Ternois, "Le suovetaurile de Beaujeu et le linteau roman de Charlieu," *La revue du Louvre et des musées de France* 15 (1965): 249–57.

43. "Bos, vitulus, aries, agnus, capra, hircus carnibus et cruore implent altaria Judaeorum; solus Agnus Dei, qui tollit peccata mundi, altari superponitur Christianorum." Peter the Venerable, "Tractatus contra Petrobrusians," *PL* 189, col. 796. See Émile Mâle, *L'Art religieux du XIIe. siècle en France* (Paris, 1922), 420–23.

CHAPTER 7

1. "Divinae siquidem majestatis dispositio Pisanae urbis gloriam nostris tem-poribus, et Saracenorum triumphis illustrare, et saecularium rerum provectibus promovere, ut prae comprovincialibus exaltare dignata est. Eapropter et nos di-vinae pietatis prosecutores et cooperatores, eam in spiritualibus quoque glori-ficare decrevimus, sicut praedecessores nostros multis civitatibus olim fecisse scriptorum ecclesiasticorum testimoniis comprobatur." *PL* 151, col. 345. Inno-cent II also emphasized this role in a bull of April 22, 1138: " . . . ut Pisana civitas, quae coelesti favore de inimicis Christiani nominis victoriam frequenter obtinuit, et eorum urbes plurimas subjugavit, amplius honoretur." *PL* 179, col. 362.

2. Bernardo Maragone, *Gli Annales Pisani*, ed. Michele Lupo Gentile, Rerum Italicarum Scriptores VI². (Bologna, 1936), 7.

3. William Heywood, *A History of Pisa. Eleventh and Twelfth Centuries*, 130.

4. The quotation appears in Jonathan Riley-Smith, *The Crusades. A Short His-tory* (London and New York, 1987), 97–98. The translation is his. "Si prudens mercator es, si conquisitor hujus saeculi, magnas quasdam tibi nundinas indico; vide ne te praetereant. Suscipe crucis signum, et omnium pariter, de quibus corde contrito confessionem feceris, indulgentiam obtinebis delictorum. Materia ipsa si emitur, parvi constat; si devote assumitur humero, valet sine dubio regnum Dei." For the original Latin, see *S. Bernardi Opera*, vol. 8, *Epistolae*, eds. J. Leclercq and H. Rochais (Rome, 1977), 315.

5. Franco Cardini, "La société italienne et les croisades," *Cahiers de civilisa-tion médiévale* 28 (1985): 19–33; Rudolf Hiestand, "L'arcivescovo Ubaldo e i Pisani alla terza crociata alla luce du una nuova testimonianza," *Bollettino storico pisano* 58 (1989), 37–51.

6. Maragone, *Gli annales Pisani*, 68.

7. See chapter 1, note 37.

8. The date of consecration should not be construed as the date of completion, for work on the cathedral continued into the thirteenth century. For example, the bronze doors of Bonanus of Pisa were made in 1180.

9. Of fundamental importance is Max Seidel, "Dombau, Kreuzzugsidee und Expansionspolitik. Zur Ikonographie der Pisaner Kathedralbauten," *Frühmit-telalterliche Studien* 11 (1977): 340–69. See also the important study by Craig B. Fisher, "The Pisan Clergy and an Awakening of Historical Interest in a Medieval Commune," *Studies in Medieval and Renaissance History* 3 (1966): 143–219. The inscriptions are transcribed and discussed in Giuseppe Scalia, "Epigrafica pisana. Testi latini sulla spedizione contro le Baleari del 1113–15 e su altre im-prese anti-saracene del sec. XI," *Miscellanea di studi ispanici* 6 (1963): 234–86, esp. 234–64. Unlike Scalia, Fisher does not see continuity in the Pisans' activities, but rather a rebirth. See also Scalia, " 'Romanitas' pisana," 791–843.

10. M. A. Di Paco Triglia, *La chiesa del Santo Sepolcro di Pisa* (Pisa, 1986).

11. On the latter, see, for example, Paolo Zovatto, "Il Santo Sepolcro di Aquileia e il dramma liturgico medievale," *Atti dell'Accademia di scienze, lettere e arti di Udine* 6 (1954–57): 127–51. On copies of the Holy Sepulchre in general, see Geneviève Bresc-Bautier, "Les imitations du Saint-Sépulcre de Jérusalem (IX^c – XV^c siècles). Archéologie d'une dévotion," *Revue d'histoire de la spiritualité* 50 (1974): 319–42. See also Robert Ousterhout, "The Church of Santo Stefano: A 'Jerusalem' in Bologna," *Gesta* 20 (1981): 311–21; Ousterhout, "Loca Sancta and the Architectural Response to Pilgrimage," *The Blessings of Pilgrimage*, ed. R. Ousterhout, Illinois Byzantine Studies I (Urbana and Chicago, 1990), 108–24.

12. D. Stiaffini, "La chiesa e il monastero di S. Paolo a Ripa d'Arno," *Rivista dell'Istituto nazionale d'archeología e storia dell'arte*, 3d ser., 6–7 (1983–84): 237–84, esp. 271–72.

13. See Richard Krautheimer, "Introduction to an Iconography of Medieval Architecture," *Journal of the Warburg and Courtauld Institutes* 5 (1942): 1–33 and Seidel, "Dombau, Kreuzzugsidee und Expansionspolitik," 348–50.

14. Scalia, "Epigrafica pisana," 269–72. Fisher, "The Pisan Clergy," 166–69, suggests that an analogy with Roman and Byzantine triumphal gates was intended.

15. Likewise, Genoa's renowned historian, Caffaro, was also a layman. For an introduction to Caffaro's work, see Richard D. Face, "Secular History in Twelfth-Century Italy: Caffaro of Genoa," *Journal of Medieval History* 6 (1980): 169–84. For the relationship between notarial activity and literacy in Genoa, see Gabriella Airaldi, "Leggere, scrivere, far di conto a Genova nel medioevo," in *La storia dei genovesi. Atti del Convegno di studi sui ceti dirigenti nelle istituzioni della repubblica di Genova. Genova 6-7-8 novembre 1981* (Genoa, 1982), vol. 2, 177–97. Bruno Migliorini notes that in the eleventh century, foreigners marvelled at the fact that laypersons in Italy had the opportunity to study. See his *The Italian Language*, rev. by T. Gwynfor Griffith (London, 1966), 57.

16. Colin Morris, "San Ranieri of Pisa: The Power and Limitations of Sanctity in Twelfth-Century Italy," *Journal of Ecclesiastical History* 45 (1994): 588–99. Réginald Grégoire, *San Ranieri di Pisa (1117-1160) in un ritratto agiografico inedito del secolo XIII*, Biblioteca del bollettino storico pisano, Collana storica 36 (Ospedaletto, 1990).

17. Raynerius also made a pilgrimage to Santiago de Compostela. See Grégoire, *San Ranieri di Pisa*, 127, lines 650–53.

18. André Vauchez, "A Twelfth-Century Novelty: The Lay Saints of Urban Italy," *The Laity in the Middle Ages. Religious Beliefs and Devotional Practices*, ed. Daniel E. Bornstein, and trans. Margery J. Schneider (Notre Dame, Ind., 1993), 51–72.

19. Western Tuscany is not unique in this respect, for vast numbers of Italian medieval monuments bear inscriptions. On Tuscany, in general, see Vannucci, "La firma dell'artista." On a neighboring province, the Emilia-Romagna, see

Christine B. Verzár, "Text und Bild in der norditalienischen Romanik: Skulpturen, Inschriften, Betrachter," in *Studien zur Geschichte der Europäischen Skulptur im 12./13. Jahrhundert*, eds. Herbert Beck and Kerstin Hengevoss-Dürkop (Frankfurt am Main, 1994), vol. 1, 495–504; Verzár, "Text and Image in North Italian Romanesque Sculpture," in *The Romanesque Frieze and its Spectator*, ed. Deborah Kahn (London, 1992), 121–40. Additionally, there are a number of other pertinent studies on medieval inscriptions. See especially: Augusto Campana, "La testimonianza delle iscrizioni," in *Lanfranco e Wiligelmo. Il Duomo di Modena* [Modena, 1984], 363–73; Peter Cornelius Claussen, "Früher Künstlerstolz. Mittelalterliche Signaturen als Quelle der Kunstsoziologie," in *Bauwerk und Bildwerk im Hochmittelalter. Anschauliche Beiträge zur Kultur- und Sozialgeschichte*, eds. K. Clausberg et al. (Giessen, 1981), 7–35; Albert Dietl, " 'In Arte Peritus.' Zur Topik mittelalterlicher Künstlerinschriften in Italien bis zur Zeit Giovanni Pisanos," *Römische historische Mitteilungen* 29 (1987): 75–125; Dietl, "Künstlerinschriften als Quelle für Status und Selbstverständnis von Bildhauern," in *Studien zur Geschichte der Europäischen Skulptur im 12./13. Jahrhundert*, eds. Herbert Beck and Kerstin Hengevoss-Dürkop (Frankfurt am Main, 1994), vol. 1, 175–91.

20. HOC OPUS QUOD CERNIS BIDUINUS DOCTE PEREGIT. On Biduinus's signatures, see chapters 4 and 5.

21. See above, chapter 3, for the inscriptions at San Bartolomeo in Pantano, Pistoia.

22. NE TIMEA(S) ZACHARIAS QUUM EXA[AUDITA ESSET] ORA[TIO TUA]; [ELI]SABET UXOR TUA [PARIET FILIUM].

23. CENANS DISCIPULIS CHRISTUS DAT VERBA SAL[UTIS CENANS NO]VAM TRIBUIT LEG(em) VETEREM QUOQUE FINIT.

24. The lintel from San Silvestro at Pisa, now in the Museo Nazionale di San Matteo in that city, is, in my view, later; it will be the subject of a future study.

25. Katzenellenbogen, "The Central Tympanum at Vézelay". See chapter 3, pp. 23–24.

26. R. C. Smail, "The International Status of the Latin Kingdom of Jerusalem, 1150–1192," in *The Eastern Mediterranean Lands in the Period of the Crusades*, ed. P. M. Holt (Warminster, England, 1977), 24.

27. Renato Bordone, "Memoria del tempo negli abitanti dei comuni italiani all'età del Barbarossa," in *Il tempo vissuto. Percezione, impiego, rappresentazione. Gargnano, 9–11 settembre 1985* (Bologna, 1988), 47–62, esp. 47.

28. Pertusi, "Ai confini tra religione e politica," *passim*.

29. See chapter 5, note 39.

30. "Accipe hunc baculum sustentationis itineris ac laboris vie peregrinationis tue. . . ." Kenneth Pennington, "The Rite for Taking the Cross in the Twelfth Century," *Traditio* 30 (1974): 429–35, esp. 430–31.

31. Emile Mâle, *Religious Art in France, The Twelfth Century. A Study of the*

Origins of Medieval Iconography, ed. Harry Bober, and trans. Marthiel Mathews, Bollingen Series XC:1 (Princeton, 1978), 126–53; Otto Pächt, *The Rise of Pictorial Narrative in Twelfth-Century England* (Oxford, 1962), 33–59.

32. Sandro Sticca, *The Latin Passion Play: Its Origins and Development* (Albany, 1970); Robert Edwards, *The Montecassino Passion Play and the Poetics of Medieval Drama* (Berkeley and Los Angeles, 1977); Patrick J. Collins, *The N-Town Plays and Medieval Picture Cycles*, Early Drama, Art and Music Monograph Series, 2 (Kalamazoo, Mich., 1979). For a stimulating, recent essay, see Pamela Sheingorn, "Medieval Drama Studies and the New Art History," *Mediaevalia* 18 (1995) (for 1992): 143–62.

33. Clifford Davidson, *Drama and Art. An Introduction to the Use of Evidence from the Visual Arts for the Study of Early Drama*, Early Drama, Art and Music Monograph Series, 1 (Kalamazoo, Mich., 1977), 13; Paola Ventrone, "On the Use of Figurative Art as a Source for the Study of Medieval Spectacles," *Iconographic and Comparative Studies in Medieval Drama*, eds. Clifford Davidson and John H. Stroupe (Kalamazoo, Mich., 1991), 6.

34. John Wesley Harris, *Medieval Theatre in Context: An Introduction* (London and New York, 1992), 45.

35. The relationship between medieval theater and Italian Romanesque sculpture at the cathedral of Modena has been explored by Chiara Frugoni, "Le lastre veterotestamentarie e il programma della facciata," in *Lanfranco e Wiligelmo. Il duomo di Modena* (Modena, 1984), 422–31. I plan to undertake a more extensive study of the issues, especially in central and northern Italy.

36. Collins, *The Production of Medieval Church Music-Drama*, 257–69, esp. 260. See also Young, *The Drama of the Medieval Church*, vol. 2, 245–50. Pistoia's local historian of medieval drama, Alberto Chiappelli, is of no help. Ignoring Sant'Andrea, he simply notes that while there is no doubt that drama took place at the cathedral of Pistoia, the earliest documents are from the fourteenth century. See his *Storia del teatro in Pistoia dalle origini alla fine del sec. XVIII* (Pistoia, 1913), 8.

37. Collins, *The Production of Medieval Church Music-Drama*, 262, suggests that "Joachim" is a scribal error for "Zechariah" because the intention could not have been to depict Mary's father. Collins does not treat the monuments discussed here.

38. For the text, see Young, *The Drama of the Medieval Church*, vol. 2, 248. Young, vol. 2, 247–48, notes that the rubrics of the coeval *Annunciation* play from Cividale state that the play is to be performed in the public forum outside the church.

39. See above, chapter 3, note 27.

40. Harris, *Medieval Theatre in Context*, 42–43.

41. Tydeman, *The Theater in the Middle Ages*, 59, notes that two main locations, probably at either end of the crossing, were involved in the production of the *Son of Getron*: Marmorinus's court and Excoranda, Getron's home.

42. Collins, *Medieval Church Music-Dramas. A Repertory of Complete Plays*, 462.

43. Processions on ordinary Sundays were not common until the twelfth century. See Terence Bailey, *The Processions of Sarum and the Western Church*, Pontifical Institute of Mediaeval Studies, Studies and Texts, 21 (Toronto, 1971), 104. For the use of statues in processions, see Ilene H. Forsyth, *The Throne of Wisdom. Wood Sculptures of the Madonna in Romanesque France* (Princeton, 1972), 40–45.

44. Young, *The Drama of the Medieval Church*. vol. 1, 90–99; Sticca, *The Latin Passion Play*, 40.

45. Joan Evans, *Cluniac Art of the Romanesque Period* (Cambridge, 1950), notes the element of impersonation in the Palm Sunday procession. On liturgical processions, see Aimé Georges Martimort, "Les diverses formes de procession dans la liturgie," *La Maison-Dieu* 43 (1955): 43–73. On mimetic processions, see John F. Baldovin, S.J., *The Urban Character of Christian Worship. The Origins, Development, and the Meaning of Stational Liturgy*, Orientalia Christiana Analecta, 228 (Rome, 1987), 234–38.

46. *Le pontifical romain au moyen-âge*, vol. 1: *Le pontifical romain du XIIe siècle*, ed. Michel Andrieu, Studi e Testi 86 (Vatican City, 1938), 210–14; Giusti, "L''Ordo officiorum' della cattedrale di Lucca," 543–55; *De Sancti Hugonis Actis Liturgicis*, ed. Mario Bocci, Documenti della chiesa volterrana, 1 (Florence, 1984), 97–98.

47. On communal memory in the Middle Ages, see Renato Bordone, "Memoria del tempo negli abitanti dei comuni italiani all'età del Barbarossa"; James Fentress and Chris Wickham, *Social Memory* (Oxford and Cambridge, Mass., 1992).

48. Glynne Wickham, *The Medieval Theater*, 3d ed. (Cambridge, 1987), 39.

49. The importance of such processions in the life of a community has been examined recently in two significant studies: Gerhard Wolf, *Salus Populi Romani. Die Geschichte römischer Kultbilder im Mittelalter* (Weinheim, 1990); Bram Kempers, "Icons, Altarpieces, and Civic Ritual in Siena Cathedral, 1100–1530," in *City and Spectacle in Medieval Europe*, eds. Barbara A. Hanawalt and Kathryn L. Reyerson, Medieval Studies at Minnesota, 6 (Minneapolis and London, 1994), 89–136.

50. Quoted in Frances A. Yates, *The Art of Memory* (Chicago, 1966), 58.

Afterword

1. "Altri monumenti di tale barbarissimo stile." Sebastiano Ciampi, *Notizie inedite della sagrestia pistoiese de'belli arredi del campo santo pisano e di altre opere di disegno dal secolo XII. al XV*, 23.

2. Charles C. Perkins, *Tuscan Sculptors. Their Lives, Works and Times* (London, 1864), vol. 1, 55.

3. David A. E. Lindsay, 27th Earl of Crawford and 10th Earl of Balcarres, *The Evolution of Italian Sculpture* (London, 1901), 24.

4. David Cast, "Reading Vasari Again: History, Philosophy," *Word and Image* 9 (1993): 29–38.

5. Erwin Panofsky, *Renaissance and Renascences in Western Art*, The Gottesman Lectures, 7 (Stockholm, 1960).

6. *Le voyage in Italie d'Eugène Viollet-le-Duc 1836–37. L'Ecole nationale supérieure des Beaux-Arts* (Paris, 1980).

7. The squabble concerning the Porta della Pescheria at the cathedral of Modena is typical of this approach. For the relevant literature prior to 1980, see Glass, *Italian Romanesque Sculpture*, 161–67.

EXCURSUS

1. The two primary proponents of this view are: Borg, "Observations on the Historiated Lintel of the Holy Sepulchre"; and Folda, *The Art of the Crusaders in the Holy Land, 1098–1187*, 214–29. The literature on the figurative lintel is extensive. Among recent studies, see H. Buschhausen, "Die Fassade der Grabeskirche zu Jerusalem," in *Crusader Art of the Twelfth Century*, ed. J. Folda, B.A.R. International Series, 152 (Oxford, 1982), 71–96; N. Kenaan-Kedar, "The Figurative Western Lintel of the Church of the Holy Sepulchre in Jerusalem," in *The Meeting of Two Worlds: Cultural Exchange Between East and West during the Period of the Crusades*, eds. V. P. Goss and C. V. Bornstein, Studies in Medieval Culture, 21 (Kalamazoo, Mich., 1986), 123–31,; M. Lindner, "Topography and Iconography in Twelfth-Century Jerusalem," in *The Horns of Hattin, Proceedings of the Second Conference of the Society for the Study of the Crusades and the Latin East, Jerusalem and Haifa 2-6 July 1987*, ed. B. Z. Kedar (Jerusalem and London, 1992), 81–98. There is a second lintel composed of an inhabited vine motif. See L. Y. Rahmani, "The Eastern Lintel of the Holy Sepulchre," *Israeli Exploration Journal* 26 (1976): 120–29; B. Kühnel, "Der Rankenfries am Portal der Grabeskirche zu Jerusalem und die romanische Skulptur in den Abruzzen," *Arte medievale* 2d ser. 1 (1987): 87–125. Kühnel sees relationships between this lintel and sculpture in the Abruzzo. Kühnel also examines the affiliation between Crusader sculpture and south Italian medieval sculpture in her *Crusader Art of the Twelfth Century, A Geographical, an Historical, or an Art Historical Notion?* (Berlin, 1994), 42–46.

2. The following discussion is based primarily on two scenes on the Holy Sepulchre lintel: the *Raising of Lazarus* and *Christ and His Disciples Meet Mary Magdalene and Martha*. The other scenes are too greatly damaged to warrant detailed analysis.

SELECTED BIBLIOGRAPHY

Abulafia, David S. H. "The Pisan *Bacini* and the Medieval Mediterranean Economy: A Historian's Viewpoint." *Papers in Italian Archaeology IV: The Cambridge Conference*, part iv, *Classical and Medieval Archaeology*, eds. Caroline Malone and Simon Stoddart, 287–302. B.A.R. International Series, 246. Oxford: 1985. Reprinted in *Italy, Sicily and the Mediterranean, 1100–1400*. London: 1987.

Airaldi, Gabriella, and B. Z. Kedar. *I comuni italiani nel regno crociato di Gerusalemme*, Collana storica di fonti e studi. Genoa: 1986.

Airaldi, Gabriella. "Leggere, scrivere, far di conto a Genova nel medioevo." *La storia dei genovesi. Atti del convegno di studi sui ceti dirigenti nelle istituzioni della repubblica di Genova. Genova 6–7–8 novembre 1981*. Vol. 2, 177–97. Genoa: 1982.

Albrecht, Otto E. *Four Latin Plays of St. Nicholas from the 12th Century Fleury Play-book*. Philadelphia: 1935.

Amari, M., and C. Schiaparelli, eds. *L'Italia descritta nel Libro del Re Ruggero compilato da Edrisi*. Atti della Reale Accademia dei Lincei, 274 (1876–77). Rome: 1883.

Ambrosi, Augusto C. "Il culto di S. Nicolao in Garfagnana e in Lunigiana." *Archivio storico per le province parmensi* 4th ser., 19 (1967): 35–53.

Andreucci, S. "La strada romea et peregrina in territorio lucchese." *La Provincia di Lucca* 11, no. 3 (July–September 1971): 73–82.

Andrieu, Michel, ed. *Le pontifical romain au moyen-âge*. Vol. 1: *Le pontifical romain du XIIe siècle*, Studi e Testi, 86. Vatican City: 1938.

———. *Les ordines Romani du haut moyen âge*, Spicilegium sacrum Lovaniense, Etudes et documents, fasc. 29. Louvain: 1961.

Angeletti, Colombo. *S. Leonardo. Abate di Noblat*. Rome: 1966.

Angeli, Adolfo. "Carrara nel medioevo." *Atti della società ligure di storia patria* 54, fasc. 2 (1929): 5–29.

Anrich, Gustav. *Hagios Nikolaos. Der Heilige Nikolaos in der griechischen Kirche*, 2 vols. Berlin: 1913–17.

Armanini, Maria Grazia. "Resti scheletrici umani rinvenuti in località S. Leonardo al Frigido." *Giornale storico della Lunigiana e del territorio lucense*, n.s. 37 (1986): 75–81.

Ascani, V. "Biduino." *Enciclopedia dell'arte medievale*, vol. 3, 502–6. Rome: 1992.

Ashley, Kathleen M. "The Fleury 'Raising of Lazarus' and Twelfth-Century Currents of Thought." In *The Fleury Playbook. Essays and Studies*, eds. Thomas P.

Campbell and Clifford Davidson, 100–19. Early Drama, Art, and Music Monograph Series, 7. Kalamazoo, Mich.: 1985.

Bacci, Pèleo. "Gruamonte ed altri maestri di pietra che lavorarono alle facciate di S. Giovanni Forcivitas in Pistoia. Note e documenti (secoli XII–XIV)." *Rivista d'arte* 3 (1905): 57–76.

———. "La chiesa di S. Giovanni 'Forcivitas' di Pistoia e i suoi ultimi restauri." *Bollettino d'arte* 1, fasc. 11 (1907): 23–30.

Bailey, Terence. *The Processions of Sarum and the Western Church.* Pontifical Institute of Mediaeval Studies, Studies and Texts, 21. Toronto: 1971.

Balboni, D. "Il rito della benedizione delle palme (Vat. lat. 4770)." In *Collectanea Vaticana in honorem Anselmi M. Card. Albareda*, 55–74. Studi e Testi, 219. Rome: 1962.

Baldelli, Ignazio. "Le iscrizioni latine e volgari nelle porte di Bonanno Pisano." In *Le porte di bronzo dall'antichità al secolo XIII*, ed. Salvatorino Salomi, vol. 1, 389–97. Rome: 1990.

Baldovin, John F., S.J. *The Urban Character of Christian Worship. The Origins, Development, and the Meaning of Stational Liturgy*, Orientalia Christiana Analecta, 228. Rome: 1987.

Banti, Luisa. "Pisae." *Atti della Pontificia accademia romana di archeología* ser. 3, *Memorie* 6 (1943): 67–141.

Banti, Ottavio. " 'Cantarinus, Pisanae Urbis Cancellarius' (ca. 1140–1147). Fu lo strumento della preminenza politica di un vescovo in regime consolare?" *Bollettino storico pisano* 40–41 (1971–72): 23–29.

Baracchini, Clara, and Maria Teresa Filieri, eds. *Il Volto Santo. Storia e culto. Catalogo della mostra.* Lucca: 1982.

Baracchini, Clara, Antonino Caleca, and Maria Teresa Filieri. "Architettura e scultura medievali nella diocesi di Lucca: criteri e metodi." In *Romanico padano, romanico europeo. Convegno internazionale di studi. Modena-Parma 26 ottobre–1 novembre 1977*, 289–304. Parma: 1982.

Baracchini, Clara, and Maria Teresa Filieri. "I pulpiti." *Niveo de Marmore. L'uso artistico del marmo di Carrara dall'XI al XV secolo*, ed. Enrico Castelnuovo, 120–25. Genoa: 1992.

Barbacci, Alfredo. "Il restauro della facciata del Sant' Andrea di Pistoia." *Bollettino d'arte* ser. 3, 29 (1935): 506–9.

Baumstark, A. "La solennité des palmes dans l'ancienne et la nouvelle Rome." *Irenikon* 13 (1936): 3–24.

Beani, Gaetano. *La cattedrale pistoiese. L'altare di S. Jacopo e la sacrestia de'belli arredi. Appunti storici documentati.* Pistoia: 1903.

———. *La pieve di S. Andrea apostolo in Pistoia. Memoria storica.* Pistoia: 1907.

———. *S. Bartolomeo Ap. La chiesa e l'abbazia in Pistoia.* Pistoia: 1907.

Belli Barsali, Isa. "Adeodato." *DBI* 1, 273–74.

———. "Biduino." *DBI* 10, 365–67.

————. "Contributo alla topografia medioevale di Rome. 1. La Via Francigena presso la città leonina." *Studi romani* 21 (1973): 451–68.

————. *Lucca. Guida alla città*, 2d ed. Lucca: 1988.

————. "Sui recenti studi di topografia, urbanistica e architettura medioevale pisana." *Bollettino storico pisano* 46 (1977): 537–48.

Benedict of Peterborough. *Ex Gestis Henrici II et Ricardi I*, MGH SS, XXVII. Hannover: 1885.

Benjamin ben-Jonah of Tudela, *The Itinerary of Rabbi Benjamin of Tudela*, 2 vols. in 1. Trans. and ed. A. Asher. New York: 1841.

Benvenuti, Gino. *Storia della Repubblica di Pisa*, 4th ed. Pisa: 1982.

Berlière, Ursmer. "Anciens pèlerinages bénédictins au Moyen Age." *Revue liturgique et monastique* 11 (1926): 205–13, 247–53.

S. Bernardi Opera, vol. 8, *Epistolae*, eds. J. Leclercq and H. Rochais. Rome: 1977.

Bertaux, Emile. *L'art dans l'Italie méridionale*. 1903. Reprint, Paris: 1968.

Bertelli, Lino. "Gli ospitalieri di Altopascio in Italia e in Europa." In *Atti del primo congresso europeo di storia ospitaliera, 6–12 giugno 1960*, 151–67. Reggio Emilia: 1962.

————. "L'ordine dei cavalieri di Altopascio." *Giornale storico della Lunigiana e del territorio lucense*, n.s. 16 (1965): 39–45.

————. "L'ospizio e il paese di Altopascio (dalle origini all'anno 1239)." In *Atti del primo congresso italiano di storia ospitaliera. Reggio Emilia 14–17 giugno 1956*, 60–72. Reggio Emilia: 1957.

Berti, Graziella, and Liana Tongiorgi. *I bacini ceramici medievali delle chiese di Pisa*. Rome: 1981.

Berti, Graziella, and Paola Torre. *Arte islamica in Italia: i bacini delle chiese pisane: 26 maggio–25 settembre 1983, Roma, Palazzo Brancaccio*. Pisa: 1983.

Bertolini Campetti, L., et al. *Museo di Villa Guinigi, Lucca. La villa e le collezioni*. Lucca: 1968.

Bertozzi, Massimo. *Massa*. Genoa: 1985.

Berzolla, Pietro and Armando Siboni. *Guida all'architettura romanica nel piacentino*. Piacenza: 1966.

Biagotti, Dante. "La Magione dei Cavalieri di Altopascio." *Atti della R. Accademia Lucchese di Scienze, Lettere ed Arti*, n.s. 5 (1942): 247–65.

Biehl, Walther. *Toskanische Plastik des frühen und hohen Mittelalters*, Italienische Forschungen, Kunsthistorisches Institut in Florenz, n.s. 2. Leipzig: 1926.

Blaschke, Karlheinz. "Nikolaipatrozinium und städtische Frühgeschichte." *Zeitschrift der Savigny-Stiftung für Rechtsgeschichte* 84, *Kanonistische Abteilung* 53 (1967): 273–337.

Bless-Grabher, Magdalen. *Cassian von Imola: die Legende eines Lehrers und Märtyrers und ihre Entwicklung von der Spätantike bis zur Neuzeit*, Geist und Werk der Zeiten, 56. Bern: 1978.

Boeck, Urs. "Der Pisaner Dom zwischen 1089 und 1120. Beobachtungen zu Bautechnik und Bauausführung der ersten Baustufe." *Architectura* 11 (1981): 1–30.

Boeckler, Albert. *Die Bronzetür von San Zeno*, Die frühmittelalterlichen Bronzetüren, 3. Marburg: 1931.

———. *Die Bronzetüren des Bonanus von Pisa und des Barisanus von Trani*, Die frühmittelalterlichen Bronzetüren, 4. Berlin: 1953.

Bonacchi Gazzarrini, Giuliana. "Schede storiche." In *Pistoia. Leggere una città*, eds. Giovanni Michelucci and Aurelio Amendola. Pistoia: 1988.

Bonaventura, Arnaldo. *I Bagni di Lucca, Coreglia e Barga*, Italia artistica, ser. I, 75. Bergamo: 1914.

Bordone, Renato. "Memoria del tempo negli abitanti dei comuni italiani all'età del Barbarossa." *Il tempo vissuto. Percezione, impiego, rappresentazione, Gargnano, 9–11 settembre 1985*, 47–62. Bologna: 1988.

Borelli, G. *Fondazione e progressi della venerabile abbazia di S. Bartolomeo in Pistoia*. Pistoia: 1754.

Borg, Alan. "The Holy Sepulchre Lintel." *Journal of the Warburg and Courtauld Institutes* 35 (1972): 389–90.

———. "Observations on the Historiated Lintel of the Holy Sepulchre, Jerusalem." *Journal of the Warburg and Courtauld Institutes* 32 (1969): 25–40.

Bottineau, Yves. *Les Chemins de Saint-Jacques*. Paris: 1964.

Boulet, Noële Maurice-Denis. "Le dimanche des rameaux." *La Maison-Dieu* 41 (1955): 16–33.

Brakel, Cyriakus Heinrich. "Die vom Reformpapsttum geförderten Heiligenkulte." *Studi gregoriani* 9: 239–311. Rome: 1972.

Brandt, Michael, and Arne Eggebrecht, eds. *Bernward von Hildesheim und das Zeitalter der Ottonen. Katalog der Ausstellung. Hildesheim 1993*, 2 vols. Hildesheim: 1993.

Braun, Oskar. "Der Palmsonntag in Jerusalem zur Zeit der Kreuzzüge." *Historisch-politische Blätter für das katholische Deutschland* 171 (1923): 497–512.

Brenk, Beat. "Sugers Spolien." *Arte medievale* 1 (1983): 101–7.

Bresc-Bautier, Geneviève. "Les imitations du Saint-Sépulcre de Jérusalem (IXe–XVe siècles). Archéologie d'une dévotion." *Revue d'histoire de la spiritualité* 50 (1974): 319–42.

Brezzi, Paolo. "Alessandro III, papa." *DBI* 2, 183–89.

Brockett, Clyde W. "'Persona in Cantilena': St. Nicholas in Music in Medieval Drama." In *The Saint Play in Medieval Europe*, ed. Clifford Davidson, 11–29. Early Drama, Art, and Music Monograph Series, 8. Kalamazoo, Mich.: 1986.

Brunelli, Enrico. "Appunti sulla storia dell'arte in Sardegna: Gli amboni del duomo di Cagliari." *L'Arte* 4 (1901): 59–67.

Brunetti, Giulia. "Indagini e problemi intorno al pulpito di Guido da Como in S. Bartolommeo a Pistoia." In *Il romanico pistoiese nei suoi rapporti con l'arte romanica dell'occidente. Atti del I Convegno internazionale di studi medioevali di storia e d'arte (Pistoia-Montecatini Terme, 27 sett.–3 ott. 1964)*, 371–77. Pistoia: 1966.

Bruschi, Mario. *Il complesso abbaziale di S. Bartolomeo in Pistoia*. Pistoia: 1981.

———. "Note d'archivio per la storia della pieve di S. Andrea." *Bullettino storico pistoiese* 3d ser., 19 (1984): 93–106.

Burger, Stefan. "L'architettura romanica in Lucchesia ed i suoi rapporti con Pisa." *Annali della scuola normale superiore di Pisa* 2d ser. 23 (1954): 121–28.

Buschhausen, Helmut. "Die Fassade der Grabeskirche zu Jerusalem." In *Crusader Art of the Twelfth Century*, ed. J. Folda, 71–96. B.A.R. International Series, 152. Oxford: 1982.

Buselli, Franco. *S. Andrea Apostolo. Duomo a Carrara*. Genoa: 1972.

Cachiagi, Giuseppe. *Pisa*, 4 vols. Pisa: 1970.

Caleca, Antonino. *La Dotta Mano. Il Battistero di Pisa*. Bergamo: 1991.

Calzecchi, Carlo. "Sculture romaniche del duomo di Pistoia, rinvenute durante recenti lavori." *Arti* 2 (1939): 104–6.

Campana, Augusto. "La testimonianza delle iscrizioni." *Lanfranco e Wiligelmo. Il duomo di Modena*, 363–73. [Modena: 1984].

Campbell, Thomas P., and Clifford Davidson, eds. *The Fleury Playbook. Essays and Studies*. Early Drama, Art, and Music Monograph Series, 7. Kalamazoo, Mich.: 1985.

Camposanto Monumentale di Pisa. Pisa: 1977.

Canestro Chiovenda, Beatrice. *L'ambone dell'isola di San Giulio*, Monografie e studi d'arte antica e moderna, 10. Rome: 1955.

Cardini, Franco. "La società lucchese e la prima crociata." *Actum Luce* 8 (1979): 7–30.

———. "La société italienne et les croisades." *Cahiers de civilisation médiévale* 28 (1985): 19–33.

———. "Toscani verso Gerusalemme." In *'De Finibus Tuscie'. Il medioevo in Toscana*, 76–102. Politica e storia, 8. Florence: 1989.

Carli, Enzo. *Il duomo di Pisa*. Florence: 1989.

———. *Volterra nel Medioevo e nel Rinascimento*. Pisa: 1978.

Carratori, L., and B. Hamilton. "Daiberto." *DBI* 31, 679–84.

Cast, David. "Reading Vasari Again: History, Philosophy." *Word and Image* 9 (1993): 29–38.

Castelnuovo, Enrico. "Maestranza pisana di Biduino, capitello figurato." In *Da Biduino ad Algardi. Pittura e scultura a confronto*, ed. G. Romano. Turin: 1990.

———, ed. *Niveo de Marmore. L'uso artistico del marmo di Carrara dall'XI al XV secolo*. Genoa: 1992.

Castelnuovo-Tedesco, Lisbeth. "Romanesque Sculpture in North American Collections. XXII. The Metropolitan Museum of Art. Part II: Italy (1)." *Gesta* 24/1 (1985): 61–76.

Cattalini, Doriana. "Un capitello da Roma a San Piero a Grado." *Prospettiva* fasc. 31 (Oct. 1982): 73–77.

Caturegli, Natale, ed. *Regestum Pisanum*. Rome: 1938.

Caucci von Saucken, Paolo. "La Via Francigena e gli itinerari italiani a Compostella." In *Europäische Wege der Santiago Pilgerfahrt*, ed. Robert Plotz, 119–29. Jakobus Studien, 2. Tübingen: 1990.

———. "Le chemin italien de Saint-Jacques." In *Saint-Jacques de Compostelle*, 63–75. Turnhout: 1985.

———. "The 'Via Francigena' and the Italian Routes to Santiago." In *The Santiago de Compostela Pilgrim Routes*, 59–63. Council of Europe, Architectural Heritage Reports and Studies, 16. Strasbourg: 1989.

Le Ceramiche medievali delle chiese di Pisa. Contributo per una migliore comprensione delle loro caratteristiche e del loro significato quale documento di storia. Bollettino storico pisano, Collana storica, 25. Pisa: 1983.

Chevallier, Raymond. *Roman Roads*. Trans. N. Field. 1976. Rev. ed., London: 1989.

Chiappelli, Alberto. *Storia del teatro in Pistoia dalle origini alla fine del sec. XVIII*. Pistoia: 1913.

Chiellini Nari, Monica. *Le sculture nel battistero di Pisa. Temi e immagini dal medioevo: i rilievi del deambulatorio*. Ospedaletto: 1989.

Chronica Monasterii Casinensis, ed. H. Hoffmann. MGH SS, 34. Hannover: 1980.

Ciampi, Sebastiano. *Notizie inedite della sagrestia pistoiese de'belli arredi del campo santo pisano e di altre opere di disegno dal secolo XII. al XV*. Florence: 1810.

Cignitti, B., and C. Colafranceschi. "Leonardo da Nobiliacum." In *BS* 7, cols. 1198–1208.

Cioffari, Gerardo. "La vita." In *San Nicola di Bari e la sua basilica. Culto, arte, tradizione*, ed. Giorgio Otranto, 20–36. Milan: 1987.

———. "L'origine del culto di S. Nicola in Puglia." *Nicholaus* 11 (1983): 145–53.

———. *S. Nicola nella critica storica*. Bari: 1987.

Cipollaro, P., and C. Notarianni. *L'Arno*. Florence: 1974.

Clare, Edward G. *St. Nicholas, His Legends and Iconography*. Florence: 1985.

Classen, Peter. *Burgundio von Pisa. Richter-Gesandter-Übersetzer*. Sitzungsberichte der Heidelberger Akademie der Wissenschaften, Philosophisch-historische Klasse. Heidelberg: 1974.

Claussen, Peter Cornelius. "Früher Künstlerstolz. Mittelalterliche Signaturen als Quelle der Kunstsoziologie." In *Bauwerk und Bildwerk im Hochmittelalter. Anschauliche Beiträge zur Kultur- und Sozialgeschichte*. eds. K. Clausberg, et al., 7–35. Giessen: 1981.

Cohen, Esther. "Roads and Pilgrimage: A Study in Economic Interaction." *Studi medievali* 3d ser., 21/1 (1980): 321–41.

Collins, Fletcher, Jr. *Medieval Church Music-Dramas. A Repertory of Complete Plays*. Charlottesville: 1976.

———. *The Production of Medieval Church Music-Drama*. Charlottesville: 1972.

Collins, Patrick J. *The N-Town Plays and Medieval Picture Cycles*, Early Drama, Art and Music Monograph Series, 2. Kalamazoo, Mich.: 1979.

Coolidge, W.A.B. *Swiss Travel and Swiss Guide-books*. London: 1889.

Corsi, Domenico. *La pace di Lucca con Pisa e Firenze negli anni 1181 e 1184*, Accademia lucchese di scienze, lettere e arti, Studi e Testi, 12. Lucca: 1980.

Corsi, Pasquale. *La traslazione di San Nicola: le fonti*, Centro studi nicolaiani, Studi e Testi, 8. Bari: 1987.

Coturri, Enrico. "La canonica di S. Frediano di Lucca dalla prima istituzione (metà del sec. XI) alla unione alla congregazione riformata di Fregionaria (1517)." *Actum Luce* 3 (1974): 47–80.

———. "L'ospedale di S. Jacopo di Altopascio in Toscana lungo la via Francesca." In *Atti del Convegno internazionale di studi. Pistoia e il cammino di Santiago. Una dimensione europea nella Toscana medioevale. Pistoia, 28–29–30 settembre 1984*, ed. Lucia Gai, 331–42. Naples: 1987.

Crawford, Mary Sinclair. *Life of St. Nicholas*, Publications of the University of Pennsylvania Series in Romanic Languages and Literatures, 12. Philadelphia: 1923.

Crichton, G. H. *Romanesque Sculpture in Italy*. London: 1954.

Cristiani Testi, Maria Laura. "Biduino e la chiesa dei S.S. Casciano e Giovanni." In *Cascina*, vol. 4: *L'arte medievale a Cascina e nel suo territorio*, 93–121. Ospedaletto: 1987.

———. "'Classico' e 'Romanzo' nell'incompiuto Fonte di Calci." *Critica d'arte* 45, fasc. 172–74 (July–December 1980): 107–32.

———. "Sculture nel campanile pisano." *Critica d'arte* 41, fasc. 147 (1976): 14–30.

Curatola, Giovanni, ed. *Eredità dell'Islam. Arte islamica in Italia. Venezia, Palazzo Ducale. 30 ottobre 1993–30 aprile 1994*. [Milan, 1993].

Dal Canto, Giuseppe. "La vecchia chiesa curata di S. Giacomo di Altopascio nell'inventario del 1740." *La provincia di Lucca* 11, no. 4 (October 1971): 61–70.

Davidson, Clifford. *Drama and Art. An Introduction to the Use of Evidence from the Visual Arts for the Study of Early Drama*, Early Drama, Art and Music Monograph Series, 1. Kalamazoo, Mich.: 1977.

De Sancti Hugonis Actis Liturgicis, ed. Mario Bocci. Documenti della chiesa volterrana, 1. Florence: 1984.

Del Re, Niccolò, and Maria Chiara Celletti. "Nicola (Nicolò), vescovo di Mira." In *BS* 9, cols. 923–48.

Delehaye, Hippolyte. *Les passions des martyrs et les genres littéraires*. Brussels: 1921.

Della Pace, Alfredo. *Il duomo di Barga e le terre robbiane di Barga*. Barga: 1927.

Delplace, Christiane. *Le griffon de l'archaïsme à l'époque impériale. Étude iconographique et essai d'interprétation symbolique*, Études de philologie, d'archéologie et d'histoire anciennes, L'Institut historique belge de Rome, 20. Brussels and Rome: 1980.

Demus, Otto. *The Mosaics of San Marco in Venice*. I. *The Tenth and Eleventh Centuries*. Vol. 1: *Text*, Vol. 2: *Plates*. Chicago: 1984.

Denny, Don. *The Annunciation from the Right from Early Christian Times to the Sixteenth Century*. Outstanding Dissertations in the Fine Arts. New York and London, 1977.

Deschamps, Paul. "Tables d'autel de marbre exécutées dans le midi de la France au Xe et au XIe siècle." In *Mélanges d'histoire du Moyen Age offerts à M. Ferdinand Lot par ses amis et ses élèves*, 137–68. Paris: 1925.

Dietl, Albert. "*In Arte Peritus*. Zur Topik mittelalterlicher Künstlerinschriften in Italien bis zur Zeit Giovanni Pisanos." *Römische historische Mitteilungen* 29 (1987): 75–125.

———. "Künstlerinschriften als Quelle für Status und Selbstverständnis von Bildhauern." In *Studien zur Geschichte der Europäischen Skulptur im 12./13. Jahrhundert*. eds. Herbert Beck and Kerstin Hengevoss-Dürkop, vol. 1, 175–91. Frankfurt am Main: 1994.

Di Paco Triglia, Maria Antonietta. *La chiesa del Santo Sepolcro di Pisa*. Pisa: 1986.

Doberer, Erika. "Il ciclo della passione sul pontile di Modena." In *Romanico padano, romanico europeo. Convegno internazionale di studi. Modena-Parma 26 ottobre–1 novembre 1977*, 391–98. Parma: 1982.

Dodds, Jerrilynn D., ed. *Al-Andalus. The Art of Islamic Spain*, New York: 1992.

Dodge, Hazel. "Ancient Marble Studies: Recent Research." *Journal of Roman Archaeology* 4 (1991): 28–50.

Donati, Fulvia, and Maria Cecilia Parra. "Pisa e il reimpiego 'laico': La nobiltà di sangue e d'ingegno, e la potenza economica." *Colloquio sul reimpiego dei sarcofagi romani nel medioevo. Pisa 5–12 September (sic) 1982*, eds. Bernard Andreae and Salvatore Settis, 103–19. Marburger Winckelmann-Programm, 1983. Marburg: 1984.

Dondaine, Antoine. "Hugues Ethérien et Léon Toscan." *Archives d'histoire doctrinale et littéraire du moyen âge* 27 (1952): 67–134.

Dreves, Guido Maria. *Liturgische Hymnen des Mittelalters aus Handschriften und Wiegendrucken*, Analecta Hymnica Medii Aevi, 22. Leipzig: 1895.

Dünninger, J. "Leonhard von Noblac." *LCI* 7, cols. 394–98.

Il Duomo e la civiltà pisana del suo tempo. Pisa: 1986.

Edwards, Robert. *The Montecassino Passion Play and the Poetics of Medieval Drama*. Berkeley and Los Angeles: 1977.

Egbert, Virginia Wylie. "St. Nicholas. The Fasting Child." *Art Bulletin* 46 (1964): 68–70.

Emerton, Ephraim. "Altopascio—A Forgotten Order." *American Historical Review* 29 (1923–24): 1–23.

Emminghaus, J. H. "Verkündigung an Maria." *LCI* 4, cols. 422–37.

Esch, Arnold. "Spolien. Zur Wiederverwendung antiker Baustücke und Skulpturen im mittelalterlichen Italien." *Archiv für Kulturgeschichte* 51 (1969): 1–64.

Evans, Joan. *Cluniac Art of the Romanesque Period.* Cambridge: 1950.

Face, Richard D. "Secular History in Twelfth-Century Italy: Caffaro of Genoa." *Journal of Medieval History* 6 (1980): 169–84.

Falkenhausen, Vera von. "Bari bizantina: profilo di un capoluogo di provincia (secoli IX–XI)." In *Spazio, società, potere nell'Italia dei comuni*, ed. Gabriella Rossetti, 220–27. Naples: 1986.

Fanfani, Amintore. "Note sull'industria alberghiera italiana nel medioevo." *Archivio storico italiano* 22 (1934): 259–72.

Fantappiè, Renzo. "La chiesa di S. Giovanni Forcivitas e i suoi rapporti con la propositura di Prato." *Bullettino storico pistoiese* 3d. ser. 6 (1971): 79–124.

Favreau-Lilie, Marie-Luise. *Die Italiener im Heiligen Land vom ersten Kreuzzug bis zum Tode Heinrichs von Champagne (1098–1197).* Amsterdam: 1989.

Felletti Maj, Bianca Maria. "Il fregio commemorativo dell'arco di Susa." *Pontificia accademia romana di archeologia, Rendiconti* 33 (1960–61): 129–53.

Fentress, James, and Chris Wickham. *Social Memory.* Oxford and Cambridge, Mass.: 1992.

Fernie, Eric. "Notes on the Sculpture of Modena Cathedral." *Arte lombarda* 14/2 (1969): 88–93.

Ferrali, Sabatino. *L'apostolo S. Jacopo il Maggiore e il suo culto a Pistoia.* Pistoia: 1979.

Fiorentini, Fausto Ersilio. *Le chiese di Piacenza.* Piacenza: 1985.

Fisher, Craig B. "The Pisan Clergy and an Awakening of Historical Interest in a Medieval Commune." *Studies in Medieval and Renaissance History* 3 (1966): 143–219.

Flanigan, C. Clifford. "The Fleury *Playbook*, the Traditions of Medieval Latin Drama, and Modern Scholarship," In *The Fleury 'Playbook'. Essays and Studies*, eds. T. P. Campbell and C. Davidson, 1–25. Early Drama, Art, and Music Monograph Series, 7. Kalamazoo, Mich.: 1985.

Fletcher, R. A. *Saint James's Catapult. The Life and Times of Diego Gelmírez of Santiago de Compostela.* Oxford: 1984.

Folda, Jaroslav. *The Art of the Crusaders in the Holy Land, 1098–1187.* Cambridge and New York: 1995.

———. *The Nazareth Capitals and the Crusader Shrine of the Annunciation*, College Art Association of America, Monographs, 42. University Park and London: 1986.

Fonseca, Cosimo Damiano. "Canoniche e ospedali." *Atti del I Congresso europeo di storia ospitaliera*, 482–89. Reggio Emilia: 1962.

Fontana, Paolo. "I marmi antichi nelle chiese medioevali di Toscana." *Saggi sull'architettura etrusca e romana. Atti del III Convegno nazionale di storia dell'architettura (Roma, 9–13 ottobre 1938)*, 201–5. Rome: 1940.

Formentini, Ubaldo. "Le tre pieve del Massese e le origini della città di Massa." *Atti e Memorie della Deputazione di storia patria per le antiche provincie modenesi*, 8th ser. 2 (1949): 97- 112.

Forsyth, Ilene H. *The Throne of Wisdom. Wood Sculptures of the Madonna in Romanesque France.* Princeton: 1972.

————. "The 'Vita Apostolica' and Romanesque Sculpture: Some Preliminary Observations." *Gesta* 25 (1986): 75–82.

Fraipont, Max de. "Les origines occidentales du type de saint Michel debout sur le dragon." *Revue belge d'archéologie et d'histoire de l'art* 7 (1937): 289–301.

Francovich, Géza de. *Benedetto Antelami. Architetto e scultore e l'arte del suo tempo*, 2 vols. Milan and Florence: 1952.

Franz, Adolph. *Die kirchlichen Benediktionen im Mittelalter*, 2 vols. 1909. Reprint, Graz: 1960.

Frazer, Alfred. *Samothrace. The Propylon of Ptolemy II*, Bollingen Series, LX:10. Princeton: 1990.

Frugoni, Chiara (*see also* Settis Frugoni, Chiara). "Le lastre veterotestamentarie e il programma della facciata." In *Lanfranco e Wiligelmo. Il duomo di Modena*, 422–31. [Modena: 1984].

Gai, Lucia. *L'altare argenteo di San Iacopo nel Duomo di Pistoia. Contributo alla storia dell'oreficeria gotica e rinascimentale italiana.* Turin: 1984.

————. "Testimonianze jacobee e riferimenti compostellani nella storia di Pistoia dei secoli XII–XIII." *Pistoia e il cammino di Santiago. Una dimensione europea nella Toscana medioevale, Atti del Convegno internazionale di studi. Pistoia, 28–29–30 settembre 1984*, ed. Lucia Gai, 119–230. Naples: 1987.

Gai, Lucia, Rosalia Manno Tolu, and Giancarlo Savino. *L'apostolo San Jacopo in documenti dell'Archivio di Stato di Pistoia.* Pistoia: 1984.

Gambacorta, Antonio. "Culto e pellegrinaggi a San Nicola di Bari fino alla prima Crociata." In *Pellegrinaggi e culto dei santi in Europa fino alla 1a Crociata, 8–11 ottobre 1961*, 485–502. Convegni del centro di studi sulla spiritualità medievale, 4. Todi: 1963.

Garrison, Edward B. "Checklist of Tuscan Transitional Manuscripts, Second Quarter of the Twelfth Century." *Studies in the History of Mediaeval Italian Painting*, vol. 1, 176. Florence: 1953.

————. "Early Lucchese Manuscripts (to ca. 1150)." *Studies in the History of Mediaeval Italian Painting*, vol. 3, 221–59. Florence: 1957.

————. *Italian Romanesque Panel Painting. An Illustrated Index.* Florence: 1949.

————. "Three Manuscripts for Lucchese Canons of S. Frediano in Rome." *Journal of the Warburg and Courtauld Institutes* 38 (1975): 1–52.

————. "Twelfth Century Initial Styles of Central Italy: Indices for the Dating of

Manuscripts, Part II. Materials (Continued). The Late Geometrical Style in the Third Quarter of the Twelfth Century (Continued). 8. The Pistoiese Region." *Studies in the History of Mediaeval Italian Painting* vol. 3, 33–46. Florence: 1957.

Garzella, Gabriella. "Cascina. L'organizzazione civile ed ecclesiastica e l'insediamento." In *Cascina*, vol. 2. *Cascina dall'antichità al medioevo*, 69–108. Pisa: 1986.

Gauthier, Marie Madeleine. *Les routes de la foi. Reliques et reliquiaires de Jérusalem à Compostelle*. Fribourg: 1983.

Geary, Patrick J. *Furta Sacra. Thefts of Relics in the Central Middle Ages*. Rev. ed. Princeton: 1990.

————. "I Magi a Milano." In *Il millennio Ambrosiano: La città del vescovo dai Carolingi al Barbarossa*, ed. Carlo Bertelli, 274–87. Milan: 1988. Reprinted in *Living with the Dead in the Middle Ages*. Ithaca and London: 1994.

Gehrt, Wolf. *Die Verbände der Regularkanonikerstifte S. Frediano in Lucca, S. Maria in Reno bei Bologna, S. Maria in Porto bei Ravenna und die 'cura animarum' im 12. Jahrhundert*. Frankfurt am Main: 1984.

Gem, Richard. "Canterbury and the Cushion Capital: a Commentary on Passages from Goscelin's 'De Miraculis Sancti Augustini'." In *Romanesque and Gothic. Essays for George Zarnecki*. Vol. I, 83–101. Woodbridge, Suffolk, and Wolfeboro, N.H., 1987.

Gerola, Berengario. "Il culto di S. Leonardo ed i suoi ex-voto nei XIII comuni." *Il Folklore italiano. Archivio trimestrale per la raccolta e lo studio delle tradizioni popolari italiane* 5 (1930): 99–125.

Giampaoli, Umberto. "Una scultura di maestro Biduino nella chiesa di S. Leonardo al Frigido." *Giornale storico della Lunigiana* 13 (1923): 113–21.

Giglioli, Odoardo H. *Pistoia nelle sue opere d'arte*. Florence: 1904.

Gilbert, Creighton E. "Last Suppers and their Refectories." In *The Pursuit of Holiness in Late Medieval and Renaissance Religion*, eds. Charles Trinkhaus and Heiko A. Oberman, 371–402. Studies in Medieval and Reformation Thought, 10. Leiden: 1974.

Giorgi, Giorgio. *S. Salvatore in Mustiola*, Le chiese di Lucca, 4. Lucca: 1981.

Giorgieri, P. *Carrara*, La città nella storia d'Italia. Rome and Bari: 1992.

Giusti, Martino. "L'antica liturgia lucchese." In *Lucca, Il Volto Santo e la civiltà medioevale. Atti. Convegno internazionale di studi. Lucca, Palazzo Pubblico 21–23 ottobre 1982*, 21–44. Lucca: 1984.

————. "L''Ordo officiorum' della cattedrale di Lucca." In *Miscellanea Giovanni Mercati*. Vol. II. *Letteratura medioevale*, 523–66. Studi e Testi, 122. Vatican City: 1946.

Glass, Dorothy F. *Italian Romanesque Sculpture: An Annotated Bibliography*. Boston: 1983.

————. *Romanesque Sculpture in Campania. Patrons, Programs, and Style*. University Park, Penn.: 1991.

Gómez-Moreno, Carmen. "The Doorway of San Leonardo al Frigido and the Problem of Master Biduino." *Bulletin of the Metropolitan Museum of Art* 23 (June 1965): 349–61.

Gordini, Gian Domenico. "Cassiano di Imola." In *BS* 3, cols. 909–11.

———, and Angelo Maria Raggi. "Magi, adoratori di Gesú, santi." In *BS* 8, cols. 494–528.

Grabar, André. *Ampoules de terre sainte (Monza-Bobbio)*. Paris: 1958.

Gräf, Hermann J. *Palmenweihe und Palmenprozession in der lateinischen Liturgie*. Steyl: 1959.

Greenhalgh, Michael. "'Ipsa ruina docet': l'uso dell'antico nel Medioevo." In *Memoria dell'antico nell'arte italiana*. vol. 1. *L'uso dei classici*, ed. Salvatore Settis, 113–67. Biblioteca di storia dell'arte, n.s. 1. Turin: 1984.

———. *The Survival of Roman Antiquities in the Middle Ages*. London: 1989.

Grégoire, Réginald. *San Ranieri di Pisa (1117–1160) in un ritratto agiografico inedito del secolo XIII*, Biblioteca del bollettino storico pisano, Collana storica, 36. Ospedaletto: 1990.

Grimaldi, Jacopo. *Descrizione della basilica antica di S. Pietro in Vaticano. Codice Barberini Latino 2733*. ed. Reto Niggl, Codices e Vaticanis Selecti, 32. Vatican City: 1972.

Guntheri Poetae Ligurinus. Ed. Erwin Assmann, MGH, Scriptores Rerum Germanicarum, LXIII. Hannover: 1987.

Gy, Pierre. "L'influence des chanoines de Lucques sur la liturgie du Latran." *Revue des sciences religieuses* 58 (1984): 31–41.

Hager, Hellmut. *Die Anfänge des italienischen Altarbildes. Untersuchungen zur Entstehungsgeschichte des toskanischen Hochaltarretabels*. Munich: 1962.

Hamann, Richard. *Die Abteikirche von St. Gilles und ihre künstlerische Nachfolge*. 3 vols. Berlin: 1955.

———. "Das Lazarusgrab in Autun." *Marburger Jahrbuch für Kunstwissenschaft* 8–9 (1936): 182–328.

Harris, John Wesley. *Medieval Theatre in Context: An Introduction*. London and New York: 1992.

Hartmann, K. A. Martin. "Ueber das altspanische Dreikönigsspiel." Ph.D. diss., University of Leipzig, 1879.

Haskins, Charles H. *Studies in the History of Mediaeval Science*. 2d ed. Cambridge, Mass.: 1927.

Haug, Ingrid. "Erscheinungen Christi (E. vor den Jüngern)." *RDK* 5/2, cols. 1327–50.

Heimann, Adelheid. "The Capital Frieze and Pilasters of the Portail Royal, Chartres." *Journal of the Warburg and Courtauld Institutes* 31 (1968): 73–102.

Herbers, Klaus. *Die Jakobuskult des 12. Jahrhunderts und der 'Libri Sancti Jacobi'*. Historische Forschungen 7. Wiesbaden: 1984.

Herde, Peter. "Christians and Saracens at the Time of the Crusades." *Studia Gratiana* 12 (1967): 359–76.

Herlihy, David. *Medieval and Renaissance Pistoia. The Social History of an Italian Town, 1200–1430.* New Haven: 1967.

——. *Pisa in the Early Renaissance. A Study of Urban Growth.* Yale Historical Publications, Miscellany 68. New Haven: 1958.

Heydasch-Lehmann, Susanne. *Der 'Taufbrunnen' in San Frediano in Lucca und die Entwicklung der toskanischen Plastik in der 2. Hälfte des 12. Jahrhunderts,* Europäische Hochschulschriften, ser. 28, Kunstgeschichte, 123. Frankfurt am Main: 1991.

Heywood, William. *A History of Pisa, Eleventh and Twelfth Centuries.* Cambridge: 1921.

Hiestand, Rudolf. "L'arcivescovo Ubaldo e i Pisani alla terza crociata alla luce di una nuova testimonianza." *Bollettino storico pisano* 58 (1989): 37–51.

Hödl, Ludwig. "Abendmahl, Abendmahlstreit." In *Lexikon des Mittelalters* 1, cols. 22–27. Munich and Zurich: 1980.

Hofmann, Hans. *Die Heiligen Drei Könige. Zur Heiligenverehrung im Kirchlichen, gesellschaftlichen und politischen Leben des Mittelalters,* Rheinisches Archiv, 94. Bonn: 1975.

Hohler, Christopher. "The Proper Office of St. Nicholas and Related Matters with Reference to a Recent Book." *Medium Aevum* 36 (1967): 40–48.

Huygens, R.B.C., ed. *Peregrinationes Tres. Saewulf. Iohannes Wirziburgensis. Theodericus.* Corpus Christianorum, Continuatio Mediaevalis, CXXXIX. Turnhout: 1994.

Jacobus of Voragine. *The Golden Legend. Readings on the Saints.* trans. William G. Ryan, 2 vols. Princeton: 1993.

Janson, H. W. *Apes and Ape Lore in the Middle Ages and the Renaissance.* London: 1952.

Johnstone, Mary A. "The Griffin, the Coat-of-Arms of Perugia." *Studi etruschi* 2d ser., 30 (1962): 335–52.

Jones, Charles W. *The Saint Nicholas Liturgy and Its Literary Relationships (Ninth to Twelfth Centuries).* University of California English Studies, 27. Berkeley and Los Angeles: 1963.

——. *Saint Nicholas of Myra, Bari and Manhattan. Biography of a Legend.* Chicago: 1978.

Juhel, Vincent. "Le bain de l'Enfant-Jésus. Des origines à la fin du douzième siècle." *Cahiers archéologiques* 39 (1991): 111–32.

Jullian, René. *L'éveil de la sculpture italienne. La sculpture romane dans l'Italie du nord,* 2 vols. Paris: 1945.

Kaftal, George. *Iconography of the Saints in Tuscan Painting.* Florence: 1952.

Kapitän, G. "Church Wreck off Marzamemi." *Archaeology* 22 (1969): 122–33.

Kaster, G. "Zacharias, Vater Johannes' des Täufers." *LCI* 8, cols. 634–36.

Katzenellenbogen, Adolf. "The Central Tympanum at Vézelay. Its Encyclopedic Meaning and Its Relation to the First Crusade." *Art Bulletin* 26 (1944): 141–51.

———. "The Sarcophagus in S. Ambrogio and St. Ambrose." *Art Bulletin* 29 (1947): 249–59.

———. *The Sculptural Programs of Chartres Cathedral. Christ, Mary, Ecclesia.* Baltimore: 1959.

———. "The Separation of the Apostles." *Gazette des beaux-arts* 6th ser., 35 (1949): 81–98.

Kazhdan, A. P. "Saint Nicholas, Saint George and the Cretans' Attacks." *Byzantion* 54 (1984): 176–82.

Kehr, Paul F. *Italia Pontificia*, vol. 3: *Etruria.* 1908. Reprint, Berlin: 1968.

Kehrer, Hugo. *Die Heiligen Drei Könige in Litteratur und Kunst,* 2 vols. Leipzig: 1908–9.

Kemp, Brian. "The Miracles of the Hand of St. James." *Berkshire Archaeological Journal* 65 (1970): 1–19.

Kempers, Bram. "Icons, Altarpieces, and Civic Ritual in Siena Cathedral, 1100–1530." In *City and Spectacle in Medieval Europe*, eds. Barbara A. Hanawalt and Kathryn L. Reyerson, 89–136. Medieval Studies at Minnesota, 6. Minneapolis and London: 1994.

Kenaan-Kedar, Nurith. "The Figurative Western Lintel of the Church of the Holy Sepulchre in Jerusalem." In *The Meeting of Two Worlds: Cultural Exchange Between East and West during the Period of the Crusades*, eds. V. P. Goss and C. V. Bornstein, 123–31. Studies in Medieval Culture, 21. Kalamazoo, Mich.: 1986.

———. *Marginal Sculpture in Medieval France: Towards the Deciphering of an Enigmatic Pictorial Language.* Aldershot: 1995.

———. "The Margins of Society in Marginal Romanesque Sculpture." *Gesta* 31/1 (1992): 15–24.

King, Norbert. *Mittelalterliche Dreikönigsspiele,* 2 vols. Freiburg: 1979.

Kinney, Dale. "Spolia from the Baths of Caracalla in S. Maria in Trastevere." *Art Bulletin* 68 (1986): 379–97.

Klapisch-Zuber, Christiane. *Les maîtres du marbre. Carrare 1300–1600.* Paris: 1969.

Kobler, Friedrich. "Das Pisaner Affenkapitell in Berlin-Glienicke." In *Munuscula Discipulorum. Kunsthistorische Studien Hans Kauffmann zum 70. Geburtstag 1966*, eds. Tilmann Buddensieg and Matthias Winner, 157–64. Berlin: 1968.

Koeppel, Gerhard M. "Die historischen Reliefs der römischen Kaiserzeit. I. Stadtrömische Denkmäler unbekannter Bauzugehörigkeit aus augusteischer und julisch-claudischer Zeit." *Bonner Jahrbuch* 183 (1983): 61–144.

———. "Die historischen Reliefs der römischen Kaiserzeit. IV. Stadtrömische Denkmäler unbekannter Bauzugehörigkeit aus hadrianischer bis konstantinischer Zeit." *Bonner Jahrbuch* 186 (1986): 1–90.

Kranz, Peter. *Jahreszeiten-Sarkophage. Entwicklung und Ikonographie des Motivs der Vier Jahreszeiten auf Kaiserzeitlichen Sarkophagen und Sarkophagdeckeln,* Die antiken Sarkophagreliefs, 5/4. Berlin: 1984.

Krautheimer, Richard. "Introduction to an Iconography of Medieval Architecture." *Journal of the Warburg and Courtauld Institutes* 5 (1942): 1–33. Reprinted in his *Studies in Early Christian, Medieval, and Renaissance Art.* New York and London: 1969.

Kretzenbacher, Leopold. "Die Ketten um die Leonhardskirchen im Ostalpenraume. Kulturhistorische Beiträge zur Frage der Gürtung von Kultobjekten in der religiösen Volkskultur Europas." In *Kultur und Volk. Beiträge zur Volkskunde aus Österreich, Bayern und der Schweiz. Festschrift für Gustav Gugitz zum achtzigsten Geburtstag,* ed. Leopold Schmidt, 165–202. Vienna: 1954.

Krey, August C. *The First Crusade. The Accounts of Eye-Witnesses and Participants.* 1921. Reprint, Gloucester, Mass.: 1958.

Kühnel, Bianca. *Crusader Art of the Twelfth Century. A Geographical, an Historical, or an Art Historical Notion?* Berlin: 1994.

———. "Der Rankenfries am Portal der Grabeskirche zu Jerusalem und die romanische Skulptur in den Abruzzen." *Arte medievale* 2d ser. 1 (1987): 87–125.

Ladner, Gerhart B. "The Gestures of Prayer in Papal Iconography of the Thirteenth and Fourteenth Centuries." In *Didascaliae. Studies in Honor of Anselm M. Albareda Prefect of the Vatican Library, Presented by a Group of American Scholars,* ed. Sesto Prete, 245–75. New York: 1961. Reprinted in his *Images and Ideas in the Middle Ages. Selected Studies in History and Art,* vol. 1, 209–37. Storia e letteratura, Raccolti di studi e testi, vol. 155. Rome: 1983.

Lamy-Lassalle, Colette. "Enseignes de pèlerinages de Saint Léonard." *Bulletin de la société nationale des antiquaires de France* (1990): 157–67.

Lanzoni, Francesco. *Le diocesi d'Italia dalle origini al principio del secolo VII (AN. 604),* Studi e Testi, 35. Vatican City: 1927.

———. "Le leggende di San Cassiano d'Imola." *Didaskelion,* n.s. 3, fasc. 2 (1925): 1–44.

Lauer, Rolf. "Dreikönigenschrein." In *Ornamenta Ecclesiae. Kunst und Künstler der Romanik in Köln. Katalog zur Ausstellung des Schnütgen-Museums in der Josef-Haubrich-Kunsthalle,* vol. 2, 216–25. Cologne: 1985.

Lavagnini, Luigi. "Il duomo di Carrara." *Atti e memorie della Deputazione di storia patria per le antiche provincie modenesi* ser. 10, 5 (1970): 147–65.

Lawrence, Marion. "A Gothic Reworking of an Early Christian Sarcophagus." *Art Studies* 7 (1929): 89–103.

Le Goff, Jacques. "The Symbolic Ritual of Vassalage." *Time, Work, and Culture in the Middle Ages,* 237–87. Chicago and London: 1982.

Lechner, M. "Heimsuchung Mariens." *LCI* 2, cols. 229–35.

Lefrançois, J. A. "James (Son of Zebedee), St." *New Catholic Encyclopedia* 7, 809. New York: 1967.

Lehmann-Hartleben, Karl, and Erling C. Olson. *Dionysiac Sarcophagi in Baltimore.* Baltimore: 1942.

Lentini, Anselmo. "La leggenda di S. Nicola di Mira in un'ode di Alfano cassinese." In *Mélanges Eugène Tisserant,* 333–43. Studi e Testi, 232. Vatican

City: 1964. Reprinted in *Medioevo Letterario Cassinese. Scritti vari*, ed. Faustino Avagliano, 247–58. Miscellanea Cassinese, 57. Montecassino: 1988.

Lentini, Anselmo, and Avagliano, Faustino, eds. *I carmi di Alfano I, Archivescovo di Salerno*. Miscellanea Cassinese, 38. Montecassino: 1974.

Lera, Guglielmo. "La chiesa dei cavalieri di Altopascio e le sue opere d'arte." *Giornale storico della Lunigiana e del territorio lucense*, n.s. 16 (1965): 56–64.

Leyser, Karl. "Frederick Barbarossa, Henry II and the Hand of St. James." *English Historical Review* 90 (1975): 481–506.

Liber Pontificalis, 2 vols., ed. L. Duchesne. Paris, 1886–92.

Lilie, Ralph Johannes. *Handel und Politik zwischen dem byzantinischen Reich und den italien Kommunen Venedig, Pisa und Genua in der Epoch der Komnenen und der Angeloi (1081–1204)*. Amsterdam: 1984.

Lindner, Molly. "Topography and Iconography in Twelfth-Century Jerusalem." In *The Horns of Hattin, Proceedings of the Second Conference of the Society for the Study of the Crusades and the Latin East, Jerusalem and Haifa, 2–6 July 1987*, ed. B. Z. Kedar, 81–98. Jerualem and London: 1992.

Lindsay, David Alexander Edward, 27th Earl of Crawford and 10th Earl of Balcarres. *The Evolution of Italian Sculpture*. London: 1901.

Liotta, Filippo. "Burgundione da Pisa." *DBI* 15, 423–28.

——, ed. *Miscellanea, Rolando Bandinelli, Papa Alessandro III*. Siena: 1986.

Little, Charles T. "The Magdeburg Ivory Group: A Tenth Century New Testament Narrative Cycle." Ph.D. diss. New York University: 1977.

Loomis, Laura Hibbard. "The Table of the Last Supper in Religious and Secular Iconography." *Art Studies* 5 (1927): 71–88.

Lori Sanfilippo, Isa, ed. *Federico I Barbarossa e l'Italia nell'ottocentesimo anniversario della sua morte. Atti del convegno. Roma, 24–26 maggio 1990* (= *Bullettino dell'Istituto storico italiano per il medio evo e archivio Muratoriano* 96). Rome: 1990.

Lucca e la Tuscia nell'alto medioevo. Atti del V Congresso internazionale di studi sull'alto medioevo, 1971. Spoleto: 1973.

Lucca, il Volto Santo e la civiltà medioevale: Atti, Convegno internazionale di studi, Lucca, Palazzo Pubblico, 21–23 ottobre 1982. Lucca: 1984.

Lucchesi, Emiliano. *I monaci benedettini e Vallombrosani nella diocesi di Pistoia e Prato. Note storiche*. Florence: 1941.

Lucchesi Palli, E., and L. Hoffscholte. "Abendmahl." *LCI* 1, cols. 10–18.

Maetzke, Anna Maria. *Il Volto Santo di Sansepolcro. Un grande capolavoro medievale rivelato dal restauro*. Milan: 1994.

Magoun, Francis P., Jr. "The Pilgrim Diary of Nikulas of Munkathvera: the Road to Rome." *Mediaeval Studies* 6 (1944): 314–54.

Mai, Angelo. *Spicilegium Romanum*. vol. 4. Rome: 1840.

Mâle, Emile. *Religious Art in France, The Twelfth Century. A Study of the Origins of Medieval Iconography*, ed. Harry Bober, and trans. Marthiel Mathews.

Bollingen series XC:1. Princeton: 1978. Originally published as *L'Art religieux du XIIe siècle en France* (Paris: 1922).

Malherbe, George. "La dramatisation médiévale de la procession des Rameaux." *Bulletin paroissial liturgique* (1933): 99–108.

Mallardo, D. "Giovanni diacono napoletano." *Rivista di storia della chiesa in Italia* 2 (1948): 317–37.

Malmstrom, Ronald. "The Colonnades of High Medieval Churches at Rome." *Gesta* 14 (1975): 37–45.

Manselli, Raoul. "La Repubblica di Lucca." In *Comuni e signorie nell'Italia nordorientale e centrale: Lazio, Umbria e Marche, Lucca*, Storia d'Italia, ed. Giuseppe Galasso, VII², 610–731. Turin: 1987.

———. "Lucca e Lucchesi nei loro rapporti con la prima crociata." *Bollettino storico lucchese* 12 (1940): 158–68. Reprinted in his *Italia e Italiani alla prima crociata*, 125–35. Rome: 1983.

Mansi, Giovanni Domenico. *Sacrorum Conciliorum*, vol. 22. Venice: 1778.

Maragone, Bernardo. *Gli Annales Pisani*, ed. Michele Lupo Gentile. Rerum Italicarum Scriptores, VI². Bologna: 1936.

Marchetti Pollina, Antonella. "La chiesa di S. Andrea di Carrara negli antichi documenti lucchesi." *Atti e memorie della Deputazione di storia patria per le antiche provincie modenesi*, ser. 10, 5 (1970): 173–81.

Marcucci, Maria Adelaide. *Guida storica ed artistica delle chiese di Massa*. [Massa: 1987].

Martimort, Aimé Georges. "Les diverses formes de procession dans la liturgie." *La Maison-Dieu* 43 (1955): 43–73.

Martini, Mario Ermolao. *La Pieve di Calci (Guida per il visitatore)*. 2d ed. Calci: 1990.

Matteoni, Giovanni Antonio. *Guida delle chiese di Massa Lunense*. Massa: 1879.

Matteucci, Benvenuto. "Attone (Atto), vescovo di Pistoia." In *BS* 2, cols. 573–76.

Mazzarosa, Antonio. *Guida di Lucca e dei luoghi più importanti del ducato*. Lucca: 1843.

Mazzi, Maria Cecilia, ed. *Museo civico di Pistoia: catalogo delle collezioni*, Catalogo del Museo Civico, 3. Florence: 1982.

McArdle, Frank. *Altopascio. A Study in Tuscan Rural Society, 1587–1784*. Cambridge and New York: 1978.

McCann, Anna Marguerite. *Roman Sarcophagi in the Metropolitan Museum of Art*. New York: 1978.

McDermott, William Coffman. *The Ape in Antiquity*, The Johns Hopkins University Studies in Archaeology 27, ed. David M. Robinson. Baltimore: 1938.

Medding, W. "Erscheinung Christi (6) vor den Aposteln." *LCI* 1, cols. 671–72.

Meisen, Karl. *Nikolauskult und Nikolausbrauch im Abendlande: eine kultgeographisch-volkskundliche Untersuchung*. 1931. Reprint, Quellen und Abhandlungen zur mittelrheinischen Kirchengeschichte, 41. Mainz: 1981.

Melczer, William. *La porta di Bonanno nel duomo di Pisa. Teologia ed immagine.* Pisa: 1988.

Mende, Ursula. *Die Bronzetüren des Mittelalters, 800–1200.* Munich: 1983.

Mercati, Giovanni. "Usi liturgici non romani in Toscana?" *Rassegna gregoriana* 2 (1903): cols. 23–26.

Meurer, H. "Lazarus von Bethanien." *LCI* 3, cols. 33–38.

Migliorini, Bruno. *The Italian Language*, rev. by T. Gwynfor Griffith. London: 1966. Originally published as *Storia della lingua italiana.* Florence: 1960.

Mombritius, Boninus. *Sanctuarium seu Vitae Sanctorum*, ed. Monks of Solesmes. 2 vols. Paris: 1910.

Moretti, Italo, and Renato Stopani. *La Toscana*, Italia romanica, vol. 4, Già e non ancora, arte, vol. 19, Milan: 1982.

Morris, Colin. "San Ranieri of Pisa: The Power and Limitations of Sanctity in Twelfth-Century Italy." *Journal of Ecclesiastical History* 45 (1994): 588–99.

Muciaccia, F. "I cavalieri dell'Altopascio (con documenti inediti)." *Studi storici* 6 (1897): 33–92; 7 (1898), 215–32; 8 (1899), 347–97.

Müller, Renate. *Die Entwicklung der Naturwerksteinindustrie im toskanischen Apennin als Funktion städtebaulicher Gestaltung.* Frankfurt am Main: 1975.

Munz, Peter. "Frederick Barbarossa and the 'Holy Empire'." *Journal of Religious History* 3 (1964–65): 20–37.

Muratori, Ludovico Antonio. *Antiquitates Italicae Medii Aevi*, vol. 4. Milan: 1741.

Nasalli Rocca, Emilio. "Pievi ed ospedali." *Atti del primo congresso italiano di storia ospitaliera. Reggio Emilia 14–17 giugno 1956*, 493–507. Reggio Emilia: 1957.

Nolan, Kathleen. "Narrative in the Capital Frieze of Notre-Dame at Etampes." *Art Bulletin* 71 (1989): 166–84.

Ohler, Norbert. *The Medieval Traveller*, trans. Caroline Hillier. Woodbridge: 1989. Originally published as *Reisen im Mittelalter* (Munich: 1986).

Olivari, Maria Teresa. "Ancora su Guido Bigarelli." *Arte lombarda* 11, pt. 2 (1966): 31–38.

———. "Le opere autografe di Guido Bigarelli da Como." *Arte lombarda* 10, pt. 2 (1965): 33–44.

O'Meara, Carra Ferguson. *The Iconography of the Façade of Saint-Gilles-du-Gard.* Outstanding Dissertations in the Fine Arts. New York and London: 1977.

Opll, Ferdinand. *Das Itinerar Kaiser Friedrich Barbarossas (1152–1190).* Vienna: 1978.

Osten, Gert von der. "Zur Ikonographie des ungläubigen Thomas angesichts eines Gemäldes von Delacroix." *Wallraf-Richartz Jahrbuch* 27 (1965): 371–88.

Otten-Froux, C. "Les pisans en Orient de la première croisade à 1406," 2 vols., Ph.D. diss. Paris: 1981.

Ousterhout, Robert. "The Church of S. Stefano: A 'Jerusalem' in Bologna." *Gesta* 20 (1981): 311–21.

———. "Loca Sancta and the Architectural Response to Pilgrimage." In *The Blessings of Pilgrimage*, ed. R. Ousterhout, 108–24. Illinois Byzantine Studies, I. Urbana and Chicago: 1990.

Pächt, Otto. *The Rise of Pictorial Narrative in Twelfth-Century England*. Oxford: 1962.

Palmer, Anne Marie. *Prudentius on the Martyrs*. Oxford: 1989.

Palmieri, Arturo. "Le strade medievali fra Bologna e la Toscana." *Atti e memorie della Regia deputazione di storia patria per le provincie di Romagna* 4th ser., 8 (1918): 25–47.

Panofsky, Erwin. *Renaissance and Renascences in Western Art*, Gottesman Lectures, 7. Stockholm: 1960.

Parra, Maria Cecilia. "Pisa e Modena: spunti di ricerca sul reimpiego 'intorno' al Duomo." In *Lanfranco e Wiligelmo. Il duomo di Modena*, 355–60. [Modena: 1984].

———. "Rimeditando sul reimpiego: Modena e Pisa viste in parallelo." *Annali della Scuola normale superiore di Pisa. Classe di lettere e filosofia* 3d ser., 13 (1983): 453–83.

Partner, Peter. *The Lands of St. Peter. The Papal State in the Middle Ages and the Early Renaissance*. Berkeley and Los Angeles: 1972.

Il patrimonio artistico di Pistoia e del suo territorio. Catalogo storico descrittivo. Pistoia: 1967–70.

Penco, Gregorio. *Storia del monachesimo in Italia dalle origini alla fine del medio evo*. Rome: 1961.

Pennachi, Joseph, and Victor Piazzesi, eds. *Acta Sanctae Sedis*. 1884. Reprint, New York: 1968.

Pennington, Kenneth. "The Rite for Taking the Cross in the Twelfth Century." *Traditio* 30 (1974): 429–35.

Pensabene, Patrizio. "Amministrazione dei marmi e sistema distributivo nel mondo romano." In *Marmi antichi*, ed. Gabriele Borghini, 43–54. Materiali della cultura artistica, 1. Rome: 1989.

———. "A Cargo of Marble Shipwrecked at Punta Scifo near Crotone (Italy)." *International Journal of Nautical Archaeology* 7/2 (May 1978): 105–18.

———. "Considerazioni sul trasporto di manufatti marmorei in età imperiale a Roma e in altri centri occidentali." *Dialoghi di archeologia* 6 (1972): 317–62.

Pèra, Luigi. *Il duomo di Barga*. I monumenti italiani. Reale Accademia d'Italia, ser. 1, fasc. 11. Rome: 1937.

———. *Il duomo di Barga e i suoi ampliamenti*. Pisa: 1938.

Perkins, Charles C. *Tuscan Sculptors. Their Lives, Works and Times*, 2 vols. London: 1864.

Pertusi, Agostino. "Ai confini tra religione e politica. La contesa per le reliquie di San Nicola tra Bari, Venezia e Genova." *Quaderni medievali* 5 (June 1978): 6–56. Reprinted in his *Saggi Veneto-Bizantini*, ed. Giovanni Battista Parente, 139–86. Florence: 1990.

Pescaglini Monti, Rosanna. "Le dipendenze polironiane in diocesi di Lucca." In *L'Italia nel quadro dell'espansione europea del monachesimo cluniacense, Atti del Convegno internazionale di storia medievale, Pescia, 26–28 novembre 1981*. Italia benedettina 8, 143–72. Cesena: 1985.

Petrucci, Armando. "La scrittura tra ideologia e rappresentazione." In *Storia dell'arte italiana*, Part 3, *Situazione, momenti, indagini*, vol. 2. *Grafica e immagine. I. Scrittura, Miniatura, Disegno*, ed. F. Zeri, 3–123. Storia dell'arte italiana, 9°, Turin: 1980.

Petzoldt, L. "Nikolaus von Myra (von Bari)." *LCI* 8, cols. 45–58.

Pfaff, V. "Hospitalaria, scholaria, pecunaria und die Päpste des späten XII Jahrhunderts." *Historische Jahrbuch* 97–98 (1978): 463–97.

Pfanner, Luigi. "I lavori della Sopraintendenza ai Monumenti e Gallerie di Pisa agli edifici monumentali della Lunigiana e Garfagnana." *Giornale storico della Lunigiana*, n.s. 7 (1956): 50–52.

———. *Le origini di Massa, la 'Taberna Frigida' e la chiesa con l'ospedale di S. Leonardo al Frigido*. Massa: 1954.

Pierotti, Piero. *Pisa e Accon. L'insediamento nella città crociata. Il porto. Il fondaco*, Ecostoria, 3. Pisa: 1987.

Pistarino, Geo. "Diocesi, pievi e parrocchie nella Liguria medievale (secoli XII–XV)." In *Pievi e parrocchie nella Liguria medievale (sec. XII–XV). Atti del VI Convegno di storia della chiesa in Italia, Firenze, 21–25 sett. 1981*, vol. 2, 625–76. Rome: 1984.

Plotino, Roberto, and Justo Fernández Alonso. "Giacomo il Maggiore." In *BS* 6, cols. 363–88.

Porter, Arthur Kingsley. *Lombard Architecture*, vol. 1. New Haven: 1917.

———. *Romanesque Sculpture of the Pilgrimage Roads*, 1923. Reprint, 10 vols. in 3. New York: 1966.

Pratesi, Alessandro. "Attone (Atto)." *DBI* 4, cols. 566–67.

Prawer, Joshua. *The Crusaders' Kingdom. European Colonialism in the Middle Ages*. New York and Washington: 1972.

———. "The Italians in the Latin Kingdom." *Crusader Institutions*, 217–49. Oxford: 1980.

Pressouyre, Léon. "Nouvelle identification d'une statue-colonne de Saint-Maur-des-Fossés." *Bulletin monumental* 122 (1964): 393–94.

———. "St. Bernard to St. Francis: Monastic Ideals and Iconographic Programs in the Cloister." *Gesta* 12 (1973): 71–92.

Prieur, Jean. "Les arcs monumentaux dans les Alpes occidentales: Aoste, Suse, Aix-le-Bains." *Aufstieg und Niedergang der römischen Welt, Geschichte und Kultur Roms im Spiegel der neueren Forschung* II, vol. 12.1: *Künste*, ed. Hildegard Temporini, 442–75. Berlin and New York: 1982.

Quintavalle, Arturo Carlo. *La cattedrale di Modena: problemi di romanico emiliano*, 2 vols. Modena: 1964–65.

———. *La cattedrale di Parma e il romanico europeo*. Parma: 1974.

———. *La strada Romea.* [Milan: 1974].

———, et al. *Romanico mediopadano. Strada, città, ecclesia.* Parma: 1983.

———. *Romanico padano civiltà d'occidente*, Raccolta pisana di saggi e studi, 25, ed. Carlo L. Ragghianti. Florence: 1969.

———. *Vie dei pellegrini nell'Emilia mediavale.* Milan: 1977.

Rahmani, L. Y. "The Eastern Lintel of the Holy Sepulchre." *Israeli Exploration Journal* 26 (1976): 120–29.

Raimundi de Aguilers. *Historia Francorum qui Ceperunt Iherusalem.* In *Recueil des historiens des Croisades, historiens occidentaux*, vol. 3, 235–309. Paris: 1866.

Rangerius of Lucca. *Vita metrica s. Anselmi Lucensis episcopi.* eds. G. Schwartz, B. Schmiedler, and E. Sackur. MGH SS, 30/2, 1152–1307. 1934. Reprint, Stuttgart: 1976.

Rauty, Natale. "Il castello di Batoni e l'antico itinerario per Modena attraverso l'Appennino pistoiese." *Bullettino storico pistoiese* 74 (3d. ser., 7) (1972): 65–86.

———. "La via consolare Cassia attraverso Pistoia." *Bullettino storico pistoise* 68 (3d. ser., 1) (1966): 3–14.

———. *L'antico palazzo dei vescovi a Pistoia.* vol. 1, *Storia e restauro*, Arte e Archeologia, Studi e Documenti, 19. Florence: 1981.

———. *Storia di Pistoia*, vol. 1: *Dall'alto medioevo all'età precomunale*, 406–1105. Florence: 1988.

Redi, Fabio. *La pieve di S. Michele in Groppoli.* Quaderni pistoiesi di storia dell'arte, 4. Pistoia: 1976.

Repetti, Emanuele. *Dizionario geografico, fisico, storico della Toscana*, vol 1. 1833. Reprint, Rome: 1969.

———. *Dizionario geografico, fisico, storico della Toscana*, vol. 5. 1843. Reprint, Rome: 1969.

Ricca, Luca, Simonetta Simonetti, and Gerardo Nolledi. *450 Anniversario della fondazione della Compagnia del S.S. Nome di Gesù.* Lucca: 1990.

Rice, David Talbot. *The Church of Haghia Sophia at Trebizond.* Edinburgh: 1968.

Ridolfi, Enrico. *Guida di Lucca.* Lucca: 1899.

Riley-Smith, Jonathan. *The Crusades. A Short History.* New Haven and London: 1987.

Riparbelli, Alberto. *Lucca romana.* Lucca: 1982.

Rodolico, Francesco. *Le pietre della città d'Italia.* Florence: 1953.

Rolland, Paul. "L'expansion tournaisienne aux XIe et XIIe siècles. Art et commerce de la pierre." *Annales de l'academie royale d'archéologie de Belgique* 72 (1924): 175–217.

Ronsjö, Einar, ed. *La vie de Saint Nicolas par Wace. Poème religieux du XIIe siècle publié d'après tous les manuscrits*, Etudes romanes de Lund, 5. Lund and Copenhagen: 1945.

Rossetti, Gabriella. "Pisa: assetto urbano e infrastruttura portuale." In *Città portuali del mediterraneo. Storia e archeologia. Atti del Convegno internazionale di Genova 1985*, ed. Ennio Poleggi, 263–86. Genoa: 1989.

Rossi-Sabatini, Giuseppe. *L'espansione di Pisa nel Mediterraneo fino alla Meliora*, Studi di lettere, storia e filosofia pubblicati dalla R. Scuola Normale superiore di Pisa, 6. Florence: 1935.

Rupprecht, Bernhard. *Romanische Skulptur in Frankreich*, 2d ed. Munich: 1984.

Ryberg, Inez Scott. *Rites of the State Religion in Roman Art*, American Academy in Rome, Memoirs, 22. Rome: 1955.

Salmi, Mario. "Il duomo di Carrara." *L'Arte* 29 (1926): 124–35.

———. *L'architettura romanica in Toscana*. Milan: 1927.

———. *Romanesque Sculpture in Tuscany*. Florence: 1928.

———. "Sant'Jacopo all'Altopascio e il Duomo di Pisa." *Dedalo* 6 (1925–26): 483–515.

Salvini, Roberto. "La scultura romanica pistoiese." In *Il romanico pistoiese nei suoi rapporti con l'arte romanica dell'occidente. Atti del I Convegno internazionale di studi medioevali di storia e d'arte (Pistoia-Montecatini Terme, 27 settembre–3 ottobre 1964)*, 165–79. Pistoia: 1966.

Sandberg-Vavalà, Evelyn. *La croce dipinta italiana e l'iconografia della passione*. Verona: 1929.

Sanpaolesi, Piero. "Alcuni edifici romanici in cotto in Toscana." In *Atti del II Convegno nazionale di storia dell'architettura. Assisi, 1–4 ottobre 1937*, 127–38. Rome: 1939.

———. *Il campanile di Pisa*. Pisa: 1956.

———. *Il duomo di Pisa*. Pisa: 1975.

———. "Ispirazioni da un modello di scultura classica in Pisa nel XII e XIII secolo." *Mitteilungen des Kunsthistorischen Institutes in Florenz* 7 (1953): 280–82.

Santi, A. de. "La Domenica delle Palme nella storia liturgica." *La Civiltà cattolica* 57, no. 1339 (1906): 3–18; no. 1340 (1906): 159–77.

Santoli, Quinto. "Pistoia ai tempi di S. Atto." *Bullettino storico pistoiese* 55 (1953): 57–75.

Sauerländer, Willibald. *Gothic Sculpture in France, 1140–1270*. New York: 1972.

———. "La cultura figurativa emiliana in età romanica." In *Nicholaus e l'arte del suo tempo. Atti del seminario tenutosi a Ferrara dal 21 al 24 settembre 1981 organizzato dalla Deputazione Provinciale Ferrarese di Storia Patria*, vol. 1, ed. A. M. Romanini, 51–92. Ferrara: 1985.

———. "Les chapiteaux de la cathédrale Saint-Jean à Besançon." In *Franche-Comté romane, Bresse romane*, ed. René Tournier, 215–28. La nuit des temps, 52. La Pierre-qui-vire: 1979.

Savio, Fedele. "Giovanni Diacono, biografo dei vescovi napoletani." *Atti della Reale accademia delle scienze di Torino* 50 (1914): 974–88.

Scalia, Giuseppe. "Epigrafica pisana. Testi latini sulla spedizione contro le Baleari del 1113–15 e su altre imprese anti-saracene del secolo XI." *Miscellanea di studi ispanici* 6 (1963): 234–86.

———. "Il carme pisano sull'impresa contro i Saraceni del 1087." In *Studi di filologia romanza offerti a S. Pellegrini*, 565–627. Padua: 1971.

———. " 'Romanitas' pisana tra XI e XII secolo. Le iscrizioni romane del duomo e la statua del console Rodolfo." *Studi medievale* 3d ser. 13/2 (1972): 791–843.

Scano, Dionigi. *L'antico pulpito del duomo di Pisa scolpito da Guglielmo d'Innsbruck*. Cagliari: 1905.

———. "A proposito del pulpito pisano dell'antica cattedrale di Cagliari." *L'Arte* 4 (1901): 204–7.

———. *Storia dell'arte in Sardegna dal XI al XIV secolo*, Biblioteca storica sarda, 1. Cagliari and Sassari: 1907.

Schiller, Gertrud. *Iconography of Christian Art*, vol. 1: *Christ's Incarnation-Childhood-Baptism-Temptation-Transfiguration-Works and Miracles*, trans. J. Seligman. Greenwich, Conn.: 1971.

———. *Iconography of Christian Art*, vol. 2: *The Passion of Jesus Christ*, trans. J. Seligman. Greenwich, Conn.: 1972.

———. *Ikonographie der christlichen Kunst*, vol. 3: *Die Auferstehung und Erhöhung Christi*. Guterslöh: 1971.

Schmarsow, August. *S. Martin von Lucca und die Anfänge der toskanischen Skulptur im Mittelalter*, Italienische Forschungen zur Kunstgeschichte, 1. Breslau: 1890.

Schmidt, H.A.P. *Hebdomada Sancta*, 2 vols. Rome: 1956.

Schmitt, Marilyn. " 'Random' Reliefs and 'Primitive' Friezes: Reused Sources of Romanesque Sculpture." *Viator* 11 (1980): 123–45.

Schreiner, Ludwig. *Die frühgotische Plastik südwestfrankreichs. Studien zum Style Plantagenet zwischen 1170 und 1240 mit besonderer Berücksichtigung der Schluszsteinzyklen*. Cologne and Graz: 1963.

Schwartzbaum, Elizabeth. "Three Tournai Tombslabs in England." *Gesta* 20/1 (1981): 89–97.

Schwarzmaier, Hansmartin. *Lucca und das Reich bis zum Ende des 11. Jahrhunderts. Studien zur Sozialstruktur einer Herzogstadt in der Toskana*, Bibliothek des Deutschen Historischen Instituts in Rom, 41. Tübingen: 1972.

———. *Movimenti religiosi e sociali a Lucca nel periodo tardo- longobardo e Carolingio (Contributo alla leggenda del Volto Santo)*, Accademia lucchese di scienze, lettere e arti, Studi e Testi, 7. Lucca: 1973.

Scudieri Ruggieri, Jole. "Il pellegrinaggio compostellano e l'Italia." *Cultura neolatina* 30 (1970): 185–98.

Secchi, Albino. "Restauro ai monumenti romanici pistoiesi." In *Il romanico pistoiese nei suoi rapporti con l'arte romanica dell'occidente. Atti del I Convegno internazionale di studi medioevali di storia e d'arte (Pistoia-Montecatini Terme, 27 settembre–3 ottobre 1964)*, 107–9. Pistoia: 1966.

Seidel, Max. "Dombau, Kreuzzugsidee und Expansionspolitik. Zur Ikonographie der Pisaner Kathedralbauten." *Frühmittelalterliche Studien* 11 (1977): 340–69.

———. "Ikonographie und Historiographie: 'Conversatio Angelorum in Silvis,' Eremiten-Bilder von Simone Martini und Pietro Lorenzetti." *Städel-Jahrbuch* 10 (1985): 77–138.

Serra, Joselita. "Un capitello del duomo di Pisa." *Commentari* 12 (1961): 245–46.

Settis, Salvatore. "Verbreitung und Wiederverwendung antiker Modelle." In *Studien zur Geschichte der Europäischen Skulptur im 12./13. Jahrhundert*, eds. Herbert Beck and Kerstin Hengevoss- Dürkop. vol. 1, 351–66. Frankfurt am Main: 1994.

Settis Frugoni, Chiara (*see also* Frugoni, Chiara). "La rappresentazione dei giullari nelle chiese fino al XII sec." In *Il Contributo dei giullari alla drammaturgia italiana delle origini. Atti del II Convegno di studi, Viterbo, 17–19 giugno 1977*, 113- 34. Città di Castello: 1978.

Ševčenko, Ihor, and Nancy Patterson Ševčenko, trans. *The Life of Saint Nicholas of Sion*, The Archbishop Iakovos Library of Ecclesiastical and Historical Sources, 10. Brookline, Mass.: 1984.

Ševčenko, Nancy Patterson. *The Life of St. Nicholas in Byzantine Art*, Centro Studi Bizantini, Bari, Monografie, I. Turin: 1983.

Sforza, G. "Massa di Lunigiana nella prima metà del secolo XVIII." *Atti e memorie della R. Deputazione di Storia Patria per le provincie modenesi* ser. 5, 5 (1907): 91–239.

Sheingorn, Pamela. "Medieval Drama Studies and the New Art History." *Mediaevalia* 18 (1995) (for 1992): 143–62.

Sheppard, Carl D. "The East Portal of the Baptistery and the West Portal of the Cathedral of Pisa. A Question of Dates." *Gazette des beaux-arts* 52 (1958): 5–22.

———. "Classicism in Romanesque Sculpture in Tuscany." *Gesta* 15 (1976): 185–92.

———. "Romanesque Sculpture in Tuscany: a Problem of Methodology." *Gazette des beaux-arts* 6th ser. 54 (1959): 97–108.

Silvestre, Hubert. "Review of Charles W. Jones, 'The Saint Nicholas Liturgy and its Literary Relationships (Ninth to Twelfth Centuries)'." *Revue d'histoire ecclésiastique* 60/1 (1965): 138–46.

Skey, Miriam Anne. "Herod's Demon-Crown." *Journal of the Warburg and Courtauld Institutes* 40 (1977): 274–76.

———. "The Iconography of Herod in the Fleury Playbook and in the Visual Arts." In *The Fleury Playbook. Essays and Studies*, eds. T. P. Campbell and C. Davidson, 120–43. Early Drama, Art, and Music Monograph Series, 7. Kalamazoo, Mich.: 1985.

Slessarev, Vsevolod. "'Ecclesiae Mercatorum' and the Rise of Merchant Colonies." *Business History Review* 41 (1967): 177–97.

Smail, R. C. "The International Status of the Latin Kingdom of Jerusalem, 1150–1192." In *The Eastern Mediterranean Lands in the Period of the Crusades*, ed. P. M. Holt, 23–45. Warminster: 1977.

Smith, Christine. *The Baptistery at Pisa*. Outstanding Dissertations in the Fine Arts. New York and London: 1978.

———. "The Date and Authorship of the Pisa Duomo Façade." *Gesta* 19/2 (1980): 185–92.

———. "East or West in 11th-Century Pisan Culture: The Dome of the Cathedral and Its Western Counterparts." *Journal of the Society of Architectural Historians* 43 (1984): 195–208.

Stiaffini, D. "La chiesa e il monastero di S. Paolo a Ripa d'Arno." *Rivista dell'Istituto nazionale d'archeologia e storia dell'arte* 3d ser., 6–7 (1983–84): 237–84.

Sticca, Sandro. "Italian Theater of the Middle Ages: from the 'Quem quaeritis' to the 'Lauda'." *Forum Italicum* 14 (1980): 275- 310.

———. "Italy: Liturgy and Christocentric Spirituality." *The Theater of Medieval Europe. New Research in Early Drama*, ed. Eckehard Simon, 169–88. Cambridge and New York: 1991.

———. *The Latin Passion Play: Its Origins and Development*. Albany: 1970.

Stocchi, Sergio. *Emilie romane. Plaine du Po*, trans. Dom Norbert Vaillant. La nuit des temps, 62. La Pierre-qui-vire: 1984.

Stopani, Renato. *La Via Francigena in Toscana. Storia di una strada medievale*. Collana di studi storico-territoriali. Aspetti e vicende umano in Toscana, 11. Florence: 1984.

———. *La Via Francigena. Una strada europea nell'Italia del Medioevo*. Florence: 1988.

———. *Le grande vie di pellegrinaggio del medioevo: le strade per Roma*. Florence: 1986.

———. *Le vie di pellegrinaggio del Medioevo. Gli itinerari per Roma, Gerusalemme, Compostella: con una antologia di fonti*, Vie della storia. Florence: [1991].

———, ed. *La Via Francigena nel senese, storia e territorio*. Florence: 1985.

———. *Storia e cultura della strada in Valdelsa nel medioevo*. Poggibonsi and S. Gimignano: 1986.

———, with G. Muzzi and T. Szabò. *La Valdelsa, La Via Francigena e gli itinerari per Roma e Compostella*. Quaderni del Centro Studi Romei, 2. Florence: 1988.

Studi storici in onore di Emilio Nasalli Rocca. Parma: 1971.

Sturdevant, Winifred. *The 'Misterio de los Reyes Magos'. Its Position in the Development of the Mediaeval Legend of the Three Kings*, Johns Hopkins Studies in Romance Literatures and Languages, 10. Baltimore: 1927.

Stussi, Alfredo. "La Tomba di Giratto e le sue epigrafi." *Studi mediolatini e volgari* 36 (1990) [1992]: 63–71.

Supino, Igino Benvenuto. *Arte pisana*. Florence: 1904.

Swarzenski, Hanns. *Monuments of Romanesque Art. The Art of Church Treasures in North-Western Europe*, 2d ed. Chicago and London: 1967.

Swiechowski, Zygmunt. *Sculpture romane d'Auvergne*, Le Bibliophile en Auvergne, 16. Clermont-Ferrand: 1973.

Szabò, Thomas. *Comuni e politica stradale in Toscana e in Italia nel medioevo*, Biblioteca di storia urbana medievale, 6. Bologna: 1992.

————. "Les routes toscanes du XIe au XIVe siècle." In *L'homme et la route en Europe occidentale au Moyen Age et aux temps modernes, Deuxièmes journées internationales d'histoire, 20–22 settembre 1980*, 267–74. Auch: 1982.

————. "Strassenbau und Strassensicherheit in Territorium von Pistoia (12.–14. Jh.). Untersuchungen zur Verkehrspolitik einer mittelalterlichen Kommune." *Quellen und Forschungen aus italienischen Archiven und Bibliotheken* 57 (1977): 88–137. Translated as "Strade e sicurezza nel territorio pistoiese (secoli XII–XIV). Ricerche sulla politica viaria di un comune medioevale," trans. M. Ronzani, in Thomas Szabò, *Comuni e politica stradale in Toscana e in Italia nel Medioevo*, 195–234. Biblioteca di storia urbana medievale, 6 (Bologna, 1992).

Tarroni, Laura. *La festa di S. Nicola nelle istituzioni scolastiche medioevali*. Bari: 1988.

Tassi, Roberto. *Il duomo di Parma. I. Il tempio romanico*. Parma: 1966.

Tedeschi Grisanti, Giovanna. "Dalle Terme di Caracalla. Capitelli reimpiegati nel Duomo di Pisa." *Atti della Accademia nazionale dei Lincei* ser. 9, 1 (1990): 161–85.

Ternois, Daniel. "Le suovetaurile de Beaujeu et le linteau roman de Charlieu." *La revue du Louvre et des musées de France* 15 (1965): 249–57.

Tholomeus of Lucca, *Annales*, ed. Bernard Schmiedler, MGH Scriptores Rerum Germanincarum, n.s. 8. Berlin: 1930.

Tigler, Guido. "Una statua romanica ad Altopascio (per il problema della scultura monumentale nel medioevo)." *Arte medievale* 2d ser., 4, no. 2 (1990): 123–33.

Tigri, Giuseppe. *Nuova guida di Pistoia e dei suoi dintorni*. Pistoia: 1896.

Tirelli, Vito. "Lucca nella seconda metà del secolo XII. Società e istituzioni." *I ceti dirigenti dell'età comunale nei secoli XII e XIII*, 157–231. Pisa: 1982.

Toesca, Pietro. *Storia dell'arte italiana*, vol. 1, Il Medioevo, 1927. Reprint, Turin: 1965.

Tolaini, Emilio. *Forma Pisarum. Storia urbanistica della città di Pisa. Problemi e ricerche*. 2d ed. Pisa: 1979.

————. *Pisa*, La città nella storia d'Italia, Bari: 1992.

Tolomei, Francesco. *Guida di Pistoia per gli amanti delle belle arti con notizie degli architetti, scultori, e pittori pistoiesi*. 1821. Reprint, Sala Bolognese: 1975.

Torsy, Jakob. "Achthundert Jahre Dreikönigenverehrung in Köln." *Kölner Domblatt* 23–24 (1964): 15–162.

Trachtenberg, Marvin. "Gothic/Italian 'Gothic': Toward a Redefinition." *Journal of the Society of Architectural Historians* 50 (1991): 22–37.

Trenta, Tommaso Felice. *Guida del forestiere per la città e il contado di Lucca.* Lucca: 1820.

Turi, Pilo. "Corpus Iscriptionum Pistoriensium." *Bullettino storico pistoiese* 77 (1975): 129–37.

———. "I restauri della chiesa di S. Bartolomeo in Pantano ed il pergamo di Guido da Como." *Bullettino storico pistoiese* n.s. 3 (1961): 317–26.

Tydeman, William. *The Theater in the Middle Ages. European Stage Conditions, c. 800–1576.* Cambridge: 1978.

Valiano, Giulio. "I restauri alla Pieve di S. Andrea." *Bullettino storico pistoiese* 34 (1932): 29–31.

Vannucci, Monica. "La firma dell'artista nel medioevo: testimonianze significative nei monumenti religiosi toscani dei secoli XI–XIII." *Bollettino storico pisano* 56 (1987): 119–38.

Vauchez, André. "A Twelfth-Century Novelty: the Lay Saints of Urban Italy." *The Laity in the Middle Ages. Religious Beliefs and Devotional Practices*, ed. Daniel E. Bornstein and trans. Margery J. Schneider, 51–72. Notre Dame, Ind.: 1993. Originally published as *Les laïcs du Moyen Age: Pratiques et expériences religieuses* (Paris: 1987).

Ventrone, Paola. "On the Use of Figurative Art as a Source for the Study of Medieval Spectacles." In *Iconographic and Comparative Studies in Medieval Drama*, eds. Clifford Davidson and John H. Stroupe, 4–16. Kalamazoo, Mich.: 1991.

Venturi, Adolfo. *Storia dell'arte italiana.* Vol. 3, *L'arte romanica.* Milan: 1904.

Verzár, Christine B. "Text und Bild in der norditalienischen Romanik: Skulpturen, Inschriften, Betrachter." In *Studien zur Geschichte der Europäischen Skulptur im 12./13. Jahrhundert*, eds. Herbert Beck and Kerstin Hengevoss-Dürkop. vol. 1, 495–504. Frankfurt am Main: 1994.

———. "Text and Image in North Italian Romanesque Sculpture." In *The Romanesque Frieze and Its Spectator*, ed. Deborah Kahn, 121–40. London: 1992.

Vikan, Gary. "Pilgrims in Magi's Clothing: The Impact of Mimesis on Early Byzantine Pilgrimage Art." In *The Blessings of Pilgrimage*, ed. Robert Ousterhout, 98–107. Illinois Byzantine Studies, I. Urbana and Chicago: 1990.

Violante, Cinzio. "Che cos'erano le pievi? Primo tentativo di studio comparato," *Critica storica* 26, nos. 2–3 (1989), 429–38.

———. *Economia, Società, Istituzioni a Pisa nel medioevo. Saggi e ricerche.* Bari: 1980.

Vitz, Evelyn Birge. "From the Oral to the Written in Medieval and Renaissance Saints' Lives." In *Images of Sainthood in Medieval Europe*, eds. Renate Blumenfeld-Kosinski and Timea Szell, 97–114. Ithaca and London: 1991.

Vogel, Cyrille, and Reinhard Elze, eds. *Le pontifical romano-germanique du dixième siècle*, Studi e Testi, 227. Vatican City: 1963.

Vogel, Cyrille. *Medieval Latin Liturgy: An Introduction to the Sources*, rev. and trans. W. G. Storey and N. K. Rasmussen, O.P. Washington, D.C.: 1986. Originally published as *Introduction aux sources de l'histoire du culte chrétien au moyen âge* (Spoleto: 1981).

Walter, Christopher. "Papal Politcal Imagery in the Medieval Lateran Palace." *Cahiers archéologiques* 20 (1970): 155–76. Reprinted in *Prayer and Power in Byzantine and Papal Imagery*. Aldershot, Hampshire: 1993.

Ward-Perkins, J. B. *Quarrying in Antiquity. Technology, Tradition and Social Change*. Proceedings of the British Academy, 57. Mortimer Wheeler Archaeological Lecture, British Academy, 1971. London: 1972.

Wehrhahn-Stauch, Liselotte. "Christliche Fischsymbolik von den Anfängen bis zum hohen Mittelalter." *Zeitschrift für Kunstgeschichte* 35 (1972): 1–68.

Weinberger, Martin. "Nicola Pisano and the Tradition of Tuscan Pulpits." *Gazette des beaux-arts* 6th ser., 55 (1960): 129–46.

Weitzmann, Kurt. "Icon Painting in the Crusader Kingdom." *Dumbarton Oaks Papers* 20 (1966): 49–83.

Werckmeister, Otto K. "The Emmaus and Thomas Pillar of the Cloister of Silos." In *El Romanico en Silos. IX Centenario de la Consagracion de la Iglesia y Claustro. 1088–1988*, 149–61. Silos: 1990.

White, John. "The Bronze Doors of Bonanus and the Development of Dramatic Narrative." *Art History* 11 (1988): 158–94.

White, T. H. *The Bestiary. A Book of Beasts*. New York: 1954.

Wickham, Chris. *Early Medieval Italy. Central Power and Local Society, 400–1200*. 1981. Reprint, Ann Arbor, Mich.: 1989.

———. *The Mountains and the City. The Tuscan Appennines in the Early Middle Ages*. Oxford: 1988.

Wickham, Glynne. *The Medieval Theater*, 3d ed. Cambridge: 1987.

Wilkinson, John, with Joyce Hill and W. F. Ryan, *Jerusalem Pilgrimage 1099–1185*. Works Issued by the Hakluyt Society, 2d ser., 167. London: 1988.

Wilpert, Giuseppe. *I sarcofagi cristiani antichi*, 3 vols. plus atlas. Rome: 1929–32.

Wolf, Gerhard. *Salus Populi Romani. Die Geschichte römischer Kultbilder im Mittelalter*. Weinheim: 1990.

Wollesen, Jens T. *Die Fresken von San Piero a Grado bei Pisa*. Bad Oeynhausen: 1977.

Yates, Frances A. *The Art of Memory*. Chicago: 1966.

Young, Karl. *The Drama of the Medieval Church*, 2 vols. Oxford: 1933.

Zech, Reinhard. "Meister Wilhelm von Innsbruck und die pisaner Kanzel im Dome zu Cagliari." Inaugural diss., Albertus-Universität zu Königsberg Pr., 1935.

Zerbi, Piero. "I rapporti di S. Bernardo di Chiaravalle con i vescovi e le diocesi d'Italia." In *Vescovi e diocesi nel Medioevo (Sec. IX-XIII). Atti del II Con-*

vegno di storia della chiesa in Italia (Roma, 5–9 sett. 1961), 219–314. Italia sacra, 5. Padua: 1964.

Zimmermann, Harald. "Eugenio III, papa." *DBI* 43, 490–96.

Zovatto, Paolo Lino. "Il Santo Sepolcro di Aquileia e il dramma liturgico medievale." *Atti dell'Accademia di scienze, lettere e arti di Udine* ser. 6, 13 (1954–57): 127–51.

Zucchi Castellini, Nicola. "La commenda di S. Leonardo e l'ospedale di S. Giovanni in Pontremoli." In *Studi storici. Miscellanea in onore di Manfredo Giuliani*, 221–37. Parma: 1965.

Zuchold, Gerd-H. *Der "Klosterhof" des Prinzen Karl von Preussen im Park von Schloss Glienicke in Berlin*, vol. 2, *Katalog der von Prinz Karl von Preussen im "Klosterhof" aufbewahrten Kunstwerke*, Berlin: 1993.

INDEX